The Social World
of Children
Learning
to Talk

◆ ◆ ◆ ◆

The Social World
of Children
Learning
to Talk

♦ ♦ ♦ ♦

by

Betty Hart, Ph.D.
Schiefelbusch Institute for Life Span Studies
The University of Kansas

and

Todd R. Risley, Ph.D.
University of Alaska at Anchorage

and

Schiefelbusch Institute for Life Span Studies
The University of Kansas

·P A U L·H·
BROOKES
PUBLISHING CO ®

Baltimore • London • Sydney

Paul H. Brookes Publishing Co.
Post Office Box 10624
Baltimore, Maryland 21285-0624

www.brookespublishing.com

Typeset by Brushwood Graphics, Inc., Baltimore, Maryland.
Manufactured in the United States of America by
Versa Press, East Peoria, Illinois.

All of the vignettes in this book are based on verbatim extracts from
transcripts of actual family interactions. In all instances, names
have been changed; in some instances identifying details have been
altered to protect confidentiality.

Second printing, November 2002.

Library of Congress Cataloging-in-Publication Data

Hart, Betty, 1927–
   The social world of children learning to talk / by Betty Hart and
Todd R. Risley.
        p.   cm.
   Includes bibliographical references (p.   ) and index.
   ISBN 1-55766-420-X
   1. Language acquisition.   2. Social interaction in children.
I. Risley, Todd R.   II. Title.
P118.H36   1999
401'.93—dc21   99-13087
                                                                      CIP

British Library Cataloguing in Publication data are available from
the British Library.

This book is dedicated with fondness and admiration to the 42 children and their families.

Contents

◆ ◆ ◆ ◆

List of Tables and Figures

◆ ◆ ◆ ◆

Preface

◆ ◆ ◆ ◆

With this book we celebrate 36 years of collabora-
tion. We first met at the University of Washington
in 1962, where we were both mentored by the great
Montrose Wolf. He guided Betty in demonstrating to the
world the power of adult attention for young children. On the
basis of that discovery, he and Todd invented "time-out" and
discovered how to teach mute children to talk. In 1965 we
joined a group that set up early intervention programs in a
low-income neighborhood in Kansas City, Kansas. The longitudinal study we describe in this book had its beginning in the
questions we asked as we worked together on language intervention, on the organization of preschool and child care programs, and on children's vocabulary growth. In 1982 we decided to search for the realities of children's early lives. We
devoted the next 3 years to monthly observations of casual
family interactions and then 10 more years to creating an immense, reliable, completely quantified database.

After 13 years of the routine, exhausting work of natural
science, we suddenly were so rich in data and discoveries that
we had to write two books. The first, *Meaningful Differences
in the Everyday Experience of Young American Children*
(Paul H. Brookes Publishing Co., 1995), reported our journey
to the most important of our discoveries, one that amazes us
still because it was so invisible during our observations of
family interactions. The longitudinal data revealed that there
are enormous, durable differences among families in the
amount that parents talk with young children and that these
differences are profoundly and lastingly related to how children turn out. We had to devote a book to establishing the in-

tegrity of this finding and discussing the implications for national policy of such huge differences in the amounts of early language experience that children bring to an increasingly technological society.

We discussed in *Meaningful Differences* the role of language experience in the intergenerational transmission of competence. In this book we describe our discovery of the pattern of that transmission. We put all of the tables and figures together in the appendixes rather than intersperse them within the chapters so that the quantification of our findings would complement and review rather than interrupt our description of the changing parent–child interactions we observed.

Equally as unexpected as our first discovery of differences among the parents was our second discovery of similar differences among the children. Before the children began talking, all of their data looked alike. All were vocalizing approximately 150 times per hour. But at 36 months old, each child's data looked like the data of that child's parent. The data revealed that as children are learning to talk, they talk more and more, and then their rates of talking level off. This leveling off occurs when they begin to talk as much as their parents had been talking to them.

When we looked at what was happening between the parents and children during the months the children were learning to talk, we saw the intergenerational transmission of the particular social dance practiced in the family. After the demands of daily living were taken care of, extra talk occurred in conversations concerning ideas, feelings, and impressions. Parents who talked a lot about such things or only a little ended up with 3-year-olds who also talked a lot, or only a little. We saw added to the huge differences in the amount of language experience we reported in our first book, huge differences in the amount that the children were practicing using language to influence and understand their everyday experience.

The data lead us to a simple message for parents. When you talk with your children a lot about things that are not important, you automatically give them experiences that are important to their cognitive and emotional learning. While your children are little, your conversation matters. Children get better at what they practice, and having more language tools, more nuances, more fluency, more steps in the social dances of life is likely to contribute at least as much to your children's future success as their heredity and their choice of friends.

Acknowledgments

❖ ❖ ❖ ❖

Our work can merely suggest the true magnitude of the gifts given us by the families who let us observe and record their daily lives. The scientific study of the social world of children learning to talk will be forever indebted to them, as we will be, personally, for our cherished memories of beautiful children, caring parents, and the warmth of families as places to live.

But we can hope that our work may fulfill the faith in its importance given in the years of financial support generously provided by the National Institute of Child Health and Human Development through Grant HD03144, in the vision and inspiration of Dick Schiefelbusch, and in the untiring help of the staff of the Schiefelbusch Institute for Life Span Studies at the University of Kansas, especially Ed Zamarripa, Paul Diedrich, and its suave director, Steve Schroeder.

All of the gifts and support would have come to nothing, though, without the hard daily work of Maxine Preuitt and Liz Haywood, who transcribed and coded 1,300 hours of observation; the persistence of Sheila Hoffman and Shirley Young, who typed 30,000 pages of raw data; the creativity of Rebecca Finney, who designed the database and the user-proof programs that built it; and the statistical expertise of Janet Marquis and David Thissen. We are profoundly and permanently grateful to each of them, as we are to each of the families, for standing by us over the years.

But the study would never have begun had it not been for Sid Bijou, who believed that there was something still to be learned about what people are doing when they are talking, and Montrose Wolf, who showed us how to look at the world in order to find out what is really going on there.

To all the gratitude we have accumulated over the years of the study, we have lately added the warmth of our appreciation for the work and help of Melissa Behm, Lois Bloom, and Cheryl Risley.

The Social World
of Children

Learning
to Talk

◆ ◆ ◆ ◆

CHAPTER 1

The Social Dance of American Family Life

◆ ◆ ◆ ◆

*I*t is often said that children take an active part in learning
to talk. The purpose of this book is to tell about that part.
In successive chapters we describe what children do as
they learn to act as partners in the social dance that is talking
between parents and children, and how interactions change as
baby talk turns into back-talk. We describe the pattern of
change as the reciprocal responses of turn taking become co-
ordinated contributions to conversation such that even when
parents and children are engaged in independent tasks, they
can stay and play in a dance of talking.

We are able to describe the gradual development of talking as a social dance because of the longitudinal data we collected on the everyday lives of young American children. Each
month for 2½ years we recorded in their homes the interactions between 42 children and their parents as the children
learned to talk. We spent 10 more years creating and verifying
an immense computer database in order both to preserve the
priceless gift of these families' willingness to be watched and
to ensure that the database would be one of a kind in the
depth and scientific integrity of its information about the
everyday experience of young American children. This book

refines what is already known about language development by giving a fuller description based on more complete data from a much larger group of children in families more varied in size, race, and socioeconomic status (SES). But more important, this book also adds information previously unknown: a description of the social world of ambient conversation and casual interaction in which language development proceeds.

We undertook the longitudinal observations to discover what was happening to children during their first 3 years of life. We could find studies of families with special needs, families having physical, marital, or mental problems, and families subject to societal intervention related to neglect and abuse. We could find astonishingly few data, however, concerning what actually goes on in the daily lives of the well-functioning families that are the stable, unremarkable majority of Americans. As specialists in clinical language intervention, we were well aware of how different children are in terms of language resources by age 4, but we found far more theories than facts that would explain why some 4-year-olds were performing so much more proficiently than others on verbal/cognitive tasks. We assumed, wrongly as it turned out, that the early experience of most children in ordinary American families was very similar to what we and our college-educated colleagues had experienced growing up. We designed a study to measure children's early experience and find out how much talking ordinary families actually do and how often and about what parents interact with 1- to 2-year-olds in the course of taking care of their household tasks.

Even after 2½ years of observing the daily lives of 42 ordinary families that all were similarly socializing their children to participate in American society, we could not see the massive differences the data revealed in the amount of talking that went on across families until we had converted our observations into quantified data. We were further surprised at how consistent the relative quantity of talking was in a family over time such that we could calculate how much experience with words a child was accumulating month by month while learning to talk. The amount that parents talked with their 1- to 2-year-old children was generally correlated with the parents' SES. But the data showed that no matter what the family SES, the more time parents spent talking with their child from day to day, the more rapidly the child's vocabulary was likely to be growing and the higher the child's score on an IQ test was likely to be at age 3.

When we analyzed what was happening in the families such that the amount of talking differed so greatly, we saw that all of the families devoted similar amounts of talk to socializing their children, getting them properly fed and dressed, and keeping them safe and appropriately engaged. The added amounts of talk we recorded in some of the more talkative families concerned topics other than the giving and getting necessary in everyday life, and it was this extra, optional talk that was highly correlated with measures of the children's verbal/cognitive competence at age 3. The data showed that when parents and children were staying to talk together with no need beyond social interaction, much more was happening than children hearing and saying words and sentences or learning reference and the names of things. Most of the optional talk occurred when parents and children were partners in mutual or parallel activities in which accomplishing something was rewarding but not imperative, doing a puzzle, for instance, or the child picking out socks to try on as the parent folded laundry. As partners in play, the children tended to be more cooperative, the parents more approving, and both of them less demanding and more likely to comment on nuances and elaborate what was said. The prohibitions required to manage the children's behavior were diluted by the amount of talk about a shared activity, and the vocabulary and concepts embedded in the talk were, without planning or effort, contributing to the accumulation of language and cognitive accomplishments that later tests would measure.

Even as we focused on the importance of the amount of experience with language and interaction parents provided their children before age 3, we knew that was only part of the story and that we would have to write this book to describe the importance of the children's contributions to the amount and kinds of experience their parents provided. In this book we have focused on the children learning from their interactions how to talk and thus influence their experience. But this too is only part of the story. The whole story is the intimate social dance between children and parents interacting as partners, listening and speaking, following and leading, locked into the ways language works between people. As children learn to talk they become increasingly heterogeneous dance partners: each learns the social dance of his or her own family culture that governs what its members talk about, how much, and in what circumstances.

The amount of time the children and parents spent dancing together above and beyond what was needed to take care of everyday necessities influenced not only the amount of language experience the parents provided but also the amount of the children's practice using language. All of the children had ample practice using words and constructions to get the objects and attention they wanted and to influence how they were dressed and cared for. The extra talk we recorded in the parents' data began to appear in the children's data when the children started using words to explore how things work and how people respond. We began to record dances devoted to persuasion and resistance as 2-year-olds, encouraged both to act independently and to conform to society's rules, began choosing to do neither. But most often we saw children exploring the words that would entice their parents into a dance and prolong it once it began. The data showed the talkativeness of the parents becoming the talkativeness of the children.

Talkativeness affected the amount the children learned more than the language development of the children: the size of the vocabulary and the range of expression more than the words and constructions the children began to use. Talkativeness affected both the frequency of the social dance and its elaboration as the children's display of increasing knowledge drew automatically more complex responses from their parents. Talkativeness provided the children with more language experience in increasingly sophisticated social dances with expert partners whose willingness to dance encouraged both the children's talkativeness and their assurance that they were important, competent, and understood. Self-confident, talkative 2-year-olds began to use their skills, though, not only to share new discoveries with their parents but also to manipulate them and weary them with a profusion of self-centered comments. Parents who had things they needed to do and other adults available to talk with began leaving the children to practice with their toys or their siblings. The parents had gotten from their investment in dancing what they would need when their children went from the safety of home to the outside world full of mysteries and temptations: children intent on exploring experience who could and would talk with their parents about what was happening to them.

Our observations showed us children growing up and learning to talk in preexisting social worlds that were continuing to develop around them. Each child was added to a family whose members each had friends, interests, and obligations that did not include the child. Learning to talk opened the gate to the more complex and exciting world on view in the family, and the children applied all of their cognitive resources to practicing until they gained full access. This book describes the pattern of the children's practice, its influence

5

on the amount of language experience their parents provided, and the increasing extent to which the children were determining their own outcomes. For the children, mastery of the social world began with taking up talking.

CHAPTER 2

Observing Children and Families Talking

◆ ◆ ◆ ◆

This book is the second to report on a unique corpus of longitudinal data from monthly, hour-long observations of families interacting in everyday situations with 1- to 2-year-old children just learning to talk. The first book, *Meaningful Differences in the Everyday Experience of Young American Children*,[1] focused on what we saw the parents doing that was related to their children's accomplishments in terms of vocabulary resources and IQ scores at age 3 and later. We summarize the findings from that book in Chapter 9 after we describe in this book what we saw the children doing that influenced what we saw their parents doing.

The corpus of longitudinal data we collected is unique both in its size, 1,300 hours of observations, and in its demographics (see Table 1). The 42 families we observed included 13 families in professional and managerial occupations, 23 working-class families, and 6 families living on welfare. Of the children, 23 were girls, 17 were African American, and 1 was Hispanic; 4 still had no siblings at age 3, and 4 had four or five siblings. The study is further unique in recording everything said by, to, and around each of the 42 children during the unstructured activities of their daily lives at home (see Figure 1).

The study is the result of a series of decisions we made before we began. Similar to all investigators, we had to decide first what we wanted to find out about. Then we had to decide how much we wanted to know about that on how solid a basis and choose the methods of study accordingly. We had to decide why we were making the effort and what we wanted to be able to tell people that is not already common knowledge. We use this chapter to discuss the what, how, and why of the longitudinal study.[2]

What: The Object of Study

Among the aims of the longitudinal study was finding out how learning to talk changes children's social worlds. How often do parents interact with infants who babble and toddlers who talk, in families with one child and in those with several children? How much talking goes on to, around, and by children learning to talk? Do interaction patterns change as children learn to talk? If so, when, how much, and in what ways? As developmental psychologists, we assumed that children play an active part in changing their social worlds, such that it was important for us to consider the nature of childhood as well as to distinguish talking from language as an object of study.

Childhood

Childhood in America is assigned to parents (by birth or in loco) who are given responsibility for socializing infants to think and act like members of the social group.[3] Socialization proceeds through continual rearrangement of the environment as each gain in maturity by the child brings changes that encourage still more mature behavior. Walking turns an infant into a toddler who gets new toys and new demands (to

8

"behave," to speak, to stop running). First words turn a non-talker into an apprentice to conversation. Parents rearrange the environment to provide the social partners needed for learning to talk and take advantage, as always, of the special combination of gifts conferred upon childhood: genetic endowment, developmental change, and a social world.

Genetic Endowment Heredity puts in place both the characteristics that will ensure the uniqueness of every child and the genetic program that predetermines a species-specific course of maturation. Genetics contributes the musculature needed to produce speech. Genetics contributes to social learning by making infants so dependent for so long on the care of other people. Evolution has provided human infants with both the physical equipment required for learning to talk and the processes that link internal biology to external experience.

The nature and extent of the genetic contribution to language acquisition is still a theoretical question. Some linguistic theories[4] propose that though experience is necessary for acquiring a lexicon and setting language-specific parameters (e.g., word order), the complexities of grammar can be acquired only if considerable knowledge is innate (instinctual). More cognitively oriented theories, such as connectionism,[5] propose that language is acquired through interactions among developing neural networks.

Readers are referred to Elman and colleagues and Lyon and Rumsey[6] for descriptions of the sophisticated techniques developed for imaging brain activity and modeling brain processes. This research promises increasing knowledge concerning the developmental changes in human brains that "get complex behaviors (in the mature animal) from a minimal specification (in the gene)."[7] We hope our research will contribute to that research once neuroscience is ready to examine relationships between actual early experience and brain function at the level of synaptic transmission.

Developmental Change The central characteristic of childhood is change. Speech perception changes within the first year spent in a speaking environment. Changes occur in coordination among hearing what is said, seeing what a mouth is doing, and exercising the muscles of speech production.[8] Linked to changes in attention, memory, and eye–hand coordination are the changes in engagement with people and objects brought about by experience. One of the most fascinating aspects of observing infants is seeing how totally and immediately all of their senses are drawn to objects, such as lint and water, that adults no longer find interesting. Biology both equips and propels children to play an active part in their own development.

Children actively socialize their parents into modes of acting and communicating; "often first children 'break in' adults as caregivers."[9] Physical development changes what children are doing, the actions and activities they bring to their parents' attention.[10] Cognitive development interacts with physical development: "recalling words from the lexicon where newly learned words are less automatic than known [frequently practiced] words, formulating a response to something someone else says, and adding complexity (negation or a subject) to an utterance all 'cost' a child"[11] increasingly less with practice. Physical and cognitive development further interact with social development to change how children recruit and maintain the participation of a social partner in practice.

Readers are referred to any of the many child development texts[12] for detailed descriptions of the developmental changes in motor, social, language, and cognitive behavior that occur as normal children mature. All of the children we observed were normal. We saw in each all of the developmental changes the literature[13] had led us to expect. These changes provided the continuing context of learning to talk;

we assumed their influence. We wanted to add to this developmental literature rather than merely replicate it.

A Social World   Societies assign to their mature members the job of socializing infants following an agenda of acceptable approximations to the adult behaviors appropriate in the group. Eating with fingers is acceptable at 6 months old, and holding a spoon overhand is acceptable at age 2, but by the time a child debuts in the social groups of public school, the child needs to hold the spoon the way adults do. The end points of socialization are the cultural givens: how people act alone and together (cultural norms of decency and deference) and how they talk, to whom, and about what (communicative competence).[14]

Socialization is the "interactional display to a novice of expected ways of thinking, feeling, [talking], and acting."[15] Infants are not only continuously exposed to models of cultural norms but also are prompted, guided, and eventually pressured by parents to "do as I do." Just as parents who cannot explain eye–hand coordination can recognize improvements in eating with a spoon, parents who deny all knowledge of grammar can recognize whether an utterance is acceptable.[16] Because parents are members of society, they have already learned what is needed to socialize the next generation.

The importance of the first 3 years of life when children are so dependent on the family lies in the power of a social group to influence what is learned. Meanings and standards are established by the culture, and "subtle interactional factors shape and socialize children to think and act like members of their own [cultural] groups."[17] Learning to talk socializes children "to use signs whose meaning is socially rather than individually determined."[18] The expression of individual genetic endowment and the changes brought about by development happen within the social world of the family. The object of our work is an empirical description of that social world.

Talking

Talking, if it is to be understood by members of a social group, requires some grasp of the language spoken by the group. Talking implies the acquisition of language, but as children with tracheostomies and children with cerebral palsy have shown,[19] language can be acquired without talking. Attempts to separate talking and language for purposes of study are seen in the terminology specialized to distinguish between them: *parole* and *langue*,[20] performance and competence,[21] learning and acquisition,[22] vocabulary and lexicon, and utterances and sentences. Talking denotes observable behavior, what people say using words or signs. Language denotes a mental system that organizes what people know about words or signs. Talking displays the vocabulary words that make sense in the situation of speaking. Language stores words in a mental lexicon along with their pronunciation and meanings. Talking produces utterances containing words in linear strings. Language systematizes the rules governing the syntax and morphology of sentences. Talking is a social activity consisting of acts of expression, conversation, and persuasion. Language is the mental organization of the knowledge that makes communication possible.

The study of talking has focused on environmental contributions, the influence of interaction context and child-directed speech on language development. The study of language has focused on how children, given sentences as input and the cognitive capacity to generate hypotheses, go about acquiring the semantics, syntax, and pragmatics of the language.[23]

Influences on Talking   Talking as social behavior is influenced by cultural norms,[24] by SES,[25] by the social[26] and material[27] context of interaction, by developmental changes in the child, and by who the social partner is, mother or father,[28] sibling,[29] or peer.[30] Studies of talking have been concerned with observing what parents do that facilitates language development.[31] A considerable literature has described interactions between white, middle-class parents and their children; increasing numbers of cross-cultural studies[32] are adding descriptions of interactions in the cultures of the South Pacific[33] and Central and South America[34] and in American subcultures.[35] These studies have shown how varied are the circumstances in which children learn to talk.

Parents in middle-class American families are described as prompting reciprocal responses from infants during games of turn taking in which they fill in the infants' turns if necessary[36] and model words at the junctures where words naturally occur.[37] They get and hold their infants' attention with the simplified, stressed speech of parentese[38] and gradually increase the complexity of what they say, "fine tuning" their talk to the children's developing abilities.[39] When their children start to talk, parents begin to imitate as a prompt for imitation[40] and respond to their children's immature utterances by extending and expanding them into more advanced and grammatical forms.[41] Parents encourage their children to display advances in learning when they accept their children's early attempts at saying words[42] and provide positive feedback more often than negative.[43] Parents talk a lot[44] so that their children will too.[45]

Interaction context influences the amount and kinds of talking that go on. Directives often call on children to do something without necessarily speaking.[46] Conversation calls on children to use the information in parent utterances to formulate a contingent reply.[47] Social monologues in which parents hold the floor to describe their own or their children's activities set the stage for the private speech that emerges in children's pretend play.[48] Studies of environmental influences have focused on conventions such as turn taking and on the models of speech from which children learn language, leaving much to be discovered about what is happening during conversations and about the influence of practice on learning to talk.

Influences on Language   Language as knowledge is influenced by the cognitive capacities that children bring to the acquisition task and the extent to which they rely on the speech they hear and on their general cognitive processing capacities for analyzing the data from the adult language.[49] Psycholinguistic studies are concerned with inferring from data what must be happening mentally in order to account for the observed changes in what children say.

Children are seen to assume readily that a particular sound wave refers to the situation they are currently observing, and they naturally represent concepts lexically and propositionally. They conceive the word as the natural domain of simple concepts, and they interpret events in a propositional structure (e.g., as agent–action).[50] As active, cognitively driven processors of experiential data, including language data, children are seen to look naturally for patterns, to formulate hypotheses about relationships among items in the data, and to test patterns and hypotheses against new data as it comes in, assimilating new data that fit the hypothesized system and, when crucial data do not fit, reorganizing the system.[51] A central problem in processing language data is that because parents speak grammatically and very rarely correct children's immature productions, the children have no firm basis (negative evidence) for knowing whether their hypotheses are right or wrong and thus whether the system they are currently using needs to be revised in order to acquire all of the complexities of the adult language.[52]

Readers are referred to the works cited in the previous paragraph for fuller (and perhaps more accurate) explanations of the work on language acquisition, and to Bloom's[53] succinct discussion of the fascinating debates and insights of psycholinguistic research. This research has elucidated for us the cognitive processes that must underlie learning to talk and has enriched our understanding of what children are attempting to say when they take up talking. But our focus is on interaction, on the child as a social partner. Therefore, we expressly do not address the question of what the children may have had in mind when speaking[54] or the important influence on interactions of children's intentions[55] and parent's purposes.[56] It would take another, quite different book to do so, and we have something important to report, first, about what children are doing and being encouraged to do as they learn to talk.

How: Methods

Whether for the study of learning to talk or of acquiring language, the source of the data is necessarily a child. Methods relate to how, when, where, and in what form records of a child's speech are obtained and to how reliable they are as a basis for knowing. Data may be collected from direct observation, from tests, or from parent report. Data may be collected in natural field settings or in laboratory settings. The form of the data collected may be quantitative or anecdotal. A great many studies combine methods so as to observe both in homes and in laboratory settings[57] or to collect data from both observation and parent report.[58]

Sampling

Whatever data are collected will always be only a sample of what a child can say; and what a child says, if appropriate, will always be at least partly determined by the circumstances of saying. A test can present pictures, and laboratory settings can limit the people, materials, and space available so as to control what children talk about. The trade-off for data on what children say in controlled circumstances is uncertainty about differences in children's familiarity with the test and laboratory materials.[59] In the natural setting of the home,

15

children can be expected to talk about what is familiar, and many of the daily circumstances for children just starting to talk are likely to be those that give rise to the words listed as "common knowledge" among toddlers.[60] The trade-off for data on what children say spontaneously is uncertainty about a child's actual skill level, for some words and constructions are so infrequently called for in everyday conversation that a child may never be heard to say them during data collection. Baby biographies and parent reports can fill in the order of acquisition of these rarely heard forms, but the trade-off is uncertainty about differences among observers. Baby biographies are often recorded by parents who are linguists[61] and thus likely to be more alert than untrained observers to the use of rare forms. Parent reports similarly depend on parents to notice and remember what their children say.

Whatever the method used to collect samples of what children say, it will have disadvantages as well as advantages and will largely determine the kinds of analyses that can be performed on the data and the conclusions that can be drawn. The literature on methodology is much too extensive even to summarize here. Instead we describe the decisions we made from reading that literature as we set out to collect the data we report in subsequent chapters. The purposes of the study itself determined for us the first four decisions.

Decisions

First, because we wanted to find out about the everyday interactions between children and parents at home, we had to collect the data in family homes. Rather than add to knowledge from parent reports of how they are raising their children[62] or from interviews and tests,[63] we wanted to fill the considerable gap in our knowledge about what actually goes on in the daily lives of ordinary people raising children. Then we could supplement the data by asking parents to report milestones and family events.

Second, because we wanted to find out how casual family interactions support and encourage children who are learning to talk, we could not structure or specify what should happen during data collection. Rather than add to knowledge concerning interactions in nuclear, white, middle-class families,[64] we wanted to find out about a range of families from the least to the most advantaged in education and financial resources. Then we could compare interactions across demographic groups and select subsamples of activities such as mealtimes.

Third, because we wanted to find out how family interactions change as children learn to talk, we had to collect data longitudinally, in the same homes over time. Then we could select subsamples to compare children at specified ages or skill levels cross-sectionally.

Fourth, because we wanted to find out about the typical pattern of change in interactions, we needed to observe families for comparable amounts of time so that we could average the data to reveal trends and relationships between partners and skills. Then we could report the data descriptively, with examples quoted verbatim from the transcriptions as we do in the subsequent chapters, and substantiate our descriptions with reliability-tested numbers.

Variability and Naturalness

The decision to observe unstructured interactions in ordinary people's homes meant planning for naturalness and variability. Laboratory settings have the advantage of constraining the variability in what people do by presenting the same situation to them all. But people are likely to show what they *can* do when given the perhaps enriched materials and uninterrupted opportunities presented in a laboratory setting rather than what they actually *do* do on a routine basis in ordinary circumstances.[65]

We decided to collect enough data so that we could average out the inevitable variability within families that are continually adapting to changes in their children and developing family relationships.[66] We decided that rather than time sample and record only at 10-second intervals, for instance, or event sample and record only when interaction was occurring, for instance, we would record continuously everything that was said in a family for a full hour every month. As it turned out, this gave us an average of 800 utterances per family per month to examine for consistency over time. We decided to observe for an hour each month because our pilot work had shown us that some 1-year-olds could be engaged by the novelty of unnatural parent behavior for as long as half an hour, but then they forced their parents either to deal with a tantrum or to behave more naturally.

Observer Effects   The issue central to naturalness is observer effects. Parents have been shown to do more and behave more appropriately during periods when they have been told that their behaviors are being recorded.[67] But after repeated observations, observers begin to record negative parent–child interactions, an indication that the parents have habituated to the presence of an observer.[68] Because informed consent is prerequisite to any study, parents must be made fully aware that their behavior is being recorded. Thus the issue is mitigating rather than eliminating observer effects.

Rather than put an observer in a home, the Bristol[69] study brought equipment to the home on one day every 3 months and put a radiomicrophone on the child. Between 9 A.M. and 6 P.M., the recorder randomly self-actuated for 90 seconds at approximately 20-minute intervals. Then that evening the resulting tape was played for the parents, who reported for each 90 seconds what the child had been doing, where, and with whom and interpreted any child utterance that was difficult to understand. As Wells noted, the data were "affected by . . . whether either of the parents had been present during the 90 seconds . . . and by their ability or willingness"[70] to recall the day's events in detail. The Bristol study provides an example of a necessary trade-off between breadth and depth of study. The Bristol study collected 27 minutes of data every 3 months from 128 children for 2¼ years. We collected 60 minutes of data every month from 42 children for 2½ years.

We decided to put the observers in the homes so that the parents could watch what the observer was doing and could ask questions or explain a situation. We assigned observers to families so as to enhance cultural match and interpersonal rapport and developed procedures that would make the purposes of the study evident to parents. The observer, carrying a tape recorder on a shoulder strap, watched the child and wrote continuous notes, using pretrained codes, about what the child was doing, where, and who was present and speaking to the child. The observers never watched or commented on interactions or events that did not involve the child being observed, and they turned away from them if they could. They looked at the parents and other people only when these people interacted with the child.

The observers never interacted with the child and never followed the child to another room without parental permission. They talked with the parent about the child only after the observation, when they commented on the interesting and novel behaviors they had seen; they never gave advice even when asked, and they never said anything derogatory about the child or agreed if the parent did. The observers worked at becoming an appreciative but neutral presence, and we consider our reward to be the willingness of all of the families to have an observer in their homes every month for 2½ years.

Taping   Care for naturalness also led us to use audiotape. Videotape is always a researcher's first choice for recording; the wealth of information it holds about what a child is looking at or acting on is especially important in order to infer reliably what a child had in mind when the child spoke. In homes, though, the observers had to follow children up and down stairs, into the yard, and down the street; they had to stand in the hall while a child was going to the toilet; and, because families who live in dangerous neighborhoods keep their shades drawn, they sometimes had to observe in darkened rooms. They found particularly useful the pretrained codes for noting speech addressed to the child by people who were not in the same room as the child and for parent talk that alternated among several children while the parent focused on a household task such as washing dishes.

Objectivity and Accuracy   Care for naturalness led us not to propose bringing additional, unfamiliar observers into the homes for reliability recordings. The observers trained together for 9 months until they achieved 90% levels of interobserver agreement on each coded behavior first on videotaped interactions and finally on audiorecordings made in two actual families recruited especially to provide settings for training and subsequent reliability recordings. Instead of bringing additional, unfamiliar observers into the homes, we placed five different checks on the objectivity and accuracy of the data at successive steps in collecting and processing it:[71] 1) an hour of independent recording by all of the observers simultaneously every 6 months in one of the homes in which the observers had trained, 2) independent transcription by a second person of a randomly selected section of 56% of the monthly audiorecordings made in the homes, 3) independent verification by a second person, word for word and line by line, of the transcriptions of two tapes per year per child, 4) independent re-coding by a second person of 22 randomly selected computer files, and 5) computation of the split-half reliability of each variable analyzed in the completed database. Furthermore, when we selected from the continuous recordings particular times and activities for special consideration,[72] we assessed the reliability of the time sampling or event sampling as we did so.

Creating a Database

To find out what was happening in family homes and how patterns of interaction were changing as children learned to talk, we needed to aggregate all of the observations into a database that could reveal which behaviors were common across all of the diverse families and which behaviors were idiosyncratic or happenstance. We needed to code for computer processing the categories of behavior we were interested in analyzing (see Table 2).

After each observation the observer transcribed the audiorecording. She wrote sequentially in standard orthography each utterance heard on the tape, meshing utterances with the contexts noted in the home. Then she added codes for the activity setting and for whether one or both parents were present plus any siblings and others (and when they entered and left the room). She added a code for the speaker of each utterance, for whether the utterance was addressed to the child or to someone else, for any nonverbal behavior that accompanied an utterance to or by the child, for the conversational status of the utterance (e.g., a response, an initiation), and for closure of an interaction by the absence of a response within 5 seconds of an utterance. Any other notes the observer made in the home were added to the transcript but not assigned codes in the first pass that created the database.

Each observer-coded transcript was then submitted to a series of interactive computer programs that prompted the user to verify or change each code as it was added to each utterance to mark syntax and to each word to mark part of speech. In order to compare our data with the literature, we used the terms and categories supplied in standard grammars and dictionaries and added codes for kinds of feedback (e.g., repetition, expansion, praise). Table 2 lists the features coded in the data; Figure 1 shows an example of a coded transcript.

21

For each observed person, the computer counted how much of each coded behavior occurred in that hour. It stored the number within that person's cumulative file within that person's family file within the 42 family files that constituted the database. After 2½ years, we had an immense and reliable database of 650,000 variables from which we could select to average and compare across time and families. The numbers provide an accurate and objective basis for knowing; the transcripts provide verbatim examples to illustrate what the numbers show. We provide an interpretation of the data from a developmental perspective and add our impressions of the daily lives of 42 American children learning to talk.

Why: Finding Answers

We wanted to find out what children and parents are doing together during the months children are learning to talk so that we could fill a gap in knowledge about how interactions change as babbling babies become members of a society of talkers. Even before we saw the size of the database, it was clear from our observations that if we were to understand what was actually happening between children and parents, then we would need to analyze the data beyond the level of the utterance. We would need to aggregate the data so that we could describe lawful changes in interaction patterns and significant categories of family experience that contribute to differences in children's accomplishments at age 3.

Analysis

We analyzed the data at the utterance level first, though, to assure ourselves that the families did not differ from the norms described in the literature. These analyses showed us that all 42 children were gaining in vocabulary size, sentence constructions, and mean length of utterance (MLU) in morphemes at ages almost identical to the norms reported in the literature[73] (see Table 3) and that their parents were using the kinds of utterances regularly recorded in studies of parent–child interactions,[74] asking questions, giving directions, and repeating and recasting their own and the children's utterances. But we decided not to compare the data with the rich literature that has categorized individual utterances in terms of their meaning,[75] intentions,[76] or communicative functions,[77] their status as speech[78] or illocutionary acts,[79] or as evidence of increasing pragmatic,[80] semantic,[81] or syntactic[82] knowledge.

As we transcribed and coded the more than 175,000 child utterances in the corpus, we encountered over and over the "seemingly lawless omission of every sort of major constituent"[83] and saw that the "semantic status of early words [seemed] as unclear and uncertain for the child as for the observer"[84] or the parent, such that "early speech should be more accurately described as views about how adults understand (or fail to understand) child speech than as views about child speech itself."[85] One parent's comment on her 15-month-old's use of "Mom" ("'Mom' is not a person. It's a verb she uses when she wants something") plus much of the data showed us that all utterances are multifunctional.[86] We saw questions, for instance, serving as both directives ("Can you put it in the trash?") and declaratives ("Was that a nice thing to do?"). The data continually recalled to us Lakoff's[87] question: Why are there so many different ways of saying the same thing if communicating information is the business of language?

Conversation

Rather than an exchange of utterances or information, what seemed to be happening in increasing numbers of the interactions we observed was conversation. We saw many interactions concerned with giving and getting things ("Here you go," "Look") and frequent occasions for children to learn to follow instructions and direct the actions of others. But in roughly half of all the contacts we recorded between parents and children, only one party spoke, usually only as much as needed to transact business. The increasing amounts of talking we recorded seemed to co-occur with increasingly longer conversations.

According to Coulthard,[88] conversation is the most basic use of language, the "small talk" that holds social groups together. Conversations are the social dances cultures use to establish and cultivate relationships rather than to convey information or to cooperate on a task.[89] To people who have learned to dance, conversation seems natural and easy, but a whole research field, ethnomethodology, is devoted to studying the complexity of what goes on in casual conversations.[90]

In conversation, as in dancing, steps must be simultaneously related, reciprocal, and complementary. In waltzing, for instance, each partner has to perform a similar pattern of steps and respond immediately to the partner's steps by stepping in the opposite direction. In conversation, each partner must say something related to a shared topic and respond immediately with an utterance that enables conversation to continue.[91] In addition, each partner in conversation has to cooperate in obeying the rules that govern the behavior of speakers and hearers.[92] Acting as speaker, each partner undertakes to say clearly and concisely something relevant and true. Acting as hearer, each partner undertakes to assume that the speaker is cooperating and therefore tries to make sense of what is said even when it is not immediately apparent.[93]

To participate in conversation, children have to listen to what their parents say to them and construct an answer that both shares the same topic and adds something to which their parents can then respond.[94] Children can learn words and utterances by listening. Observational learning,[95] rote memorization,[96] and imitation[97] are routes to an initial repertoire that, when combined with gestures, may suffice for as long as a year of essential transactions. But conversation does not seem to be learned from exposure. Children are exposed daily to the varied conversational exchanges between adults and older children and frequently to their parents' actions during games of turn taking. Yet long after they are producing words and utterances, they are still only gradually learning how to take something from what someone else says and use it to answer that person in a way that converts turn taking into conversation.[98]

As compared with the interactional contexts of directives and social monologues, conversations are likely to be occasions of maximum mutual attention. Children are likely to be listening for vocabulary content and attempting utterance forms to construct answering responses. Parents are likely to be listening, watching what their children are doing, and prompting in an effort to make sense of what the children are saying. We decided to aggregate the data so that we could examine patterns of change in parent–child interactions as the children we observed gradually gave up babbling to their toys, began recruiting partners for turns at talk, and ended by dominating conversations.

Endnotes

1. Hart & Risley (1995).
2. For details about designing the study, training the observers, recruiting families, and collecting and processing the data, see Hart & Risley (1995). Recruiting and attrition are described in Hart & Risley (1990).
3. Gleason (1988).
4. Pinker (1994).
5. Seidenberg (1997).
6. Elman et al. (1996); Lyon & Rumsey (1996).
7. Elman et al. (1996, p. 365).
8. Jenkins (1991).
9. Ochs (1986, p. 2).
10. Green, Gustafson, & West (1980).
11. Bloom (1991, p. 24).
12. Bee (1975); Carmichael (1954); Gesell (1928); Mussen, Conger, & Kagan (1974).
13. See Table 3 for comparisons of the data from the present study to data from prior studies of language development.
14. Brown & Levinson (1978); Ervin-Tripp (1971); Hart & Risley (1995); Hymes (1972).
15. Ochs (1986, p. 2).
16. Harris & Davies (1987).
17. Gleason (1988, p. 276).
18. Ryan (1974, p. 185).
19. Lenneberg (1967).
20. de Saussure (1959).
21. Chomsky (1957).
22. Lyons (1968).
23. Golinkoff & Gordon (1983).
24. Field & Widmayer (1981).
25. Gottfried (1984); Wachs (1984).
26. Chisholm (1981).
27. O'Brien & Nagle (1987).
28. Gleason (1975).

29. Barton & Tomasello (1991).
30. Wilkinson & Rembold (1982).
31. Snow (1986).
32. Schieffelin & Eisenberg (1984).
33. Schieffelin & Ochs (1983).
34. Wilhite (1983); Pye (1986).
35. Chisholm (1981); Gazaway (1969); Heath (1989).
36. Bullowa (1979). Kaye (1979, as cited in Golinkoff & Gordon, 1983) noted, though, that in his work he found that patterns of turn taking before children were 6 months old did not predict language or social development at age 2½ years.
37. Bruner (1975).
38. Harris (1992); Snow (1977).
39. Cross (1977).
40. Snow (1981).
41. Nelson (1973).
42. Ibid.
43. See Hart & Risley (1995) for definitions of positive and negative feedback and discussion of their relationship to children's accomplishments at ages 3 and 9.
44. Ellis & Wells (1980); Hart & Risley (1995).
45. Nelson (1973).
46. Ellis & Wells (1980); Newport, Gleitman, & Gleitman (1977).
47. Bloom, Rocissano, & Hood (1976).
48. Smolucha (1992).
49. Bloom (1991).
50. Gleitman & Wanner (1982).
51. Peters (1986).
52. Pinker (1988).
53. Bloom (1991).
54. Locke (1988).
55. Bloom, Margulis, Tinker, & Fujita (1996).
56. Durkin (1987).
57. Bloom (1993); Nelson (1973); Wells (1985).
58. Bates, Bretherton, & Snyder (1988).
59. Nichols (1981).

60. Fenson et al. (1992).
61. Braine (1976); Dromi (1987); Halliday (1975); Tomasello (1992).
62. Baldwin, Kalhorn, & Breese (1945).
63. Bayley & Schaefer (1964); Chase-Lansdale, Mott, Brooks-Gunn, & Phillips (1991).
64. Hoff-Ginsberg (1991).
65. Belsky, Gilstrap, & Rovine (1984).
66. Furstenberg (1985); Maccoby (1984).
67. Zaslow & Rogoff (1981); Zegiob, Arnold, & Forehand (1975).
68. Lytton (1973); Wachs (1984).
69. Wells (1985).
70. Wells (1985, p. 43).
71. Average percentages of agreement were 93 or higher for all of the reliability assessments. For a more complete description of each reliability assessment and the percentages of agreement on the categories checked, see Hart & Risley (1995).
72. See Hart & Risley (1995), pages 64–66, and Chapter 6, endnote 4, in this volume, for instance.
73. Bee (1975); Brown (1973); Gesell (1928).
74. See Snow (1986) for a review; see Hart & Risley (1995) for our analyses.
75. Bloom (1970).
76. Bates (1976).
77. Halliday (1975); Wells (1974).
78. Searle (1969).
79. Dore (1977).
80. Green (1989).
81. Bloom & Lahey (1978).
82. McNeill (1970); Pinker (1994).
83. Brown (1973, p. 140).
84. Veneziano (1988, p. 133).
85. Ryan (1974, p. 205).
86. Brown & Levinson (1978); Streeck (1980).
87. Lakoff (1977, p. 85).

88. Coulthard (1977).
89. Gardner (1984); Lakoff (1977).
90. Green (1989).
91. Streeck (1980).
92. Goffman (1971).
93. Grice (1975).
94. Bloom et al. (1976).
95. Stevenson (1972).
96. Peters (1986).
97. Speidel & Nelson (1989).
98. Bloom (1991).

CHAPTER 3

A Social World

❖ ❖ ❖ ❖

W e introduce the observational data with an informal characterization based on the observers' impressions of the daily lives of 42 children between 1 and 2 years old growing up in a land of plenty.

Children's Lives

For the children, freedom seemed to prevail in a social world that fostered independence. An observer arrived for an observation scheduled for 10 A.M. and found that the child had just woken up. The parent put a plate of eggs and toast on the dining room table, and the child alternated playing and sitting down and eating for a while, still in the tee-shirt in which the child had slept. Another parent put a handful of dry cereal on a kitchen chair so the child could return periodically from play in other parts of the house to take a few bites. All of the children were fed on demand, given a cracker, juice, or cheese between meals; many parents put fruit on the low shelves of the refrigerator so the children could help themselves to healthful food.

The children were offered frequent opportunities to choose even though they would actually have a choice only after they had learned to behave in ways acceptable to the social group. Children were asked, "Are you ready to get dressed now?" "What do you want to wear today?" "Do you want me to comb your hair?" "Are you ready to eat breakfast?" and "What do you want for dinner?" Then the children were coaxed to allow their hair to be combed, were repeatedly reminded, "Use your spoon," or were nagged to finish the amount of food they were served at mealtimes. When a parent insisted that a child get dressed even though the incentive of playing outside had been removed by rain, an argument, sometimes leading to time-out, could follow. Conversation could concern the reasons that the choice of sandals and sunsuit was unsuitable in the middle of winter.

Other than choosing and informing their parents when they were hungry or wet, the children seemed to have few responsibilities. Chiefly, they were asked to bring things (purses, brushes, combs, shoes) to the parent and put things in the trash. A common solution to the problem of picking up the children's many toys was to keep them in the child's room. One parent commented, "Now that we don't keep her room so neat anymore, she spends more time playing there." The children were free to choose what to play with or to just wander around and explore. Nearly all of the children spent time watching television. Every home had at least one television set, and whether the children watched cartoons and children's programs depended on whether older children and adults wanted to watch something else.

Freedom was cut off abruptly, though, at safety and socialization. Children were offered no choices about injuring themselves or about how toileting and talking were done in the social group. Cupboards had childproof closures on the doors; stairs were blocked by gates; infant seats and seatbelts were the rule in the car. Children learned a myriad of "Don'ts" explained with "You'll get hurt," backed up, if necessary, with "Do you want to go to the doctor and get a shot?" Parents set limits for children by repeated cautions concerning swinging too high and reaching for objects that were hot, sharp, or dirty.

Parents explained about clothing ("You'll be cold," "It won't look nice") and food ("Don't you want to grow up to be big and strong?"), but they never explained the necessity for toilet training, and no child was heard to ask, "Why?" The children may have been sufficiently impressed by the regularity with which parts of their bodies were wiped while their parents commented expressively on how disagreeable was "making a mess."

Some children chose to be toilet trained; most of them were children who had a slightly older, same-sex sibling they could join in the bathroom. In other cases the parent had a hard time motivating the child to give up the freedom of wearing diapers. Among the 42 children, toilet training was begun as early as 18 months old and as late as 30 months old. Training techniques varied. One child was set on a potty chair and was simply returned there every time he got up throughout an hour of observation. Another child was similarly set on a potty chair, but it was one with a tray on which was an array of books. For other children, parents used stickers and candy to motivate sitting on the potty even though the children said, "I don't gotta pee."

Children could choose the topics of talk and whether to talk, but if they were to avoid yet another parental "I don't understand," then talking had to be done in a certain way. Only in privacy could a cow safely be called a horse; in the presence of other people, referring to three as "two" virtually guaranteed a response. The answer to a casual "How are you?" is "Fine"; the response to "Thank you" is "You're welcome."

The children learned to talk like everyone else in the social group, just as they learned to toilet themselves and follow the rules governing safety and cooperation. Having done that, some children seemed to act as though they had learned all of

33

the rules necessary for independent living: Be careful, use the toilet, talk sense. The observers began to hear children ask why they needed to obey a parent directive and parents, after giving a series of reasons, end the discussion with, "Because I'm the mom."

We want to describe how, when, and in what ways interactions changed as the children learned to talk, but first we need to describe the data and the families. The data showed two circumstances that were similar across families: patterns of family talk and of parent–child interaction. Three circumstances differed across families: the gender of the child, the birth order of the child, and the sociability of the family.

Similar Circumstances

The social environment in which the children were learning to talk was simultaneously unique to each family and similar among all of the families. In all of the families the children were surrounded by the talk of family members, visitors, the radio, and the television: Words were everywhere. All of the children were nurtured in interactions that provided for their needs, comfort, and entertainment.

Patterns of Family Talk

Perhaps most striking of all of our findings from the observations was the sheer amount of children's exposure to talk and interaction among the people around them. Over the years of observation, we regularly recorded an average of 700–800 utterances per hour within the children's hearing (see Figure 4). Approximately half of the utterances were addressed to the children; equally often the children heard their parents, siblings, and other people such as visitors and grandparents talking with one another. All of the parents talked consistently more to the child, exceeding by 150–200 the average number of utterances they addressed to the other people present within the child's hearing. As though talking to babies was the parents' job, other people such as siblings and relatives talked relatively little to the children, even after the children had learned to talk.

The background of ambient family talk around the children remained remarkably stable. Over the years the amount and consistency of the children's exposure to other people talking provided the children considerably richer and more varied experience with words and conversations than we had expected. The amount of exposure is even more impressive when we remember that the observer always followed the child, and the amount does not represent all the family talk but only the amount said within the child's hearing. Even after the children had learned to talk and began to spend time playing outdoors and elsewhere away from their parents and were talked to less by parents and more by other children, the children were still surrounded by other people's conversations.

If the children listened to other people's conversations when they were 11–19 months old, before they were saying 100 recognizable utterances per hour themselves, then they heard talk that was somewhat different than the talk addressed to them. Their parents not only used a richer vocabulary and longer clauses when talking to other people, they said more sentences and fewer such phrases as "Hi there." More of their sentences to other people (60%) were statements (an average of 115 declaratives such as "I'll do that" per hour), in contrast to 27% to the children. Parents asked other people an average of 33 questions per hour; they asked the baby an average of 83 questions per hour. Though parents addressed equal numbers of imperatives ("Do as I say") to everyone, more of their prohibitions were addressed to the baby, an average of seven directives such as "Stop," "Quit," or "Don't do that" per hour, in contrast to an average of five to the other family children. The proportions of statements, directives, and questions in the talk of the other children and adults, both among themselves and to the baby, were almost identical to the proportions in the parents' talk.

When averaged over the 2½ years of observations in these typical American families, the number of utterances the parents said per hour to children learning to talk was surprisingly consistent, an average of 300–400 utterances per hour. This average is somewhat higher than the average of 278 utterances per hour that Wells[1] reported for the 128 families in the Bristol study. But the longitudinal data from socioeconomically diverse families in an English city revealed a similar pattern of increasing amounts of parent talk before the children were 19 months old and decreasing amounts after the children were 30 months old (see Figure 4).

Patterns of Parent–Child Interaction

Long before the children began saying words, it was clear that they had learned the social skills fundamental to interaction. They were adept at getting and holding their parents' attention, taking turns, and maintaining interaction by cooing, smiling, and babbling. But interaction was not continuous. As one parent said, "I used to think until we did this study that I talked all the time to her [the baby], and now I realize there are quiet times. She's there with me playing on the floor, and I'm fixing dinner, and if she makes a sound I'll mimic it back, but I'm not constantly communicating like I thought I did."

Rather than being continuous, interaction occurred in bouts. An interaction could contain many turns if parent and child engaged in a long question–answer exchange while looking at a catalog, or an interaction could contain only one turn if a parent, stepping over a child absorbed in play, said, "Excuse me," and moved on.

Episodes In the observational data we marked the beginning and end of each occasion that families and children directed social behavior to one another. These became episodes of social interaction; an episode was delimited by at least 5 seconds of no social behavior. We coded an episode of interaction as ending, for example, when the person addressed did not answer within 5 seconds. (Within a conversation, one need only to time a 5-second pause to realize how very long it is and get the impression that no one is going to answer.)

Episodes of social interaction occurred against a background of noninteraction. A child played with a saucepan and lids as a parent fixed dinner, each engaged in active manipulation of materials. An opportunity for interaction occurred when one of them initiated, touched, gave, or said something to the other. In some families we observed, parents initiated frequently and then persisted in touching or talking until their children responded, after which the parents worked to keep the interaction going. Episodes could be long bouts of stimulating the child through affectionate play and talk. We also observed families in which the parents seldom initiated except to provide care or to manage their children's behavior and usually said only as much as needed.

Initiations   To our surprise, the children did most of the initiating (see Figure 5). When the children were 12–19 months old, still babbling most of the time, we recorded an average of 96 interactional episodes per hour. More than half (59%) were initiated by the children touching, babbling, or offering their parents something. Over the 2½ years of observations, the children continued to initiate interaction more often than their parents; they also responded more often when initiated to. The parents were only half as likely to respond to a child initiation as the children were to a parent initiation. Even after the children were talking, their parents responded to only about three of four of their children's initiations to them.

We were also surprised to see how often initiations did not lead to conversation between people. Over the 2½ years of observations, only about half (40%–60%) of all of the children's interactions contained an exchange of words or objects between child and parent. Nearly half of the time, the parent or more probably the child initiated, said one or more utterances, gave an object, and then went on to another activity without waiting for or further prompting an answering behavior. Parents gave directions that required only compliance (a parent said, "Put your feet in here," as she put on the child's shoes), or they answered themselves (the same parent said as the child left the room, "Where you going? Oh, gonna get your doll"). The child did not answer.

Floorholding We coded a social interaction as beginning with an initiation; it could end there if other people did not notice the behavior or responded by ignoring it and the initiator did not persist. Often, though, a speaker added an explanation, an amplification, or a repetition before taking no response for an answer. We labeled such utterances floorholding. A parent, after the child did not respond to "That's yours," added, "Where's that big bear? Is it behind you?" (See the examples at the end of this chapter.) Before the children began saying words, an average of half or more of all parent utterances (200 of the 350 per hour) were coded as floorholding (see Figure 5). Parents engaged in social monologues in which they persisted in holding the baby's attention, talking, filling in the baby's turn, touching and asking questions to prompt the baby to respond, and pointing and showing the baby objects, thus exposing the baby to an incredible amount and variety of interactional behavior.

Then, after the children were talking, the children took over the floorholding. After they were 30 months old, an average of 200 of the 400 utterances they produced per hour were coded as floorholding. Parents' floorholding utterances steadily decreased in number per hour as the children's floorholding utterances steadily increased (see Figure 3). When the children's average rate of talking matched their parents' average rate and they began holding the floor as often as their parents did, their parents' rate of talking to the children decreased markedly. Parents who a few months before had been actively prompting and encouraging their children to talk began to comment to observers that as much as they enjoyed the child, "She talks too much," or, "You can't shut him up."

Responses The social behavior that remained virtually unchanged over the 2 years of learning to talk was responsiveness. We have noted that both parent and child spoke in only approximately half of all interactions. But in interactions containing utterances by both parties, child and parent were always equally likely to answer one another. During the 2½ years of observations, the average ratio of parent-to-child responses was 50:50 (see Figure 5). The number of responses recorded per hour increased as interactional episodes became longer and contained more exchanges of talk, but there was no change in the probability of getting an answer once conversation started. What changed was how much prompting (floorholding) was necessary for parents, and later on for children, to get a conversation started.

We averaged family behaviors over the 2 years that the children were learning to talk so that we could see overall patterns and how interactions changed as the children developed. For the convenience of separate chapters, we have divided the data into three successive periods. The first period, when the children were 11–19 months old, we labeled *becoming partners* because although the children were still primarily vocalizing and using words infrequently, they and their parents began acting as partners who answer one another. The second period, when the children were 20–28 months old, we labeled *staying and playing* because the children were enjoying for a brief time intensive, one-to-one conversations with an expert at prompting practice. The third period, when the children were 29–36 months old, we labeled *practicing* because the children were primarily speakers busily displaying their repertoires for feedback and elaboration by their parents as listeners. We will describe in subsequent chapters what was going on between the children and parents during each of these periods. First, however, we need to examine the differences among the 42 children learning to talk in similar family circumstances and the differences among the families themselves.

Different Circumstances

We had deliberately sought families to represent differences in size and cultural background, and we had recruited to ensure equal numbers of boys and girls. We knew that the individual attributes of children and families would affect children's cumulative experience. Among our first questions of the data was whether there were large and consistent differences among the families. Did gender and birth order, for example, just add to the variability we saw in the data, or did parents over the 2½ years of observations regularly talk longer and more often with firstborn children or with girls?

Different Children: Gender

In these contemporary American families we saw almost no signs of gender discrimination. We regularly saw fathers performing household tasks, doing laundry, or dressing the children. Boys played with dolls, and girls played with trucks. Most of the children wore shorts or pants while playing at home; boys and girls were equally likely to be invited to "help" a parent cook dinner. The data revealed no overall differences in the amount of talk addressed to girls versus boys.

Different Children: Birth Order

Birth order did make a difference, though, during all three of the periods we have labeled *becoming partners, staying and playing,* and *practicing.*

Becoming Partners In two thirds of the observations, the 11 firstborn children were alone with a parent or parents for the entire hour. Not surprisingly, two thirds of the family talk (an average of 425 utterances per hour) was addressed to the child (with the remainder addressed to the telephone, the observer, or the other parent). Whether from devotion, the absence of anyone else to talk to, or the uncertainty lent by inexperience, the parents of firstborn children talked to their 11- to 19-month-old children much more often (averaging 100 more utterances per hour) than parents talked to later-born children of similar age.

In families with more than one child, one or more siblings were present in 70%–90% of all of the observations. More talk went on in these families (an average of almost 800 utterances per hour, 200 utterances more per hour on average than in the families with a firstborn child), but less than half (an average of slightly more than 300 utterances per hour) was addressed to the baby. Between the ages of 11 and 19 months, the 18 second-born children were exposed to slightly more talk going on around them than were the 13 third- or fourth-born children, but they were talked to about the same amount.

In terms of the amount of parental attention available, firstborn children were at considerable advantage; for later-born children, having five siblings was little different from having just one. Having two parents at home also made little difference. In 27 families we could compare amounts of talk to the baby when only one parent was present and when both parents were at home. When both parents were available to interact with the baby, the baby was talked to more in 16 families and less in 11 families.

Staying and Playing When the children were 20–28 months old and engaging in increasing numbers of conversations with their parents, the average amount of parent talk to firstborn children increased only a little (to 480 utterances per hour), but the amount addressed to later-born children increased to an amount (an average of 420 utterances per hour) comparable to the amount addressed to firstborn children. The social monologues that many firstborn but few later-born children heard decreased markedly. Approximately 70 utterances per hour of the increased talk to later-born children were addressed to the children by other children and adults.

The largest increase relative to the period of becoming partners (11–19 months old) was in talk to third- and later-born children. We had expected that the more experienced parents would be more confident that talking, like walking, would begin without any special efforts on their part; they surprised us with how expertly they recognized their children's readiness and how efficiently they dropped into staying and playing. One parent of a third-born child commented, "I know what I'm doing here." Parents even drew the children's siblings into interactions to help prompt and model answers to questions.

Practicing During the period of practicing (29–36 months old), after the children were talking as much as the family, all of the parents decreased the amount they talked to the children. The largest decrease was in the amount parents talked to firstborn children, who heard about 100 fewer utterances addressed to them per hour than they had heard during the period of becoming partners (11–19 months old). The parents of second- and later-born children seemed to have "dropped in" to staying and playing and then during the period of practicing merely returned to the amount of talk they had addressed to their 11- to 19-month-old children. By contrast, the 11 parents of firstborn children (9 of whom had new babies by then) seemed to "drop out" after a period of staying and playing.

During the period of practicing, all of the children, whether first-, second-, or later-born, were talked to approximately the same amount (an average of 385 utterances per hour). Most of the talk to firstborn children was by their parents, though other children were more often invited to the house to play. For second- and later-born children, a decrease in parent talk was made up by talk from siblings, and children with two or more siblings were talked to more by their siblings (an average of 50 utterances more per hour) than were children with only one sibling.

Firstborn children enjoyed the advantage of receiving more close, personal attention and conversations especially adapted to prompting and maintaining interaction. Second- and later-born children traded this advantage for increased exposure (an average of 200 utterances more per hour) to talk by and among other people. The advantages of being born second or later lay both in the frequency of hearing how competent speakers talk to one another and in having siblings to talk to during the period of practicing.

Different Children: Accomplishments

Although birth order made a difference in how the families behaved toward the children, it did not seem to make much difference in the children's behavior. First-, second-, and later-born children all spoke an average of 200 times per hour during the period of becoming partners, and during the period of practicing they produced an average of 400 fully recognizable utterances per hour. We describe the range among the 42 children in Chapter 8; at both the high and low extremes, half of the children were girls, and at least one was a firstborn child.

To look at the children's accomplishments at age 3, we ran correlations between measures of the children's behavior averaged when they were 34–36 months old (number of utterances produced, number of different words used, Stanford-Binet IQ score, and rate of vocabulary growth).[2] We found no significant relationship between any of the measures of child behavior and child gender, birth order, or (after controlling for SES) race.

We were not surprised to find that there was no relation between these attributes of the children and the children's accomplishments. Within the 42 families the parent who talked most to the child and the parent who talked least to the child both were African American, middle-SES working mothers who had had their first child at a comparable age (23 and 25 years old). The children both were later-born (third and fourth); one was a boy. But the boy talked to most was born 8 years after the youngest of two girls, and the mother was working part time. The girl talked to least was the second girl after two boys; all four children were born within 5 years, and the mother was managing a business from the home. How the attributes of the individual child were received within a pre-existing family culture seemed to be far more important than those attributes themselves.

Different Families

Among the families into which the children happened to be born, the largest and least variable difference was how often family members talked and interacted. During the period of becoming partners, when the children were not yet contributing more than a few words, the amount of talk children heard addressed to them per hour ranged from 56 to 793 utterances. When the children were 29–36 months old, the range was from 34 to 783 utterances per hour. Parents who were talkative or taciturn during the 9 months their children were 11–19 months old continued to be talkative or taciturn during the 8 months when their children were 29–36 months old ($r = .84$). Most important, the children were as talkative or as taciturn as their parents during the period of practicing ($r = .65$).

In each child's family we saw behaviors that were common to all of the families: children and parents initiating interaction, responding to one another, and holding the floor during recurring episodes of interaction. We saw common patterns: extended early exposure to family talk, increased interaction when the children began to talk, and finally graduation to practice as just another family member. We saw these patterns common among well-functioning American families embedded naturally within the amount of talk that was socially acceptable within an ongoing social group, the individual child's family. We watched each child grow up and learn to talk within a family culture that transmitted day by day not only how people talk but how much they talk.

Examples: Families Talking to Children

In different families, as talk goes on to and around children, children are exposed to different kinds of conversations. Firstborn children may hear more child-directed talk. Second-born children may have more opportunities to hear talk modeled by a slightly older sibling and to practice competing for their parents' attention. Children with several siblings may hear more varied conversations going on within the family.

The following are verbatim examples typical of the interactions we observed in these families with one, two, and three children.

A Mother and Her Firstborn

Following is an example of the frequent parent–child interactions we observed that reminded us of the optimal interactions described in the literature, interactions in which parents prompt their babies to engage with the age-appropriate toys they provide, work to achieve joint attention, and describe what the child is doing in simple utterances.

> The mother puts the child, a 12-month-old, firstborn boy, down on the floor among his toys and sits down beside him. She initiates, "Now there's your bike." He does not respond, and she offers him a cookie, asking, "Want a cookie?" He does not respond, and she continues, "There's your bike. And your chair. There's your tool bench."
> The baby says a nonword, and his mother says, "That's yours." She holds the floor, continuing, "Where's that big bear? Is it behind you? There it is. Yeah, that's your big bear. Can you get on top of him?"
> The baby looks at the bear and says some nonwords. The mother says, "Yes, because he's a good bear. Good bear." The baby utters something, and his mother asks, "You see your dog over there too?"

The baby utters something and points to the dog. The mother says, "Yeah that baby dog." The baby, saying some nonwords, turns to pat the bear. His mother says, "Bear. You're patting the bear's head. Yes."

A Mother and Her First- and Second-Born Children

This is an example of the interactions we frequently saw when two children were competing for toys and attention and a parent was trying to interact with both. We were always impressed with an older sibling's skill and persistence in pre-empting any interactions between a parent and a second-born child that would resemble the interaction illustrated in the previous example. Observing parents interacting with an older sibling also provided us a preview of how the parent would interact with the younger child when the child began to talk.

The mother puts Conrad, a 12-month-old, second-born boy, in his walker and sits on the couch where his brother Ken, a 3-year-old, firstborn boy, is playing with a See 'n Say.

Ken says to his mother, "Come me. Come me." Ken's mother says, "Say 'help me please.'" Ken says, "Help me please." His mother says, pointing to the See 'n Say, "Look. Remember, mama told you last night. See this point right here? It's an arrow. Point that to the animal. Pull."

Conrad utters something, edging closer to the See 'n Say. His mother says, "You like that, Conrad, don't you?" Conrad fusses, pushing the walker against the couch.

Ken says to his mother, "Pull dog." His mother points and says, "Right there." She moves the See 'n Say to the edge of the couch where Conrad can see it, saying, "Let Conrad see. Pull it again." Ken says, "No no no," and tries to move the See 'n Say back. The mother says, "Well, this way Conrad can see it. He wants to see it too." Ken says, "No, let me pull it." The mother says, "Well, you can pull it. Just let Conrad see it." She adjusts the angle and then tells Ken, "Okay, pull it." Ken pulls the string, saying, "Me pull."

Conrad utters something as he reaches for the turning arrow on the See 'n Say.

A Mother and Father and Their Three Children

This is an example of the interactions we often saw when a number of people were present. Several conversations were conducted simultaneously as the parents distributed their attention to one another and among the children. But when more people were present to interact with the older siblings, the baby was more likely to get one person's entire attention.

The family has just finished dinner and is in the living room. The mother is sorting laundry; Leon, the 15-month-old boy, is sitting on the couch beside her. The father is sitting in an armchair, and the two older boys, Quincy (age 4) and Arthur (age 2½), are standing beside him.

The father pats Arthur's stomach, saying, "Well, you're getting fat. Maybe you eat too much candy, do you think?" Arthur says, "No, me eat some my candy." His father says, "Oh." Quincy says, "I ate too much pancakes." The father says, "Did you?" and turns to the mother, who is bussing Leon's arm, making burbling noises as he laughs and vocalizes. Arthur says, "I got candy in there." The father says, "I was supposed to wash tonight, wasn't I?" The mother answers the father, "Uh-huh," as Leon continues to vocalize. The father responds to the mother, "Did you already do it?" The mother answers the father, "I started it," and turns to Leon and makes humming noises. Leon continues to vocalize as his mother hums. The father responds to the mother, "Oh, well, that was good." Arthur continues,

"Me put this on the rocking chair." The mother says to the father, "Go check on the dryer. And there's some in the washer too." The father answers the mother, "Alright," and turns to say to Quincy, "You gonna learn my motorcycle, huh?"

Leon says some nonwords, and his mother resumes making noises, cooing at him. Quincy answers, "I wanna ride your motorcycle," and his father responds, "Well, you gotta have a hat. Where's your hat?" Quincy says, "Maybe somewhere." Uttering something, Leon reaches to open the panel that gives access to the knobs on the television. The father answers Quincy, "Well, you gotta have a hat when you get on a motorcycle," and the mother tells Leon, "No, shut the door, uh-uh." Quincy says, "You got one?" and his father answers, "I'm gonna get one tomorrow." Quincy says, "Get me one." Leon continues reaching for the knobs on the television, saying nonwords. Arthur says to his father, "Let me have a hat." The father says to the mother, "They're giving me a helmet. Comes with the bike." The mother answers the father, "Oh, really?" and then tells Leon, "No." Arthur continues, "Me want some hat," as Quincy asks, "Hey, can I have a helmet when I grow bigger?" Father answers, "Uh-huh," as Arthur continues, "Me wanna ride some motorcycle. Me park my motorcycle go up in there."

Leon's mother tries to distract him by offering a box of socks and saying, "You gonna play with the socks? Come here. You can play in the socks. That's gonna be fun." Leon takes the box. The father turns to Arthur and says, "Here, put this shoe over there with the rest of the others." Arthur takes the shoe, and his father continues, "Oh. Bring me a sock." Arthur gets a sock from inside the shoe, and his father says, "No, bring me one of them." He points to the clean socks Arthur's mother is sorting. Arthur goes to his mother, who says, "Just take daddy one." The father says, "Bring me one." Arthur takes a sock from the box. Leon gives the box to his mother. Arthur gives the sock to his father, who says as he takes it, "Alright, here." He turns to Quincy, saying, "Come here and put your hand in here." The mother accepts the box from Leon and says, "Thank you."

Endnotes

1. Wells (1986).
2. Terman & Merrill (1960). See Hart & Risley (1995) for definitions of the measures of the children's accomplishments at age 3, for explanation of how relationships were determined, and for discussion of the significant relationships found.

CHAPTER 4

Developmental Change

◆ ◆ ◆ ◆

*I*n the previous chapter we described the social worlds in which the children began learning to talk, surrounded by ambient talk among mature speakers in a family micro-culture of habitual patterns of initiating and responding and of stable amounts of talking and interacting. The social environment we observed in a family did not change very much even as new babies were born, parents went to new jobs, and the children learned to talk. The changes we saw were in what the children were doing as they gained the skills necessary to becoming competent speakers and in how their parents reacted to those changes.

Normal Development

The 42 children we observed were remarkably different in attributes and personalities, and their families and interaction styles were different, but all of the children learned to talk in just the way our textbooks had led us to expect. All of the children gradually, but never entirely, exchanged gibberish for identifiable words. As we observed over successive months, all of the children began to say longer and longer utterances; they began to include the required markers for plurals and tenses and to add words that qualified and made subtle distinctions such as that between "I hafta go" and "I gotta go." All of the children were "normal," competent speakers at age 3, able to say whatever they needed to get along in the family.

The children were alike in the overall sequence in which they added the categories described in grammar books (tenses, auxiliaries, clauses), and they were alike in gradually adding the categories and organizing them into recognizable utterances. Even the children who, after saying a few words, seemed to listen for months before "getting serious" about learning to talk, went through a sequence of building one skill on another. The sequence was much the same for all of the children, but the chronological age at which particular categories of speech, particular words, structures, and grammatical markers were first recorded varied tremendously.

The data reminded us of and impressed us with the warning in our textbooks about the extent of the "normal range" in skill learning.[1] Therefore, we describe the overall sequence of gaining skills in reference to the median chronological age, the age of the child who was midway within the range of all of the ages at which a particular skill was first recorded in the children's data. In nearly every case, the upper end of the range was 34–36 months of age. The description is based on the first 100 utterances recorded for each child in each observation, utterances for which MLU in morphemes was calculated by computer.[2] In order to facilitate comparison of the 42 children's data with data derived from reliability- and validity-tested protocols, each of the 100 utterances was examined for the use of an auxiliary or modal verb (see Table 4), the grammatical categories listed in the Index of Productive Syntax (IPSyn)[3] (see Table 5), and the vocabulary words listed in the MacArthur Communicative Development Inventory–Toddlers (CDI)[4] (see Appendix A and Table 7).

The examples we give for skill gains each month are quoted verbatim from the data of children who were at the median age during that observation. The examples are from those first recorded for the children rather than examples recorded after the children had been producing a particular form for several months. Almost all of the examples of longest utterances were the only utterance of that length for that child that month, so they often lacked the sophistication of the utterances of that length the child would be producing in subsequent months. The average MLU of the 42 children (Table 6) illustrates gaining skill in putting words in order in linear strings and adding nuances. "Normal" vocabulary growth[5] (see Table 7 and Figure 2) illustrates gaining skill in learning distinctions between words. The increasing numbers of utterances (see Table 6 and Figure 3) and different words the children used (see Table 7) display the pattern of developmental change as the children learned to talk.

First Words

Perhaps the most important normal development in learning to talk is saying the first words. Watching babies watching their families, the observers joked that the children acted as though their gibberish were a bona fide "language." They "talked" on and on to their toys just as their parents talked on and on to the telephone. Their parents seemed able to foresee all of the children's wants and interpret their every expression; the children might conclude that such parents certainly understood what the children were saying. In fact their parents often showed they understood by giving the babies what they "asked" for. The children did not need to talk, and gestures, laughing, fussing, and especially crying worked much better to attract parental attention than did babbling. A parent who prompted a word ("Say 'hi'") was readily satisfied with gibberish. Until the children said their first words, their parents just talked and waited, in exactly the same way they modeled walking and waited for their children to try doing it themselves. And just as they expected, attempts to walk and to say words appeared in due time.

Expectations for Words

The age at which the children said their first words, though, was often determined by whether the parent heard the child say something the parent could accept as an English word (rather than a word in Gibberish or Latin). Observers of other cultures have reported that children are not considered to have begun talking until they say specific words (among the Kaluli of New Guinea, "Mother" and "Breast").[6] We saw some similarity among the American families we observed: Most of the children's first words were "Mama" and "Dada." Some parents reported the words first as "nonspecific," as the textbooks say,[7] used without reference to a particular parent. But when their children said only two syllables ("Dada") rather than the string of "Dadadada" that was usual in their babbling, most parents eagerly assigned it the status of a first word.

We realized that the observers, like the parents, were interpreting the child's sounds through the culture and the language. We expected the children to talk about what they were doing and playing with. We expected their first words to be "See," "This," "Cookie," "Doggie," "Uh-oh," and "No," and they were. We also realized how important these expectations are because children's first attempts at words are so very difficult to identify. Parents had to recognize words within an average of 145 instances of gibberish per hour, at a time when they had become accustomed to hearing their children speak merely as an accompaniment to contented exploration. Parents had to recognize words within a string of expressive jargon and accept "Gih" for "Give" and "Dis" for "This." And they had only an instant to do so; when they thought they heard a word and asked, "What did you say?" no child ever repeated.

We saw among the 42 families how much depends on the interaction between a parent's ear and a child's pronunciation. The children ranged from those who pronounced words very clearly to a few who qualified for speech-language therapy when they got to school; the parents ranged from those who responded as though nearly everything the child said was a word to those who rarely guessed at what the child was trying to say and often guessed wrong when they did. But there was no relationship between the pairs. A parent with a tin ear was just as likely to have a child with clear pronunciation, and all of the children with poor articulation had parents who spoke very clearly.

Criteria for Words

Interacting with a parent's ear were the parent's criteria for words. Some parents seemed to hear words everywhere. One child was looking out the window at the neighbor's dog and said, "Duh." The parent turned to the observer and said, "See, she just said, 'dog.'" When another child held up a ball and said, "Ball," his parent commented to the observer, "It sounded like he said 'ball.' Do you think he really meant 'ball'?" We compared the month in which parents reported the child's first word with the month in which the observer recorded the child's first word. The month of the first word was the same for 18 of the children; for 15 children the parent reported a month prior and for 9 children the parent reported a month subsequent to the month the observer recorded the child's first word.

The observers had specific criteria for crediting words to children.[8] When a child spoke, the observer could code the behavior as words rather than gibberish only if, first, a word was clear on the audiotape, such that it could be verified out of context by an independent listener, and, second, the context in which the word was produced was appropriate, one that could be associated with an accepted sense of the word. If one of the criteria was not met, as when a word was not clearly articulated, then the child could be credited with the word if the parent recognized the word 1) by responding to it, repeating the word, or giving the child the named object, 2) by remarking to the observer that the pronunciation was the child's current version of the word, or 3) by explaining the context of a particular usage. We did not make parent recognition essential because the parents varied considerably in the extent to which they interpreted their children's sounds as words. But if there was any uncertainty about what the child had said, then the observers' rule was to code it as gibberish. If the word was in the child's repertoire, then it was sure to occur again in a later observation.

Recording Words

The observers were no more proficient at recognizing words than were the parents. They, too, had to distinguish words, mostly immaturely articulated words, within the stream of prespeech utterances they were used to hearing the children produce. The observers had two advantages, though. First, their sole task was to watch continuously what the child was doing. Unlike the observers, the parents were often attending to other tasks while talking to their children. For instance, one parent was making sandwiches at the kitchen counter. She asked her 10-month-old, who was sitting on the floor some distance away, "What are you doing? Are you getting that kitty cat?" The child, his face toward the cat, said in little more than a whisper, "Kih cah." The parent did not respond, and the words "Kitty cat" were not credited to the child until he said them again and the parent recognized them 2 months later.

The observers' second, and major, advantage over the parents was the tape recording. The parents had only an instant to recognize a word the child attempted; the observers could listen over and over and change the speed, volume, and pitch of the recording in order to hear a word more clearly. Also, the observers habitually wrote down during observation any word they thought the child might have said based on the match between the child's sounds and the activity or object with which the child was engaged. (For instance, the observer had written *"kitty cat?"* when the child whispered to the cat). Then they verified the word (or did not) on the tape during transcription by asking whether an independent listener, unaware of the child's activity, could identify it.

All of the observers, like the parents, benefited from repeated exposure to children's attempts at words. They learned to interpret what the child said at the same time that the children learned to speak more clearly. (After completing the study, the observers assessed the reliability of the transcriptions and so listened again to the tapes of the children during the period of becoming partners; at that time they found they could interpret far more words than those credited to the child at the time of original transcription.)

Words in Sentences

A special challenge were the six children who began speaking in intonational sentences uttered so rapidly that only by slowing down the tape could we hear the words clearly segmented. One 15-month-old was playing in a kitchen drawer, standing on a stool beside his mother, who was washing dishes. He picked up a tea caddy and threw it on the floor, where it broke apart. He laughed, looked at his mother, and seemed to have said (once the observer had drastically slowed the tape), "I dropped it, mommy, and got it open." His mother said, "I know it's funny."

The children's parents reported hearing sentences. One parent said, "She talks in sentences without saying any words you can understand." Another said, "I could have sworn she said, 'Give sis the chair.'" A third said, "I think she's talking more than we realize. It's just that she'll say something like, 'I'll get it'—I say that a lot when the phone rings—but after she says it, she walks out of the room." The parents sometimes asked, "What did you say?" but no child attempted to repeat any part of such a sentence.

Like the parents, we were not expecting children to say recognizable sentences, and even with several independent verifications we hesitated to credit a complete sentence to a child who as yet had only a 20-word vocabulary. The parents responded to their children's intonational sentences just as they did to gibberish, as though the sentences were little more singing while dancing, unrelated to taking up talking and entering into a social exchange between partners. We saw that gaining a speaking role in a social group requires that a child learn more than how to say words and sentences.

Basic Skills

In learning to talk, the children seemed to proceed much as they had in learning other skills. First, they learned to produce the moves, in this case the words, and how to articulate them so that the family could recognize them. Then they gained fluency, deciding ever more rapidly which moves (words) were called for in the current situation and how to produce them in an order that would make sense to the family; the challenge was to accomplish all of this within the momentary pause between parent utterances. As they gained fluency, the children gained flexibility so that they could shift rapidly among moves in order to respond to subtle shifts in focus during conversations.

Gains While Becoming Partners

We labeled as a period of becoming partners the months between the children's first words at 11 months old and the month the children became talkers who said as many or more utterances containing identifiable words as strings of gibber-ish within an hour. The children became talkers at an average age of 19 months old (range 15–27 months old). During the 8 months following the children's first words, the gains most obvious to the observers were physical and social. All of the children became proficient walkers; parents began to regulate jumping and encourage "dancing" when the children began bouncing to music. Parents began to make useful the chil-dren's practice of picking up things; they said, "Can you put that in the trash?" "Can you bring me my purse?" They gave children "babies" (dolls) to carry, cars to push, and toys (stack-ing rings) and pans so that the children could take things apart appropriately. Questions often directed the children to notice and point, such as "Where's your nose?" "Who's that?" "Where's sis?"

Socially the children shifted from vocalizing to speaking to people. Seemingly autistic monologues to themselves or to toys were gradually reallocated to responses to parent speech. The children began to imitate. They began to initiate with a word and to practice until the parent identified it. An average of 132 utterances per hour at 11 months old, 5 of which con-tained identifiable words, increased to an average of 305 utter-ances per hour at 19 months old, 167 of which contained iden-tifiable words. As average MLU increased from 1.2 morphemes at 14 months old to 1.3 morphemes at 17 months old, average vocabulary size quadrupled from 10 to 41 words. By 19 months old when the average MLU had increased to 1.4 morphemes, average vocabulary size had almost doubled, to 81 words.

Using the vocabulary gained during the period of becom-ing partners, the children at 19 months old could name the things they wanted ("Milk") or ask for the name ("What that?"). They could ask and answer questions ("Where mine?" "In there"). They could claim possession ("My ball"), defend ("Stop," "Don't"), negate ("Not up"), command attention ("Look," "See?"), and demand compliance ("Move," "Give me"). They were using an average of 44 different words per 100 utterances. An average of 70 of those 100 utterances were phrases ("Yes," "No," "Car"), 4 were imperatives ("Look"), 16 were declaratives ("Eat"), 4 were questions ("See?"), and 6 were the "Huh?" so many of the children used to keep interaction going. The longest utterances contained 4 words, such as "I have this back" and "See those there outside?"

Gains While Staying and Playing

During the period of staying and playing, when the children were 20–28 months old, increases in attention span and eye–hand coordination led the children to spend more and more time engaged with increasingly challenging materials. Sharing in the children's activities helped the parents make sense of what the children were saying and let them ask for clarification or elaboration without disrupting the children's play. Outdoor play, such as swinging and riding tricycles, became a setting for talk about "High" and "Low," "Push" and "Pull." "Hot" was elaborated from stoves to sunlit slides. Practicing fine motor skills, doing puzzles and "writing," became contexts for talk about eyes and feet, how letters are made, and how body parts are arranged.

Gains in physical skills joined with social and verbal skills to increase the children's independence. Children helped dress themselves and took charge of feeding themselves. Parents' encouraging, "You can do it," became children's assertion, "I can do it." Increasing cooperation in cleaning up and building towers accompanied increasingly skilled resistance: "No" became "Wait a minute," "Don't wanna," or "Why?" Gains in physical skills enabled running from a parent and fighting with a sibling. Gains in attention span led to trips to the zoo, the circus, a fair, or the home of relatives in another state. Mothers began taking jobs as the children showed they could play independently and socialize with a variety of adults and children.

When the period of staying and playing began, the children at 20 months old held the basic pieces of the game, the words, pragmatic functions, and simple sentences, and they could get something recognizable said in more than half of their turns. In subsequent months they seemed to be putting the pieces together gradually by adding, inserting, and replacing.

At 20 months old, children began adding an article before a noun, so "Book" became "A book," and "Dog" became "The dog."

At 21 months old, they began adding an -s after a noun to mark plural, so "Book" became "Books," or "What books?" and "The dog" became "The dogs." A typical longest utterance was now five morphemes long, such as "Mom, I want toys."

At 22 months old, children began adding adverbs so "I do" could become "I do again" or "I do now." Children began adding two words after a verb to say, "I want a book," "I see my baby," or "Get more diapers," or after a preposition to say, "Go up that street," "Ride that on the floor," or "It's for you." They began adding a verb after "I want" to make "I wanna go," or "I wanna do that." Between 20 and 23 months old, the average child's recorded vocabulary more than doubled to 215 words. At 22 months old, children were using 55 different words per 100 utterances. Average MLU was 2 words (1.7 morphemes), with the longest utterances containing 5 words, such as "It's on the floor" and "Now mom off the baby."

At 23 months old, children began adding -ing (the progressive morpheme) after verbs to say, "Dad doing that," "What they playing?" or "Going up that street." They began putting "don't" in place of "wanna" to say, "I don't do that."

At 25 months old, children began putting "can" before a verb to say, "I can do that." They began commenting on the past to say, "I did it," "I made it," and "Hit my leg." These additions led to the recording of longest utterances containing 6 morphemes, such as "I don't want any pickle," "She away writing names," and "Dad did that on lights."

At 26 months old, children began replacing "wanna" and "can" with "gonna" and "can't," to say, "I gonna do that," and "I can't do that." They began inserting an auxiliary verb or a negative before a verb to say, "I'm gonna do that," "You not getting no more," and, "What do you got?" They began adding -*s* to mark third person singular on verbs to say, "There he goes," or "He stinks." They produced their first combinations, turning "Watch me. I jump" into "Watch me jump" and "Let me. I do that egg" into "Let me do that egg in there."

At 27 months old, children began adding words to put a two- or three-word phrase before a verb or a three- or four-word phrase after a verb, saying, "The guy's gonna fix it," "A little bug go in there," "I get some more eggs," and "Look at this longer chip." They began putting in the copula and the *to* of the infinitive, saying, "This room's a mess," "I'll be careful," "I like to do exercise." They began putting the verb first in a question, saying, "Is my room neat?" "Does he tie his shoes?" They began adding -*ed* to verbs with a regular past tense, saying, "I dropped mine," and "I washed my hands."

At 28 months old, the children replaced the present auxiliary with the past to say, "I was playing with it," and "Did you find it?" In this last month of staying and playing, average MLU was 2.6 morphemes; the average longest utterance was 8 morphemes: "I wanna wipe it off with this one," "What's you gonna do with the record?" Average recorded vocabulary size was 448 words, and children were using an average of 75 different words per 100 utterances.

By 28 months old, the children had gained skill with all the grammatical morphemes to be added to nouns and verbs in order to mark possession, number, and tense. They had gained enough fluency to produce an average of 396 recognizable utterances per hour and enough flexibility to produce, in 100 utterances, 44 phrases, 37 declaratives, 10 imperatives, and 9 questions.

Gains While Practicing

During the period of practicing, when the children were 29–36 months old, they were engaged with independently exercising and elaborating their skills. They began going swimming, molding playdough, practicing baseball, and playing cards and board games with siblings. Increases in eye–hand coordination, attention span, and experience outside the home were evident in extended bouts of pretend play. Looking at a book became "reading" to an audience of dolls, a tea party became a restaurant, running trucks became towing or delivery to a bridge construction. A new sibling was mothered instead of a doll.

During the period of staying and playing, the children had become competent speakers who seemed able to say anything. What they gained in the period of practicing were skills in precision, brevity, and relevance. Most noticeable was the use of clauses. At 29 months old, the children began joining two sentences to say, "I find another and I'm getting it," and, "I know we can clean this." Then at 30 months, they introduced infinitives and wh-clauses, such as "Look what I got," "I show you how to do it," "You'll have whichever you're gonna have," and "Want me to wash my face?" At 32–33 months old, they began using wh- and relative clauses, such as "Why don't you let me go with you?" and "There was a little toy he wanted."

The children added precision with medial adverbs and brevity with negated auxiliaries, saying, "I didn't even fall," "It still won't go," and "We're just gonna play in her room." They began to replace "wanna" with "better," "hafta," "gotta," or "might," and to replace "can" with "could," "may," or "would." The "I wanna drink it" of 22 months old became at 29 months old "I think I better drink it." The "Help me" of 20 months old became the "Can't you help me do it?" of 33

65

months old, and "I want a ball" became "You need to buy me a basketball." The "Come in" of 19 months old became at 33 months old, "You can come all the way in if you wanna."

By 34–36 months old, the average MLU was 3.4 morphemes (3.2 words); one third of the average child's utterances were still phrases such as "Yes," "Hi," or the name or location of an object. Of the average of 413 utterances per hour, 10% were questions and 10% were imperatives. The average recorded vocabulary contained 700–800 words and the children were using an average of 97 different words per 100 utterances, of which 25% were nouns, adjectives, and adverbs and 31% were verbs. The longest utterances averaged 11 words.

The children who had begun at 11 months old with "Mom" and "Hi" were saying at 32–36 months old, "Mom, can I have a peanut butter and jelly sandwich after this?" "He's not supposed to smoke in the house, is he?" "I'm not going without my mom coming to get me," "When the fish are dead you can eat them," "Take off her pants so she can use the bathroom," and "This is mine because I don't have no sugar in mine because I don't like sugar in it."

But as fluent and flexible as they were, the children were clearly not finished learning. At 32–36 months old, the children were recorded by observers as saying, "Did you get the cup where I can't see it?," "Don't me look pretty?" and "I want her to sit on here but I can't sit her." Sometimes children seemed to sacrifice making sense in the interest of fluency and flexibility, saying something that ended up among the average of 70 nonword utterances the observers recorded each month. The observers commented on some children's seeming interest in making sentences as similar as possible to those of their parents and hence as long as possible. The longest utterance recorded within the 100-word subsamples was 31 words: "Then we can put them in here, and then we can put them in here, and then we can put them in there, and then we can put them in here."

At Age 3

By age 3, all 42 children had gained the skills necessary to speak the language spoken by their parents. They were using fluently a variety of grammatical forms; at least one instance of each of the 56 categories listed on the IPSyn as indices of grammatical complexity had been recorded for 2 or more of the 42 children by age 3. (Only those categories used by half or more of the children are shown in Table 5.) For the average child at age 3, a dictionary containing 360 vocabulary words had been recorded using only the first 100 utterances in each observation from 19 to 36 months old (see Table 7). Using all of the utterances in every observation from 11 to 36 months old, the average child dictionary contained 821 words. The smallest child dictionary recorded across all utterances in all observations contained 253 words; the largest child dictionary contained 1,644 words. The average parent dictionary of words addressed to the child listed 1,813 words (range 839–2,884); an average of 73% of those words were also among the 2,227 words (range 1,105–3,266) listed in the average parent dictionary of words addressed to people other than the child.

Of the words in any individual child's dictionary, an average of 86% (range 71%–94%) were words listed in the parent dictionary of words the child's parent had addressed to the child. A lesser percentage (77%) were words listed in the dictionary of words that the child's parent had addressed to people other than the child. But an average of 92% (range 86%–98%) of the words in an individual child dictionary were also listed among the average of 2,898 vocabulary words (range 749–4,293) listed in the family dictionary of words said by any family member to any other family member including the child.

The commonality of the vocabulary used within a family may be compared with the variability of the vocabulary recorded in the talk by and to the children across the families. Of the 253 words listed in the smallest child dictionary, only 94 were listed in the dictionaries of all 42 children: 7 nouns (baby, bed, dog, dad, mom, shoe, thing), 2 modifiers (big, now), 33 verbs, and 52 function words such as pronouns and prepositions. Of the dictionary of 15,533 different vocabulary words recorded across all speakers in all the families over the 2½ years of sampling everyday talk, only 531 words were addressed to the children with sufficient frequency that they were recorded in all 42 of the families.

The variability of the day-to-day talk within ordinary families may also be seen in Appendix A. Appendix A lists all 2,008 of the different words recorded for the 42 children in the 100-utterance subsamples that were used to calculate MLU and record instances of the categories from the IPSyn. Also listed are the number of children recorded as saying each word and the number of parents (if more than 10) who addressed the word to the child in any utterance in any of the 1,300 hours of observation. The frequency of use is indicated for those words recorded as said by both the children and 10 or more of the parents. Of the 2,008 different words in the 100-utterance subsamples used by one or more of the 42 children between 19–36 months of age, 603 were words listed on the CDI, words said to be "common knowledge" among toddlers, and recorded for most of the 42 children at or before age 2. Added were 1,395 words of which more than one third (39%) were recorded for only 1 child among the 42.

Appendix A makes the vocabulary data available for others to analyze and interpret beyond what we set out to do. We hope it will be useful for studies of the variability and commonalities in children's early word use and for examining relationships between the words children say and the words their parents say to them. We consider it an important resource for comparisons between the numbers and types of words children say during their everyday interactions at home and the words their parents report, on the CDI, for instance, that their children know.

Endnotes

1. See Bee (1975).
2. A computer program used Brown's (1973) rules to calculate MLU in morphemes for each observation for each child. MLU was calculated for 100 utterances (or all, if less than 100) beginning after a warm-up of 10 utterances said by or to the child.

   Using the 100 utterances for which MLU was calculated, we then listed each different word used and counted the number of phrases and sentences. We counted sentences separately for declaratives, imperatives, and questions. The resulting averages for the 100 utterances corresponded closely to the average proportions of phrases and sentence types recorded in all child utterances over the successive months. Agreement on words listed as different was assessed for three observations for three randomly selected children; percentage of agreement was 99.
3. The Index of Productive Syntax (IPSyn) (Scarborough, 1990) was developed to assess the flexibility of children's language use at successive ages and provide a score that could be used to identify children who might be having difficulty. Listed are 56 syntactic and morphological forms for noun phrases, verb phrases, questions, negations, and sentence structures.

   Scarborough (1990) noted that the grammatical categories listed are not intended to indicate a developmental sequence. We used the items because they provide a comprehensive list of clearly defined words and structures that are readily recognized in children's productions. Although Scarborough designed and normed the list for use to derive a score at a particular age only, we used it to record the age at which each item was first encountered in each 100-utterance subsample for each child.

   For each child we recorded the age at which we first found an item (e.g., an article preceding a noun) in a 100-

utterance subsample. Then in the next 100-utterance subsample, we recorded whether that item was used again.
When we had found three different uses of an item (e.g.,
the progressive tense marker -*ing* added to three different
verbs) in more than a single subsample, we listed the
child's age at the first use of the item, marking the beginning of practice rather than mastery of that item. The median and the range in chronological age at which grammatical categories listed on the IPSyn were first recorded
is shown in Table 5.

The range shown in Table 5 indicates how many successive 100-utterance subsamples were examined before
three instances of even such common usage as an article
preceding a different noun were found for all 42 children.
The effects of sampling everyday contexts of interactions
are apparent. Interesting, though, was the coders' comment that after looking for a long time for an item such as
a clause or a past-tense auxiliary, once they found a first
instance they were likely to find more in the next subsamples, as though the child were practicing using that
item.

4. The MacArthur Communicative Development Inventory–
Toddlers (CDI; Fenson et al., 1992) is a parent-report
form that lists 680 words in 22 semantic categories. The
words and categories are shown in Appendix A. See Bates
et al. (1988) for discussion of the reliability and validity of
the inventory relative to observational data. Parents are
asked to check the words on the inventory that their children "know or understand." We recorded only words the
children said; we did ask the 42 parents to report their
children's words, but the few parents who did so stopped
after they had more than about 20 vocabulary words to
report.

Each child's total recorded vocabulary was examined
for the words on the CDI, and the chronological age when
each word was first recorded was listed. Only 655 of the
680 words were used; omitted were animal sounds

(meow) and proper names, which were not listed in the vocabularies of the 42 children, and duplications (e.g., "fish" as both food and animal).

5. Dr. David Thissen, an expert in the statistical measurement of growth curves (see Thissen & Bock, 1990), used the month-by-month increments in the recorded vocabulary of each of the children to fit a nonlinear curve to each child's cumulative vocabulary growth and from these derived a "normal" curve of expressive vocabulary growth.

   Dr. Thissen's multilevel model of vocabulary growth has three parameters:

   a) A "slope" parameter reflecting the rate of vocabulary acquisition at the maximum rate of acquisition

   b) A "location" parameter reflecting the age at which a maximum rate of vocabulary growth is achieved (after some acceleration, before deceleration; the average age of the 42 children at this "location" was 29 months, range 23–32 months)

   c) An "asymptote" parameter reflecting where the rate of growth is going; the "asymptote" does not imply an end or slowing of word learning but projects a stable rate of continued vocabulary growth

   Further work with the statistical aspects of the model are reported by McFarlane (1994).

   The cumulative number of words in the "normal" vocabulary growth curve fit to the data by Dr. Thissen is shown in Table 7; the growth curve is shown in Figure 2.

6. Schieffelin (1990). A similar discussion concerning children in Samoa is presented in Ochs (1988).

7. See Bee (1975).

8. Defining what constitutes a first word is a problem common to researchers and parents alike and has been discussed by many, including Dromi (1987) and Vihman & Miller (1988). Our criteria for words were very similar to those of Vihman & Miller.

CHAPTER 5

Becoming Partners

◆ ◆ ◆ ◆

*B*efore the children said their first words at an average
age of 11 months, they had spent every day for almost
a year as listeners in a social world of people talking to
and around them. We chose to begin observing families before
the children were saying words especially so that we could see
what was going on during this period. Much that we saw in
the data was quite different from what we had expected. One
surprise was just how often the 42 children had been exposed
to spoken words before they began to talk. Another was the
subtle shift in turn taking that led children and parents to become partners in a social dance.

Our description of the period of becoming partners will
take us from our observations before the children said their
first words until they became talkers. Our earliest observations were of children who were 7 months old; the children
said their first words at an average age of 11 months old (range
8–14 months old). Children were defined as talkers when half
or more of what they said during an hour of recording contained identifiable words; the children became talkers at an
average age of 19 months old (range 15–27 months old).[1]

Nonwords

Before the children said their first words, they were highly vocal, speaking the variety of tongues their parents called babbling, gibberish, jabber, and Chinese. We will summarize all of these as nonwords and so divide the children's verbalizations during the period of becoming partners into nonword utterances and utterances containing a word or words (see Table 6 and Figures 3 and 7).

We were surprised at the amount of nonword speech we were recording before words appeared. In the month before the children said their first words, they produced an average of 109 nonword utterances during the hour of observation. Nonword utterances increased at the same time that words became more frequent (see Figure 3). At 12 months old the children produced an average of 132 nonword utterances per hour plus an average of 8 utterances containing words. At 18 months old the children produced an average of 141 nonword utterances per hour plus an average of 103 utterances containing words. The percentage of utterances that contained words increased very gradually, by about 6% per month, until at 18 months old an average of 43% of what the children said contained recognizable words.

None of the children just took up talking, simply saying fewer nonword utterances and more words with each successive month. For all of the children, both nonword utterances and utterances containing words increased in frequency, and all but seven of the children went back for a month or more to saying fewer words and more nonword utterances. There was no systematic relationship between the number of months from first word to talker tallied for a child and how regularly the child increased the use of words rather than nonwords.

Even when words predominated in the children's speech, nonword utterances did not disappear. The observers had a code, CU (can't understand), that they used for parts of utterances they could not hear or understand well enough to transcribe with certainty. In the last four observations, when the children were 33–36 months old, parent and child utterances were about equally comprehensible. The children said an average of 404 utterances per hour, of which an average of 25 (6%) contained one or more incomprehensible words indicated by a CU. The average for their parents in these four observations was 4%.

But for audible utterances that contained no words the observers could find in a dictionary, they continued to use the code for a nonword utterance. Parent noises such as "Mmm," "Pee-yoo," or "Ugh," for instance, were coded as nonwords. Such nonword parent utterances represented 6%–9% of the average parent's speech per hour during the period of becoming partners and about 1% when the children were 33–36 months old. For the children, the observers coded as nonword utterances babbling, jargon, gibberish, intonational sentences, and the unconfirmed child words they had written during observation. The children continued to produce these nonword utterances throughout the 2½ years of observations. In the last four observations when the children were 33–36 months old, the children produced an average of 71 nonword utterances per hour (18% of all utterances), often when initiating toward some newly discovered object.

Contexts of Nonword Utterances

We had expected to see parents talk a lot to their babies during the predictable routines of feeding, changing, or dressing. Most of the play with children that we saw, though, did not occur during routine care. During routine care, parents tended to be task oriented. When changing the baby's diaper, for instance, the parent gave the baby a toy to explore so that the baby would lie still. At meals, once the baby was securely strapped into a highchair and had started eating, the parent went to prepare more food or to get the older children off to school. Talk focused on encouraging cooperation in the activity: "Is that good? Ready for some more?" "Let's put on your shoes. Give me your foot," "Just lie still. I'll be through in a minute." At the end of the routine, parents usually put a happy baby down on the floor to explore the environment and left to dispose of the diaper or began cleaning up the baby's highchair.

Play with the baby was more likely to occur when a parent was attracted to the baby's happy state. A parent initiated a game of cuddling or roughhousing involving general stimulation and mutual affection and arousal, playing Peekaboo, tickling, or lifting and turning the baby over. Parents held their babies in interaction, responding to nonwords with nonwords, as though establishing play as the setting for conversation. They shared a toy such as a See 'n Say that had animals for the parent to talk about and a rotating arrow to entrance the baby.

We saw what we jokingly called 10-minute turns at talk. The child played in silence while the parent talked on the telephone, conversed with other family members, or held the floor to tell the child about what the parent or child was doing. Then when the parent stopped talking, the child began to speak, usually while looking at whatever object the child was engaged with. After one of the early observations, a parent was holding the baby up to look out a window and talking to the observer. Each time the parent paused for the observer to speak, the baby, silent throughout the parent's turn, started to babble.

Function of Nonword Utterances

Our background in learning theory[2] had led us to think that nonword speech would have function for children. We had expected to see parents respond immediately and contingently when their babies vocalized and provide the kinds of positive consequences, such as affection, approval, toys, and food, that would encourage more vocalizations and further practice of the sounds and coordinations requisite to saying the first words. But we saw parents delivering attention, like nurturing, without regard to whether their children were vocalizing. We were surprised to see how seldom parents responded to a baby's initiation of a nonword utterance as an opportunity for social interaction. Parents were more likely to respond when their children initiated a new activity that produced a noise than when their children suddenly began to babble about some new discovery during exploration.

Between 11 and 19 months of age, the babies initiated (after 5 seconds or more of no interaction) a nonword utterance almost once per minute, an average of 57 times per hour (range 27–86). Parents responded to an average of 33 of those initiations. Almost half of children's nonword initiations produced no response from the parent. But the children did likewise. Parents initiated to their children an average of 39 times per hour (range 13–79), and the children did not respond to an average of 24 initiations. Sometimes a child and a parent alternated initiating interactional episodes in which the only person who spoke was the initiator.

The parents acted as though nonwords merely signified contented exploration rather than preparation for words. If the sounds shifted to fussing, then the parents responded immediately. We could see no function for nonword utterances in children's lives, and we could see no need to begin to talk, either. All of the babies' needs and wants, physical and social, were satisfied; their parents behaved like the best of servants, readying in advance and providing at just the right moment exactly what the babies wanted. In case of delay or displeasure, crying effectively reminded people of the priorities. Even the social world worked flawlessly. The babies talked in nonwords, and the parents talked in words, and they understood one another perfectly.

Imitation of Nonwords

We had expected to see parents and children imitate one another's nonword sounds. But in the 8 months when the children were 11–19 months old, we recorded an average of only two such parent imitations per hour and zero for the children. The parent who imitated the child's sounds most often did so an average of eight times per hour; four parents and 13 children never imitated each other's nonwords during these 8 months. Except for exchanges of "Mmm," in response to food, parents and children imitated words but not sounds.

Prompting During the Period of Becoming Partners

To children who were expected only to babble in response, parents posed an average of 34 wh-questions per hour, most often "What's the matter?" "What are you doing?" and "Where are you going?" They said, "Say 'bye,'" as they waved the child's hand toward a departing sibling. They offered a cup to a child and said, "Say 'milk,'" and immediately handed the child the cup. Parents rarely waited even long enough for the baby to speak. Only once did we see a parent try to require that a child say a word (see the examples at the end of this chapter), and she ended up having to withhold the food she wanted to give the child.

We heard a parent tell a babbling baby, "Say 'hi.' Say but I'm not feeling quite up to par today." Another parent said, when the baby babbled, "Say for dinner today I'm gonna have me a little bit of ham. Aren't you? Say sweet potatoes and cabbage. And a little piece of roll. Say that's what we're gonna have for dinner. Say mom just goes out there and gets it out of the yard. Say next year I'm going out there and pick my own tomatoes. And my peaches. Say somebody took all the peaches off the peach tree while we was in Florida, and I didn't get to pick none this year." When the parent finally ceded the floor, the child babbled in response.

In the first months of observing, the observers could readily identify speech addressed to the baby because the parents shifted into the higher-pitched questioning intonation described as parentese.[3] When the children began to say words, though, their parents began talking to them the way they did to everyone else. We recorded only four parents addressing baby talk to their children, and they did so very infrequently. Parents seemed to use parentese and baby talk to coax their babies to take a turn,[4] to gesture, or to vocalize during the months before the parents could begin to expect an answer to what they said.

Taking Up Talking

About the time the children said their first words at an average age of 11 months, we saw children for whom nonwords usually signified contented exploration begin to repeat sounds such as "Uh" to demand attention. They began pointing to one object after another for their parents to name, and taking the parent's hand to lead the parent to another room or to an object out of reach.[5] New to the observers' notes was the comment that a child looked directly into the parent's face when saying a nonword utterance.

Changes

When the children said their first words, their interactions began to change. Amounts of behavior began to increase steadily, and the children's behavior increased more than their parents'. Child verbalizations (nonword utterances plus utterances containing words) more than doubled from an average of 132 per hour at 11 months old to an average of 305 per hour at 19 months old, and the percentage of utterances that contained recognizable words increased from 4% to 55% (see Figure 3). At 19 months of age, children were pointing to or reaching for objects an average of 20 times per hour, twice as often as they had at 11 months old. Child responses also more than doubled from an average of 90 per hour at 11 months old to an average of 185 per hour at 19 months old. Parent responses increased by one third during these 8 months, from an average of 74 per hour to an average of 167 per hour (see Figure 5). Parent utterances increased by less than 20%, from an average of 311 per hour to their 11-month-olds to an average of 377 per hour when the children were 19 months old.

An increasing proportion of the children's interactions took the form of conversation. By the time the children were 16 months old, an average of two thirds of their interactions with their parents involved conversation, defined as a child response to a parent utterance that was followed by a parent response to the child. More frequent conversations also began lasting longer. Conversations containing only one child response declined from 19% to 13%, and those containing seven or more child responses increased from 26% to 35% between the months when the children were 11 and 16 months old. Imitation increased from an average of 2 child imitations and 3 parent imitations per hour when the children were 11 months old to an average of 13 child and 14 parent imitations per hour when the children were 19 months old.

No Change

The steady increases in amount of interaction did not change the family style of interacting. The overall interactional environment during the period of becoming partners was remarkably similar to that in which the child would talk later on. Children who initiated often before they said their first words tended to keep doing so after they were talking. Parents who responded and prompted often when their children said nonwords continued to respond and prompt often when their children began to say words. Increasing numbers of words and interactions brought little change in the fundamental social dance pattern that we observed in a family before the child began talking.

All of the parents responded more often, but their relative responsiveness did not change. During the 8 months of the period of becoming partners, the parents responded to an average of 56% of their children's utterances, an average that ranged from a high of 60% when the children were 14 months old to a low of 50% when the children were 17 months old. Questions continued to average around 25% of all parent utterances addressed to the children. Parents and children continued to be equally as likely to respond when spoken to, with the children continuing to be slightly more responsive than the parents.

Social Partnership

When the children said their first words at an average age of 11 months old, they made clear to their parents that they were listening to what other people said and attending to what others were doing. Their parents began introducing the children to conversation as a social dance in which what each partner does at each step governs what the other does. If the children were to contribute to conversations rather than just take turns, then they needed to start answering what the parent said instead of responding with a gesture or nonwords as they usually did. When parents asked, "What's that?" the children needed to respond not with the customary nonword, or even with a label, but with a word that named "that."

Surprisingly, though, words seemed to be the focus in very few of the steadily increasing numbers of interactions we recorded. The average number of wh-questions the parents asked did not begin to increase until 6 months after the children said their first words. Until the children were 16 months old and had begun imitating an average of five times per hour, an average of only 1% of parent utterances were directives to "Say. . . ." Of the children's 103 utterances containing recognizable words at 18 months old, the parents confirmed an average of 10 by repeating or recasting them. The parents seemed unconcerned with catching their children's first words, and the children did not seem to "save" their words for face-to-face display to their parents. During the months the children were 12–16 months old, as the average number of recognizable words they said increased from 9 to 40 per hour, 25%–32% each month were either not heard or not answered by their parents.

In contrast to what we would see parents doing during the period of staying and playing, we recorded only 12 parents, once each, tell their 11- to 19-month-old children, "I don't know/can't understand what you're saying." Instead, we saw parents acting as though they did understand. Rather than try to explain what the children needed to do as partners, parents seemed to demonstrate, similar to adults who dance with children who stand on the adults' feet. We saw parents making conversations out of a series of child nonword turns (see the examples at the end of this chapter). When a 17-month-old initiated with nonwords, the parent answered, "He did what?" and replied successively to the child's next three nonword responses, "When was this?" "Where was I at?" "I was gone?" To an average of 6%–7% of their children's nonword utterances, the parents responded merely, "Really?" "Is that right?" or "Yes." (The data showed that the nonwords to which the parents responded in this way were rarely the approximations to words the observers wrote in parentheses.)

An average of 15%–18% of parent responses seemed to offer 11- to 16-month-old children opportunities for easy answers (see the examples at the end of this chapter). Parents seemed to invite imitation when they responded to children's nonword utterances by naming the objects with which the children were engaged ("Car") or to which they were pointing

("Button"). Parents who responded, "What?" or, "Huh?" to their children's nonword utterances invited the children to try again to say the word the parent seemed to half understand. Both "Huh?" and "Uh-huh" modeled acceptable, if uninformative, answers. The observers were amused to hear parents asking 11- to 18-month-olds, "Is that a flower?" "Is that your shoe?" inviting a "Yes" or "No" for the parent to then answer, "That's right," or "It is too."

Many of the children's first answers were these easy ones. Children began answering, "Huh?" or, "Yes," and their parents reliably repeated or took a reciprocal turn. Children began spontaneously repeating the last word the parent said.[6] When a parent asked, "What are those?" and the child answered, "Those," the parent said, "Those are socks," maintaining the topic rather than again prompting, "Yes, what are they?" as the parent would do during the period of staying and playing. The children began enunciating words with care, "Want-uh it-uh," and reducing their answers to a single word, saying, "Want cookie," and then holding the floor to pronounce, "Cookie." Between 16 and 19 months old, 16 of the children were recorded reducing an utterance to a single word one or more times.

Though the data contained many instances of multiword utterances recorded for the 11- to 16-month-old children and though several parents reported their children saying sentences, we saw the beginning of the "one-word" stage described in the literature.[7] It was as though the children had become partners and so had begun trying to make their answers clear and concise, reducing them to a single word the parent could easily identify. The data suggested that a shift may have occurred when the children were an average of 18 months old.

Between 11 and 17 months old, the children had gained enough skill to produce at 17 months old an average of 84 recognizable utterances per hour, they had accumulated an average of 41 vocabulary words, they were repeating themselves an average of 17 times per hour and imitating their parents an average of 6 times per hour. Then within 2 months, recognizable utterances almost doubled to an average of 167 per hour, recorded vocabulary almost doubled to an average of 81 words, self-repetitions almost doubled to an average of 33 per hour, and imitations doubled to an average of 13 per hour.

For 7 months the children seemed to be very gradually taking up talking[8] and then, almost suddenly, starting to "get serious" about saying words. During these months the parents and children rarely appeared to work at becoming partners. The parents continued to respond to the children's non-word utterances, and they left almost half of what the children said uninfluenced by any requirement or programmed consequence. They left the children to enjoy talking as usual to themselves or to objects, to practice in play and bedtime monologues[9] during which they could continue to say whatever amused them.[10] Much of what the children said remained as free to vary as it had when the children were babbling. From that unconstrained variety their parents could be sure that words would increase as the social group automatically made effective those utterances that made sense.

The Easy Way

Some parents seemed to make becoming partners easy for their children. They engaged their children in games of tickling, teasing, or roughhousing that seemed designed deliberately to demonstrate how words both lead and follow the behavior of a partner in interaction. A parent began by tickling, and when the child responded by tickling or pushing the parent away, the parent said, "Stop." At 9 months old several of the children were saying, "Stop," when the parent reached to tickle, and the parents were answering, "You stop." A parent took the child's doll, saying, "My baby." The child said, "Mine," and a series of repeats made a conversation.

At 13 months old, 5 of the 42 children were 3 months younger than the average child when they began imitating five times and more per hour. Their recorded vocabularies tripled in the subsequent 2 months, from an average of 11 words at 13 months old to an average of 36 words at 15 months old.

The Hard Way

Unlike a nonword utterance, saying a word had an observable function for children. Parents answered automatically when the children said words that the parents recognized. We thought that function would be motivation enough. Talking would bloom as a social tool and flourish as children experienced the usefulness of words for getting attention and directing other people's actions. But we saw that function could be a trap if a child used words to control a parent's response but did not answer with words that were governed by that response.

During the observations from 11 to 13 months old, one of the children averaged 198 utterances per hour; 166 were nonwords, and 32 contained words. All but four of the words were, "Huh?" and his mother responded to half by repeating what she had just said. Another child from 12 to 15 months old averaged 165 utterances an hour; 102 were nonwords, and 63 contained words. All but two of the words were, "This," said as he pointed to an object that the parent then named.

Each of the parents intervened. When the first child said, "Huh?" his parent began answering, "What did I just say?" The child usually responded, "Huh?" The parent of the second child began answering the child's "This," with "What is that? Can you say . . .?" The child usually pointed to something else and said, "This." Each parent virtually stopped answering. The parent of the first child, who had in the 3 prior months responded an average of 130 times per hour, responded to the child only 22 times during the observation when the child was 15 months old. The parent of the second child, who had been responding to an average of two of every three initiations by the child, responded to fewer than one of three. In the month that their parents almost stopped responding, both children almost stopped speaking, but after another month they started again.

Late Starters

The average child became a talker at 19 months old. The average parent seemed to wait and accept nonword utterances until the child was ready to take up talking. But in two highly sociable families, the parents became quite concerned when their children were well past a year old and "still not talking." Both children had said words, though, and their parents had responded to them; the observers had coded the children's first words at 9 and 10 months old.

One of the children stopped attempting words and began to maintain interaction and keep her mother talking by saying, "Uh," whenever her mother paused, as though she had decided to spend a few months just listening. She began trying words again when her grandparents came to stay; the only change the observer noticed was how often her grandmother interpreted what the child said.

In the other family we saw what happens when children do not do their part. When the child was 19 months old, his mother said, "He still doesn't talk. Last year, when he was just 9 months old, he would say, 'Pretty,' and he'd say, 'Uh-oh.' But he doesn't say words any more. He doesn't say, 'Mommy daddy.'" The child, though, had never stopped saying words. His parents just responded much more reliably when he pointed and said, "Uh." When the child had said, "Pretty," during the observation when he was 11 months old, his mother had responded immediately, saying, "Pretty." But then she commented that it was the father who told her that the child said, "Pretty," adding, "I don't say that to him," and, "I think it is a little early for him to start talking."

Over the next months the child continued to say words, and the parent continued to respond. The child handed the mother a rolled newspaper and said, "Do this," and his mother took it, asking, "What do you want me to do?" Looking at a book, the child pointed and said, "Ball," and his mother said, "That's the ball. Where's the teddy bear?" A few turns later she said, "Where's the ball?" The child pointed and said, "There." The mother said, "That's not it," and pointed to the ball, saying, "Ball. Say 'ball.' Say 'ball.'" The child did not answer.

At 17 months old, the child held out his toast at breakfast and said very quickly in a high, soft voice between two parent utterances addressed to his older brother, "Want jelly." The parent responded, "Okay, what do you want?" The child said, "Uh," and his brother said, "He wants jam on it." The parent said, "Jelly? You want this jelly? If you'd just tell me jelly, I'd get it. But I got it without you telling me, so it worked, didn't it?" The child pointed and said, "Bread." The parent gave him the toast, saying, "There you go."

The parent and the child had no difficulty communicating; they appeared to be talking to one another exactly as we observed in all of the other families. They were responsive to one another; they just were not dancing together, like couples who follow the same music but perform the steps separately, with neither party leading or following. But similar to the other child whose parent was concerned that she was not talking, everything came together. When the child was 23 months old, the observer arrived to find that the parent and the child had apparently agreed to become partners. The only suggestion of a turning point was the parent's comment that in the intervening month the child had suddenly started to imitate.

These families impressed us with how persistently most children pursue admission to the social world of talkers, and how tolerant are interactional environments of children's fumbling approaches and parents' varied styles. We had thought that late starters might be at risk for language delays, just as we had thought that the children who started early and whose parents were highly responsive, read books, and played games to elicit words from their children might be off to accelerated development. But how early children said their first words made no difference; the children who started late just caught up.[11] None of our measures of IQ, vocabulary growth, syntactic development, or even how soon a child became a talker was significantly related to the age at which the child said his or her first words.

Examples: Taking Up Talking

Before half of what their children said contained recognizable words, parents prompted words but readily accepted babble, gibberish, or silence as a response. They seemed willing to make conversation out of whatever the children said and persisted in offering the children the easy routes to taking up talking: naming, agreeing, and imitating.

The following are two verbatim examples of the interactions we observed when parents gave their children food. The first is the single instance we saw of a parent holding out for a word; the second illustrates the usual prompting we saw parents do.

A Parent Making Food Contingent on a Word

Only once did we see a parent make food contingent on a word before the child became a talker. The lack of success of this parent, who used the high-demand conditions of mealtime to make food contingent on a child (who was neither a talker nor food-deprived) producing a word, may evoke memories among people in intervention programs and may be instructive to parents (because we never saw this parent try it again).

The child, Calvin, is 18 months old and has a recorded vocabulary of 48 words; of the 352 utterances he produces in this hour of observation, 36% contain identifiable words.

Calvin is sitting in his highchair; his sister, Georgetta, age 4, is seated at the dining room table. Their mother is serving them both lunch. She gives Calvin a sandwich and returns to the kitchen.

When Calvin's mother returns carrying milk, Calvin initiates, "Mommy." His mother says, "Want some milk? Say 'milk.'" Calvin answers the first question, "Uh-huh." His mother says, "Do you want milk?"

89

Calvin says, "Milk." His mother says, "What? I'm sorry. Say it louder. I didn't hear you." Calvin says, "Uh," and his mother says, "Say 'milk.' Do you want milk?" Calvin nods. His mother says, "Say 'milk.'" Calvin says, "Uh," and reaches. His sister initiates, "Gagagoogoo," and Calvin babbles, "Gagagaga." His mother puts the glass of milk on the tray of the highchair and returns to the kitchen.

His mother comes back with a bag of potato chips and says to Georgetta, "Want a chip, sister?" Georgetta answers, "Chips," and the mother turns to Calvin, saying, "Chips. See, sister can say 'chips.' You want chips, you gotta say 'chips.'" Calvin says, "Uh," and his mother says, "Sister said 'chips.'" Calvin says, "Uh," and points to his plate. His mother says, "Yeah, I know where you want them, but I wanna hear you say 'chips.'" Calvin pulls his sandwich apart, and his mother says, "No, we don't take it apart. We eat it like that. You want chips?" Calvin nods. His mother says, "Say 'chips.' These are chips."

Calvin points to the bag and says, "Uh." Georgetta tells him, "Say 'chips,' and you'll get them." The mother says, "You want chips?" Calvin continues to reach to the bag, saying, "Uh," and his mother says, "Say 'chips.' Chips."

Calvin's mother takes his sandwich, removes some bread crust, puts it back together, and returns it. Calvin says, "Mine." His mother says, "Yeah, that's yours," and then shows him a potato chip, saying, "You don't want this?" Calvin nods, and his mother says, "What are those?" Calvin says, "Those," and his mother says, "What are they?" Calvin points and says softly, "Chip"; the "ch" sound is barely audible. His mother says, "They're what?" Calvin says, "Me," and his mother says, "Chips?" Calvin says, "Uh-huh." His mother says, "Well, say 'chips.' I know you can say 'chips.' I heard you say it before. Say 'chips.' Chips. Chips." Calvin says, "Uh."

The mother tries twice more without success, and Calvin finishes lunch and gets down from his highchair without having had any chips. His mother comments to the observer, "He can say it. Like I know he can say 'chips' and 'please.' But getting him to do it is another thing."

The Usual Prompting We Observed
When a Parent Gave a Child Food

This is an example of a parent offering a child an opportunity for an easy answer ("yes" or "nana").

The child, Norma, is 15 months old and has a recorded vocabulary of 12 words; of the 157 utterances she produces in this hour of observation, 6% contain identifiable words.

Norma is lying on the living room floor drinking from a bottle, and her older sister, Lenore, 2½, is watching *Sesame Street.* Their mother comes in from the kitchen carrying a plate with peeled bananas on it. When her mother enters Norma makes a low sound. Her mother says, "Sit up. You can't. . . Sit up." Norma utters something and sits up. Her mother gives her a tissue, saying, "Here, keep this so you can wipe your hands when you get through." Norma takes the tissue, and then her mother offers the plate of bananas, saying, "Here."

As Norma reaches to take a banana from the plate, her mother says, "Banana. Banana. Nana. Want some nana? Huh? Nana?" Norma says a nonword and mother says, "Nana. Want some nana?"

Lenore takes the plate and joins in, saying, "Say 'nana,'" as she holds out the plate with the rest of the bananas. The mother tells Lenore, "No, she'll grab yours. Don't leave yours in there."

Lenore continues to Norma, "Say 'nana.'" Norma utters something, reaching to take another banana from the plate. Lenore withdraws the plate, saying, "No, say 'nana' first. Say 'nana' first. Say 'banana.'" Norma says

91

some nonwords, and Lenore prompts again, "Banana first. Say 'nana' first. Banana."

Norma begins to eat the banana she is holding. Lenore resumes watching *Sesame Street*, and their mother goes back into the kitchen.

Demonstrating Conversation

This is an example of a parent who acts as though what the child says makes sense and so makes a conversation out of a series of the child's nonword utterances.

The child, Ray, is 14 months old and has a recorded vocabulary of 41 words; of the 231 utterances he produces in this hour of observation, 18% contain identifiable words.

Ray is sitting on a bigwheel in the living room. His mother initiates, "You testing them wheels out? Huh? You testing them wheels out to see if they work?" Ray says a nonword, and his mother says, "You not? What you doing? What you doing?" Ray utters something, and his mother asks, "What?" Ray says some nonwords, and his mother answers, "Oh, okay. Okay. I see what you saying." Ray utters something, and his mother says, "Okay." Ray says more nonwords. His mother asks, "Huh?" and Ray utters yet more nonwords. His mother replies, "Yeah, that's what I thought. You was too." Ray does not respond.

Endnotes

1. We explored matching the 42 children at the month of becoming talkers. We realigned the data to match the children at the first of 3 successive months in which the child was recorded as using identifiable words in half or more of all utterances in an hour. The resulting averages showed the same pattern of increasing numbers of utterances, of responses and floorholding, and of different words used, as shown when the children were matched by chronological age. But realigning the data at the month in which each child became a talker left us with decreasing numbers of children in the months before the children were 15 months old and after the children were 25 months old. Averaging by chronological age gave us a more representative sample of the pattern of change as the children learned to talk.
2. See Mowrer (1954).
3. Harris (1992).
4. Schaffer (1977).
5. This change in children's behavior has been interpreted as the beginning of intentional communication (see Bates, 1976). Piaget (1970) described this change as marking sensorimotor stage 5 when, prior to the development of symbols, children begin to understand causality and that adults can be used as agents.
6. Bloom et al. (1976) also reported children's use of imitation as an early, "easy" strategy for maintaining topic.
7. See McNeill (1970) for discussion of "holophrastic speech" and the suggestion that children's single-word utterances are equivalent to the full sentences of adults.
8. Snow wrote, "[It] is striking . . . how fragile are the early 10–15 words, and with what difficulty they are acquired. Only after a lexicon of 40–50 words is attained do children really become efficient word learners" (1988, p. 348). Our data suggest that these early months may be

concerned chiefly with creating the interactional conditions conducive to efficient word learning.

9. Baltaxe & Simmons (1977); Weir (1962).
10. Keenan (1974).
11. Thal, Tobias, & Morrison (1991) also found that children
    who were assessed as late talkers no longer showed evi-
    dence of delays when visited a year after the assessment.

CHAPTER 6

Staying and Playing

◆ ◆ ◆ ◆

The 42 children spent an average of 8 months from when, at 11 months old, they said their first word to when, at 19 months old, they succeeded in replacing nonwords and gibberish with identifiable words in half or more of their utterances. They began to speak as social partners, answering, "Yes," or repeating the last word the parent said. They became fluent enough to produce 100 or more recognizable utterances per hour. They began reducing their utterances to a single, carefully articulated word. Their parents began to recognize and automatically make effective more and more words within the steady stream of nonword production that they were used to accepting as communication. Both children and parents became more and more responsive as the children gradually took up talking.

We have labeled as *staying and playing* the period from 20 months old, when half or more of the average child's utterances contained identifiable words, to 28 months old, when the average child was regularly producing utterances containing plurals and tense markers. During these months the children began to take an active part in dressing and feeding themselves, and many were learning to use the potty. We saw children learning to propel a tricycle, handle a crayon, turn a puzzle piece around, and answer relatives and strangers.

Parents and children engaged in increasing numbers of interactions that seemed best described as staying and playing. After dressing a child, the parent, instead of putting the child down as usual, held the child up to chat for a minute about the poster on the wall. When a child said, "Look," a parent paused to talk about the stack of blocks the child had made. A child brought a See 'n Say or dumped a puzzle, and the parent sat down to help. We saw children helping sort laundry and sitting on a kitchen counter while their parents made sandwiches or washed dishes. Parents and children engaged each other in activities such as looking at books and catalogs, reading the mail, and poring over family photographs.

The trend of increasing amounts of talk that was seen in the period of becoming partners continued, but family patterns of interaction remained much the same. Many interactions still concerned just taking care of business. In 40% of the parent–child interactions we recorded, only one party spoke. Child initiations and responses continued to exceed parent initiations and responses by 20 or more per hour, even as the probability of a parent–child response remained 50:50 once conversation started. The average number of utterances recorded for the children per hour continued to increase more than the average number recorded for the parents. Between the ages of 20 and 28 months old, the number of recognizable utterances the children said per hour doubled from an average of 183 to an average of 396. Parent utterances, which averaged 348 per hour when the children were 20 months old, reached a maximum average of 402 per hour when the children were 24–25 months old (see Table 6).

The most change seen during the period of staying and playing was in the amount of elaborating the children did. The average number of floorholding utterances that were recorded doubled during the months in which the children were 20–28 months old. When the children were an average of 20 months old, we recorded an average of 181 responses and 59 initiations, plus an average of 101 floorholding utterances that repeated, recast, or added words or nonwords to the response or the initiation. When the children were an average of 28 months old, we recorded an average of 213 responses and 56 initiations, plus 222 floorholding utterances. More floorholding utterances (an average of 179) were recorded for the children than for the parents (an average of 160) when the children were an average of 26 months old. In every subsequent month after the children were an average of 26 months old, the average number of child floorholding utterances exceeded the average number recorded for the parents (see Figure 5).

All of the children, and the later-born children especially, began receiving more one-to-one attention from their parents. All of the children appeared to become increasingly skilled at producing an immediate response of some kind that would hold their parents in conversation. One parent, naming animals with a 21-month-old, told the child, "If you don't know what it is, you just call it a camel. That's a lobster." The parents seemed to enjoy the sudden surprises afforded by their children's unhesitating display. A parent reported taking the children to the state fair, where the youngest "was yelling at the top of his lungs he sees a kangaroo. I could not convince him it was a goat." For the children, staying and playing seemed to be about answering and getting an answer, keeping their parents' attention focused on them. For the parents, staying and playing seemed to be about listening to their children and renewing the wonder of childhood. For both, staying and playing seemed to be about encouragement.

Encouragement

Most of what we heard parents say during conversations with their children seemed to be said primarily to encourage the children to tell about things. We never saw parents suspend the criteria for proficiency held by the social group. They did not increase pauses between their own utterances to give children more time to produce an answer, and they recognized only utterances that made some sort of sense in the situation. Instead, they readily supplied the answers, simplified their prompts, asked easier questions, and sometimes filled in with praise so that conversation could continue.

Praise

During the months when parents were encouraging their 9- to 18-month-old children to speak in babble, words, or gibberish, we had seen parents regularly answering even when they did not understand and occasionally imitating when they did. But we never heard a parent praise a child for babbling or tell a child, "Good talking." Parents said, "Good," most often to describe the food they gave the children. They said, "Good girl/boy," most often when children followed directions, including directions to "Say. . . ." Between the ages of 13 and 24 months old, the children were told, "Good," an average of once every other hour.

Parents did not often say, "Right," or, "That's right" (but they said, "Wrong," even less frequently, usually to say, "That's the wrong foot"). Five parents were never heard to tell their children that the children were "right," and another five told their children "Right" only once in the 2½ years of observations. The parents of the other 32 children said, "Right," an average of three times per hour in the first 3 months after their children became talkers when half or more of their utterances contained identifiable words. A child said, "Baby," and the parent said, "Right," or a child said, "Paper," and the parent said, "That's right, paper." Parents seemed always to be responding to the sense of what children said, regardless of grammaticality. When one child said, "Her have claws on his foot, on her foot," the parent responded, "Yeah, she has claws on her foot, right."

Imitation

Imitation[1] made conversation easy. The children seemed to use imitation to rehearse vocabulary and fill a turn when time was short. The parents seemed to use imitation to confirm the correctness of the children's pronunciation and verify the sense of what the children said. Parent imitation provided a model of (usually) improved pronunciation and prompted a child to try to match it. As child imitations increased, parents began pruning their prompts. At first, parents said, "What's that? Say 'shoe.'" Once the children were regularly answering, the parents abbreviated the prompt to, "What's that? A shoe," and the children imitated, "A shoe." Eventually the parents could say, "That's a shoe," and the children would imitate, "A shoe," or, "That's a shoe." Imitation prepared the children to start a conversation by saying, "That's a shoe."

At first, when the children were novices at conversation, they needed the easy answers imitation offered. By 22 months old, though, they had an average vocabulary of 176 words, enough to begin answering with a complement of their own devising. Child imitations peaked at an average of 19 per hour when the children were 22 months old. The following month child imitations dropped to an average of 13 per hour, beginning a steady decline. But the mean length of the children's utterances at 22 months was only two words, and their pronunciation was still immature. Parents continued to need to confirm the sense of the children's contributions if they were to move the conversation forward. Parents imitated an average of 2–7 times more often per hour than their children did (see Figure 6) every month between the months in which the children were 23 and 36 months old.

Restatement

An average of one to five times per hour, a parent restated a child's utterance rather than imitating it.[2] A parent extended the child's utterance by adding a word or a phrase or expanded the child's utterance into a more grammatically standard form. A parent extended a child's "Zoo," by saying, "At the zoo," or answered a child's "Sock," by saying, "Your sock." A parent expanded a child's "What that?" or, "That a car" by answering, "Yes, what's that?" or, "That's a car, yes." A parent recast a child's "That mom cup" by answering, "Is that mom's cup?" or, "Not mom's cup, yours."

We saw no evidence that parents used expansions to correct their children's utterances.[3] During the period of staying and playing, parents began to comment on the recognizability of what the children said ("I don't understand what you're trying to say"), but never on grammaticality. Sometimes they seemed to restate children's utterances to give the children an opportunity to add something. A parent restatement could appear as a "filler" that carried the trace of a first child statement into a following one. For instance, a child said, "Drink it," the parent answered, "Are you drinking it?" and the child said, "Drink my juice." Eventually the child would hold the floor and the two child statements would appear as a response plus an elaboration.

The children also used restatement. Between 19 and 25 months old, an average of 20% of the children's utterances per hour were repetitions, extensions, expansions, or revisions of their own immediately preceding utterances. Between 19 and 25 months old, as children more than doubled (from 167 to 355) the average number of recognizable utterances they produced in an hour, an average of 33–50 of those utterances were immediate repetitions of themselves; 11–19 were immediate repetitions of the parent; and 6–19 were an extension, expansion, or recast of their own immediately preceding utterance.

Children sometimes seemed to practice building a succession of utterances around a restated word. When a parent asked a 24-month-old child, "Where's your pop? Is it all gone?" the child answered, "More," then extended to,

"Some more," repeated once, then further extended to, "Want some more," repeated twice, and finally extended to, "I want some more," after which the parent poured him more pop. Another 24-month-old, when asked to tell about feeding ducks at a pond, said, "Took. The hand. Took the hand. It bite."

When the children were an average of 22 months old, they began expanding their own utterances, correcting themselves in a next statement. A child said, "What that?" and when the parent said, "What?" the child expanded to "What's that?" or changed "That a dog" to "That's a dog" or "Two dog" to "Two dogs." When asked, "What's way on the top?" of the Christmas tree, a 24-month-old answered, "April." The parent said, "What is it?" and the child corrected, "No, angel." Between 22 and 27 months of age, children immediately corrected their own utterances an average of once per hour (range zero to five).

Imitation and restatement never disappeared from the children's talk; they were just incorporated as part of normal conversation. For example, a 36-month-old child was telling about a movie that showed flying foxes. When she reported seeing a wolf, her parent asked, "Did you see a flying wolf?" The child said, "No," and the parent confirmed with an imitation, "No." Later in the hour the parent commented, "You like purple everything. Would you like your room painted purple?" The child said, "Uh-huh. You got purple paint?" The parent said, "I don't have purple paint, though," and the child said, "You make it with red paint then." The parent said, "Red and blue paint," and the child imitated, "Red and blue paint," before adding, "You got that color?"

To the observers, parent imitation and restatement were especially noticeable because they suddenly appeared in the data when the children began to talk. The observers had not recorded parents imitating or restating the utterances of other people. But the behaviors may have been more salient to the

101

observers than to the children. Parent imitation and restatements peaked at an average of 20 per hour when the children were 24–25 months old, when they constituted 5% of the 402 utterances the parents addressed to the children.

Staying and playing did not change a parent's style of speaking. Throughout the 2½ years of observations, roughly one third of all of the utterances the parents said to the children were statements (declaratives) and slightly more than one fourth (28%) were questions. Between the time the children were 11 and 36 months old, the proportions of statements and questions in parent talk increased somewhat as directives ("Do as I say") and phrases (naming) decreased. But the increase in questions seen during the period of staying and playing reflects not an increased proportion of questions in parent talk but an increase in the amount of talk the parents addressed to the children. Between the months in which the children were 16–17 and 24–25 months old, the amount of time that parents and children spent interacting per hour increased by 12% to an average of 30 minutes.[4] Bouts of conversation could be long or short, depending on the children's attention and engagement with materials, and were interspersed with frequent "breaks." But to the children, perhaps most encouraging and noticeable about staying and playing was the increase in the time and attention their parents focused on them.

Prompts

Parent praise, imitation, and restatement all served as prompts for children to say something more, but by far the most frequent prompt was a question. Parents prompted relative to the objects and activities with which the children were engaged and the topics their children chose (see the examples at the end of this chapter). We saw some parents devote a series of rephrasings to drawing appropriate and precise answers from children just beginning to talk; parents accepted as cor-

rect and communicative a single word related to some peripheral but remembered aspect of an experience or object. Many
parents, though, asked, "What's that?" repeated the question
once, and then simply told the child the answer.

We saw parents prompting children to listen and isolate
words when they asked, "Can you say 'green'?" An average of
15% of all parent wh-questions during the period of staying
and playing were "What?" or "Huh?" simple requests that the
children remember and repeat what they had just said, perhaps more clearly. Then parents moved on to asking children
to recall and select only part of an utterance in answer to
"You want what?" or "He did what to you?"

As the children began answering correctly more and more
of their parents' requests to tell about things by naming and
describing, parents began to use conversations to direct children's attention to what the children should notice and try to
remember in order to participate in family conversations. We
saw parents' questions concerned more and more often with
the things parents really wanted to know. Parents began asking children to notice their own behavior and respond to questions such as "Did you hit her?" and "Did you wash your
hands?" They began asking, "Who gave you that?" and "What
happened?" At first, they accepted anything a child could remember. A parent asked a 23-month-old, "What happened to
Marlon?" When the child did not answer, the parent gave a
hint, "What does he have on his arm?" The child said, "Cast."
The parent confirmed, "A cast," and returned to "What happened to his arm?" The child said, "Cast." The parent then
supplied the answer she would expect (and the child would be
able to give) at 36 months old, "Yes, the cast is on because he
broke his arm. He fell and broke his arm."

We saw parents using conversations to remind children of
social standards and to prompt compliance. A parent asked a
29-month-old, "And you know what else made me real sad?
What did you do the other night?" The child said, "I don't

know. I just teared it up." The parent said, "Yes, you did. We don't tear up books, do we? Aren't books our friends?" But we also saw interactions that seemed devoted merely to practicing dancing together: parents holding their children in "idle" conversation (see the examples at the end of this chapter).

Parents could ask children hard questions because they remained ready to maintain interaction by supplying the answers themselves. Before the children became talkers, when an average of only 15% of their answers to parent wh-questions were correct, their parents told them the answer to an average of 10% of all the wh-questions the parents asked. When the children were 19–28 months old and an average of 52% of their answers to parent wh-questions were correct, their parents still told them the answer to an average of 11% of the wh-questions the parents asked. Even after the children were 28 months old and an average of 59% of their answers were correct, their parents told them the answer to 13% of the wh-questions the parents asked.

Responsiveness

To our surprise, parents became less rather than more responsive after their children became talkers. At 19 months, when an average of 53% of the children's speech contained words, parents responded to an average of 54% of what their children said, but at 27 months, when an average of 80% of what the children said contained identifiable words, parents answered an average of only 38% of their children's utterances. Moreover, parents began to respond slightly more often when their children said nonwords than when the children said words. We realized that parents had begun responding to the words they did not understand rather than to those they did.

Parents responded automatically to their children's utterances and never seemed to plan or monitor their own utterances.[5] To a child's statement, "That's a horse," parents seemed to answer naturally with a reciprocal statement, "That's right," or, "No, it's a cow." When a child demanded, "Give me," the parent gave or refused to give. When a child asked, "Where mine?" the parent named a location: "Right there." We saw that the parents' responses frequently served to confirm the pragmatic function of the strings of words the children produced, displaying in effect, "Yes, that is the utterance form that this social group responds to as a statement, a demand, or a question."

But parents did not always respond to children's well-formed utterances; they regularly ignored talk that was socially inappropriate. They often did not answer when children spoke while the parents were conversing with someone else. Parents ignored what they called whining for attention. After responding once or twice to a child's "Look, mom," "Huh?" or "This," parents stopped answering repetitions. Also, parents often ignored a child demand such as "Come here" rather than prompting a more socially appropriate form of request. They also ignored children's failures. A parent prompted, "Say 'Can I have some, mom.' Ask me. Say 'Can I have some.' Unruly little old girl, you suppose to ask." The child said, "Ask." The parent did not respond.

More often parents waited to respond until the child had explained or elaborated, restated, or added something to a prior utterance. When a 20-month-old initiated, "I want this," her mother did not respond. The child extended to "I wanna see this" and then specified, "I wanna turn the TV on." Then her mother said, "No, you can't turn on the TV." The observers were impressed with how many and how varied were the utterances parents got from their children just by waiting. We had expected parents to respond immediately and contingently, making their children's utterances effective. Instead, we saw parents apparently ignoring many of their children's first attempts to produce utterances and waiting for the children to persist and work at adding to and varying what they said.

Most often, though, we saw parents respond with a prompt for an elaboration or an improvement. Most frequent were prompts for clarity; parents responded, "What?" or, "Huh?" But they also prompted for missing information, as when a child initiated, "Where is it?" and the parent responded, "What are you looking for?" Parents let children know that adults may ask for the names of things they already know, but children may not. We saw the names that the parents expected their children to have learned when a parent answered a child's "What's that?" with "Yeah, what is that?" Parents also began to invite children to deal with indirectness. A child said, "I want a cookie," and the parent responded, "It's almost time for lunch," or a child pushed the parent and said, "Move," and the parent responded, "Who you telling to move?"

The Curriculum

As in all good learning environments, the curriculum was determined and advanced by the children's display of developing skills and changing interests. Parents' priorities seemed to be socialization ("Be sure and tell me when you need to go potty") and keeping the children occupied ("I'm sorry, but I can't hold you while I'm doing this. Go play"). Socialization in feeding, changing, bathing, and dressing routines offered the children increasing opportunities to talk about spoons and shoes and to explore with words the complexities of putting in, on, off, and around. When the children began to walk and could less often be left alone to explore, parents brought toys and played with the children to demonstrate the satisfactions to be found in engagement with puzzles or blocks. They began planning outings to the zoo and the circus and to visit relatives.

The parents and children talked chiefly about what they were doing at the moment. Nurturing involved conversations about food, diapers, bottles, and body parts. Socialization provided opportunities for practicing greetings, rehearsing politeness routines, and following directions. Parents who had followed an infant's short attention span and just named the objects the infant pointed to or picked up began answering and encouraging talk about what the children were doing with cars and dolls. Conversations concerned safety on a slide or swing, speed on a tricycle, or the height of a tower. Naming turned to talk of relationships: "That's dad's toothbrush," "It's hot. Blow on it for a minute," "No, you are not playing with the table. If you do it again, I'm gonna spank." Outings led to conversations about past events ("What did we see?"), social obligations ("Did you say thank you?"), and, frequently, "Remember?" As experience became more varied and complex, so did conversations.

The regularity of the developmental changes in the children made it appear that there was a sequenced curriculum and that parents were tracking the children's skill gains, asking progressively more difficult questions. But the data revealed that the parents had been asking difficult questions all along. Before the children were saying more than a few words, parents were asking, "What happened?" "Why did you do that?" and, most often, "What's the matter?" The change with time and development was less in the questions and more in the frequency and seriousness with which they were asked. In conversation, too, the parents seldom seemed to plan what they said or adapt to the children's skill level. They, similar to the children, seemed content to keep conversation going with an uninformative statement ("There you go"), a repetition, or a recast. Or, they asked one of their many rhetorical questions. For instance, one parent asked a 20-month-old, "Oh, you know what I think you want?" and another asked a 21-month-old, "Shall we get the scissors and give the plant a haircut?"

Moreover, we rarely saw parents educating their children. Counting and naming colors or body parts seemed to be more a dance between social partners than a planned lesson between pupil and teacher. Not only did parents not correct their children's grammar, but they also missed innumerable opportunities to inform the children about the world around them. The parent who said, "Red and blue paint," for example, did not tell the child that red and blue make purple. A 29-month-old child said, "There duck," and the parent said, "Oh, I don't think that's a duck, is it?" The child answered, "That's a bird," and the parent said, "That's right," and did not mention that a duck is a bird. A 31-month-old child said, "Oh, there's a potato bug. How it get in there?" and the parent said, "Well, I don't know. They just live there. That's where they like to be."

Conversation: Telling About Things

We realized that the parent's role was not that of a teacher, whose task is to improve a learner's skills, but that of a chaperon, whose partnership serves to protect an immature speaker from straying too far from what the social group accepts as spoken English. Even as parents focused on arranging more frequent practice and encouraging their children to tell about more varied experiences in more precise detail, the parents casually personified the proprieties of conversation. They presented no strong consequences or conditions during conversations so that immediate, incidental aspects of activities could evoke continual variability in what was said. They seemed to demonstrate effortlessly how an increasing variety and sophistication of words and utterances remain governed by whatever impromptu dialogue the social partners are constructing together.

At 24 months old, the children were saying an average of 338 utterances per hour, thus almost 5,000 utterances in a 14-

hour waking day and almost 142,000 in the month before the observer came to record again. Given that amount of child practice talking in continually changing contexts about ever-varying experience, parents might have found it unnecessary to plan their responses. Rather, they might have relied on what seemed their natural attraction, as agents of socialization, to behaviors that were more mature and to conversations that were more like those they had with other people.

Examples: Prompting Practice

Once children were fluent enough that half or more of their utterances contained identifiable words, their parents began encouraging them to talk more and more and to tell their parents about ever more varied experiences in increasing detail and specificity.

Parents and Children Prompting

Some parents were quick to pick up on a child's topic and use it to prompt. Many of them had children who became skilled at keeping the prompting going.

Orrin, 24 months old, initiates a request for a piggyback ride; his mother takes him on her back, trots around the dining room, and then stops at the window. Typically, she first directs Orrin's attention, then asks a wh-question before prompting with a yes/no question. She tells Orrin, "Peek out the window. What do you see? Do you see trash where the doggie tore up our trash?" Orrin says, "Uh-huh." His mother responds, "Are you gonna help mama pick it up when it gets a little warmer? Mama is chicken to go out in the cold. I'm gonna wait 'til it's warmer." Orrin says, "Cold."

Orrin's mother puts him down and repeats his topic, "Cold. It's cold, isn't it? It gets cold on our toes when we go outside." Then she asks, "What do we wear when we go outside?" Orrin says, "Socks." His mother extends, "Our socks?" and Orrin imitates, "Our socks." His mother continues, "What else do we wear when it's cold and we go outside?" Orrin says, "Shoes." His mother says, "Shoes?" and holds the floor to make the question more specific: "What else do we put on just to go outside?" Orrin says, "Jackets," and his mother says, "Jackets. What do we put on our heads?" Orrin says, "Hat," and his mother says, "Hats? And what do we put on our hands?" Orrin says, "Mittens," and his mother closes the test session with, "Mittens. That's right."

Orrin continues, "And me too." His mother answers, "Who too?" and Orrin says, "And auntie too." His mother says, "Oh, auntie does too?" and Orrin says, "And sissy too." His mother takes the opportunity, saying, "Sissy too? What about daddy? Does daddy put on a jacket? Does he?" Orrin says, "Uh-huh," and his mother corrects him, "I don't think he does. Daddy doesn't even have a jacket. Daddy usually puts on one of his furry shirts." Orrin imitates, "Furry shirts." His mother says, "Uh-huh," and Orrin repeats, "Furry shirts." His mother says, "Uh-huh," and Orrin says, "Furry shirts. Furry shirts." His mother turns to asking Orrin to name body parts.

Prompting a Specific Answer

In some families casual conversations seemed like working sessions in which the child was challenged to remember and put experience into words and the parent was challenged to devise the prompts and hints that might draw details and descriptions from a child who had barely started talking.

Simon, 25 months old, is listening to tapes. His mother initiates, "How are you feeling, Simon?" Simon answers, reaching to his head, "I'm feeling Simon." His mother says, "Feeling Simon?" and Simon repeats, "Feeling Simon." His mother answers, "Is that Simon's head? Is it right there? How does it feel inside your head? Is it hurting, or is it fine?" Simon points to his finger and says, "Look at my owie's gone." His mother answers, "Your owie's gone, yeah." Simon answers, "Hurts. My owie gone for mommy. Mommy, my owie's gone for mommy." His mother says, "Your owie's gone from mommy?" Simon says, "No, mommy, look at owie. Look at." His mother says, "Which one?" Simon shows the finger on which he had a blood blister, and his mother says, "Oh yeah, it came off, didn't it? You got that at Maxine's house, didn't you?"

When Simon says, "Yes," his mother begins to prompt, starting with the general question she will ask most often in the future: "What happened?" and then narrows it to "What were you doing when you got that? Do you remember?" Simon answers the general question, "A owie." His mother responds, "Yes, but how did you get it? Can you tell me?" Simon begins, "I was at Maxine's house." His mother prompts, "You were at Maxine's house, and what were you doing there? You remember?" Simon says, "A owie." His mother says, "Yes, I know, but what were you doing there when it happened?" She gives a hint: "Were you playing on something?" Simon says, "Oh, Maxine's house," and mother repeats the hint: "Yes, but were you playing on something?" and follows with a more specific hint: "Were you climbing on something? You remember?" Simon responds, "On the . . . I climb on the Maxine's horsie." His mother confirms, "On Maxine's horsie, right. Right, exactly right." Simon remembers, "And then I got a owie." His mother confirms, "And that's how you got the owie," and ends by modeling a report of the specific circumstances: "You got pinched by the spring, right?"

Just Dancing

Some conversations, though, seemed merely to encourage a child to engage in the kinds of "small talk" in which telling about things is secondary to maintaining social closeness.

Tyrone, 21 months old, is lying on the living room floor watching a television commercial. He turns to his mother, who is sitting on the couch holding his baby sister. He initates, "Popcorn," and repeats once. His mother says, "Ain't no popcorn." Tyrone repeats, "Popcorn," twice, and his mother imitates. Tyrone says again, "Popcorn," and his mother asks, "Want some popcorn?" Tyrone says, "Uh-uh," and his mother says, "Why you ask for some then?" Tyrone does not answer.

After a minute he gets up on the couch beside his mother and says four times, "Popcorn." His mother asks, "You want some?" Tyrone gets down and stands in front of his mother and says, "Pop." His mother says, "Ain't no pop." Tyrone says, twice, "Popcorn," and his mother says, "What do you want?" Tyrone says, "Popcorn," and his mother says, "You want some popcorn?" Tyrone says, "Pop," and his mother says, "Yeah."

A minute later Tyrone initiates again, pulling on his mother's arm, and saying some nonwords. His mother asks, "What you want?" Tyrone says, "Pop. Popcorn." His mother says, "You want some popcorn?" Tyrone says, "Uh-uh," and his mother says, "You don't? You said uh-uh."

After another minute, Tyrone initiates again, "Popcorn." His mother says, "You want some popcorn?" Tyrone says, "Uh-uh. Popcorn. Popcorn. Popcorn." His mother says, "You want some?" Tyrone repeats four times, "Popcorn." His mother says, "You want some?" and Tyrone says, "Uh-uh." His mother says, "Why you asking for some?" and Tyrone says, "Mom." His mother says, "What?" Tyrone says, "You pop popcorn." Mother says, "You want some popcorn?" Tyrone says, "Pop." His mother says, "What you want?" and Tyrone says, "Popcorn." His mother says, "You want some?" Tyrone repeats, "Popcorn," twice, and his mother repeats, "You want some?" Tyrone says, "Popcorn. Yeah," and his mother gets up and goes to the kitchen and makes some popcorn.

❖❖❖❖

Seth, 25 months old, is playing in the living room when his father comes home from work. His father initiates, "Come here. What happened to your face, boy? Let me see." Seth goes to his father and says, "This." His father asks, "Who did it?" and Seth names his 3-year-old brother: "Chauncey there." His father repeats his question: "Who did it?" and Seth names his oldest brother, Otis. The boys' father refers the question to their mother, who is cooking dinner. She explains that Seth fell down the basement stairs.

The father asks whether there are any cookies left and then coaches Seth as he pulls his father's boots off.

After 5 minutes, when Seth initiates, "Dad," his father says, "Come here and let me see your face. Come on. Let dad see your hurt, where you hurt your face." Seth says, "Chauncey do." His father says, "I wanna know who did it." Seth says, "Did it." His father says, "Oh, Chauncey did it. Let me see. Who hurt that boy?" Seth says, "Me." His father says, "Did Otis do it? Who did it?" Seth says, "Otis did it." His father says, "Are you lying about it?" and Seth repeats, "Otis did it." His father says, "Did Otis do it?" and Seth does not answer.

Endnotes

1. The role of imitation and its variations has been the subject of much study; see Speidel & Nelson (1989).
2. Recasts of this kind have been presented in intervention programs to help children use more advanced language; see Nelson (1989).
3. Long ago Brown & Hanlon (1970) observed that parents almost never correct their children's grammar. Corrections are almost entirely for accuracy of reference ("No, it's not a horse").
4. See Hart & Risley (1995), pages 64–66. We listened to six tape recordings of each family early, in the middle, and late in the 2½ years of observations and noted at 30 randomly spaced instants whether we heard someone talking. We checked the transcript to code whether talk heard was addressed to the child and whether a moment of silence was within an ongoing interaction.
5. For every child, we examined the first 50 (each) recorded imperatives, declaratives, and questions and noted the parent's reaction to them as 1) immediate confirmation, 2) confirmation only after the child had added an utterance, 3) unrelated response, or 4) no response within 5 seconds. Reliability was assessed by having two coders independently categorize 500 utterances from three children; percentage of agreement was 95. We found no differences in the relative frequency of the four reactions across parents, whether they had completed only high school or had an advanced college degree. The similarity of all of the parents' reactions suggests ways that societies may "naturally" shape cooperation in conversation.

CHAPTER 7

Practicing

❖ ❖ ❖ ❖

*F*or an average of 9 months, we watched the 42 children staying and playing at conversation with their parents. We watched the children gain fluency in using grammatical structures and flexibility in elaborating and describing what they were doing and had done in the past. Therefore, we were not surprised to see the families begin to interact as though the children had learned to talk well enough and to see the babies whom we had seen cared for, catered to, and attentively prompted graduate to being just "other children" in the family, expected to take care of many of their needs themselves and ask when they wanted help. In some families graduation came with a new baby, a younger sibling to be cared for and socialized in the same way the "other children" had been. In all of the families, though, we noticed the change, as parents began to permit independence and demand conformity and children began to choose to play outside or in rooms away from parent monitoring. In the data we saw the children match and then exceed the amount of talk their families addressed to them.

We describe first how we saw the children change from babies learning to talk to children expected to participate in and conform to the ways of the social group. Then we describe the ensuing period when the children, like their families, were practicing their craft. This period of practicing takes us from the time the children were about 29 months old, regularly using grammatical sentences and morphemes appropriately, until they were 36 months old and our monthly observations ended.

Matching the Family

The observers remarked how marvelous is the life of a baby, and how persistently the children sought to leave this idyllic state. Babies' comfort and happiness were a family focus; every need was satisfied. Babies were free to explore objects and behaviors forbidden to older children and adults. Babies were centers of attention and interaction who could engage and entertain the family merely by smiling and babbling. Crying or screaming gave them power to influence family affairs and to control what happened to them. Yet the babies appeared eager to leave this Garden of Eden and get a share in the haphazard world of the family and social group.

From birth the babies had been exposed to the behaviors of the powerful and important people around them, and they were active participants in interactions. They were not equal partners, though. They responded to other people's initiations of interaction more often than other people responded to theirs. In the social hierarchy of the family, in which elders were answered first, babbling babies were usually answered last and often not all. The babies' role was often to be entertained during interaction, responsive to the words and actions of other people. As we watched the babies watching the varied activities of the people towering over them and stepping around them, we thought that to the naive, becoming like those people must seem incredibly attractive.

Motivation to Grow Up

As our training in social learning theory[1] had led us to expect, we began to see children trying to copy the actions of the important people in their lives. We saw parents encouraging them to do so. They gave children toy telephones, tea sets, and trucks. They accommodated children who insisted on sitting at the dinner table with the family rather than sitting in a highchair, and they gave children a role fetching and throwing things away for the family. But parents also actively socialized the children, following an agenda that demanded conformity with societal standards for eating with a spoon, using the potty, and wearing shoes. Parents modeled the criterion behaviors, instructed, prompted, and encouraged the children's efforts. If the children did not perform willingly in imitation of the family, parents used physical guidance, a last resort unavailable to socializing talking.

In socializing talking, parents had little choice but to wait and rely on the children to watch and listen to what other people were doing and attempt to do the same. The parents modeled words and sentences in reference to objects and activities, just as they modeled appropriate ways of eating and dressing. They began treating the children as social partners as soon as the children showed signs of trying to use words. They prompted and encouraged imitation and made the children's words socially effective. In staying and playing they engaged the children in conversations that subtly but steadily pressured conformity to family standards for how and when words are said appropriately. Then, just as with walking, eating, and dressing, there came a time when the family seemed to consider that the children now behaved well enough to graduate from instruction and be admitted as practicing members of the social group.

Making the Grade

In the data we saw the children meet and pass one hurdle after another before getting an equal share of family talk. First, they managed to match the amount of their social/vocal behavior to the amount of parent talk addressed to them. By responding or initiating and then holding the floor talking, using gibberish or nonwords if necessary, they managed to produce as much speech, with or without recognizable words, in an hour as their parents addressed to them (see Figure 7).

In each child's data we saw the steep, regular increase from 11 to 19 months old in the amount of social/vocal behavior per hour that marked the children's efforts to become talkers who could produce identifiable words in half or more of their utterances. Their parents steadily increased the number of their responses and the amount they talked to the children, from an average of 311 utterances when the children said their first words at 11 months old to an average of 377 utterances when the children became talkers at 19 months old. Once the children had become talkers who could produce 100 or more recognizable utterances per hour, the parents paused. When the children were 20 months old, the parents' average dropped from 377 to 348 utterances per hour as though the parents were inviting the children to try to say more. The next month, at an average age of 21 months old, the children spoke an average of 365 times and matched the average of 364 utterances their parents addressed to them in that hour. Even though the children could as yet include an identifiable word in only 233 of the 365 utterances, they showed they could speak as often in an hour as their highly flexible and fluent parents did. Then, as though once the parents had established an acceptable amount of verbal interaction they could begin to address its content, the parents started to stay and play for a while.

Parent talk containing wh-questions, other questions, and different words steadily increased, as did parent imitations and recasts of the children's utterances. Parents accepted from the children gibberish and immature utterances, self-repetitions, and imitations, even as the parents modeled more mature forms and encouraged the children to elaborate and tell them more. Parent prompting behaviors peaked when the children were 25 months old, when the children were using articles, plurals, and a tense marker (-*ing*). The children had begun saying, "I doing this," "I don't do this," "I can do this," and commenting on the past, "I did this."

Then when the children were an average of 26 months old, the parents again paused; the average number of utterances they addressed to the children dropped from 400 to 370 an hour and remained there for the next 2 months, as though the parents had settled down to listen to what the children could do without support. What the children could do at 28 months was say as many recognizable utterances in an hour as their parents addressed to them. At 28 months old the children matched their parents' average of 372 utterances per hour with an average of 396 of their own (with 86 nonword utterances added just in case).

Then, at 30 months old, the children went on to match the family when they produced an average of 377 recognizable utterances to match the average of 370 utterances the family addressed to them. But only 306 of the 370 utterances addressed to the children at 30 months old were spoken by their parents. After the 28-month-old children matched the amount of talk their parents addressed to them, the parents abruptly decreased the number of utterances they spoke to the children, from an average of 372 utterances at 28 months old to an average of 328 at 29 months old. The following month, parent talk to the children dropped still further to an average of 306 utterances per hour and the month after that to an average of 295 utterances per hour. Only 11 parents talked more than their children in 4 or more of the median of 12 months of subsequent observations.

Independence

The steady decline in parent talk was seen in all of the families, and the initial decrease was so abrupt as to suggest that the parents might somehow be recognizing when their children had learned to talk fluently enough. It seemed unlikely, though, that during their everyday interactions the ordinary parents we observed were using some intuitive standard to evaluate the maturity of what their children were saying. We went to the data to look at what was happening during the 3 months before a child first said as many utterances in an hour as the parent said to the child.[2]

If what a fluent conversational partner can do is answer, say as much as is needed, tell about things spontaneously, and clarify what is said, then the data showed that in the 3 months before the children matched the amount their parents talked to them, the children were displaying increasingly recognizable fluency. They were regularly telling their parents about things without prompting. The children were introducing an average of 6–7 of the average of 10 different topic nouns and modifiers that the parent as well as the child said during interactions. The children were elaborating and clarifying their own utterances such that 26%–29% of their utterances continued into one or more floorholding utterances.

But if parents were attracted naturally to more adult-like conversation, they would have talked more with fluent children, not less. The data showed, though, that more than just conversation was going on during interactions. The month before one child matched the amount the parent talked, the parent summarized, "She's started just defying me." The observers began to record children insisting, "I can do it myself," refusing to eat or get dressed, and being sent to time-out. They began to record parents responding, "You're boring today," "You getting on my nerves start talking smart," "I don't want to play. I want to do the dishes." As though there were societal consensus that 2-year-olds no longer needed close minding, a third of the mothers were pregnant at the month the children said as much in an hour as their parents said to them.

In the data from the 3 months before a child matched the amount of parent talk, we saw children begin using their increasing fluency to ignore or to discourage parent prompts (see the Examples at the end of this chapter). The answer to "Can you say . . . ?" was increasingly often "No." But only once did an observer notice an abrupt change in the pattern of interaction, in an observation that turned out to be the one in which the child first matched the amount the family talked. The mother asked the 25-month-old to tell about the movie they had gone to see. When the child named the movie, the mother prompted, "What did we see?" The child answered, "It's a lady. It's . . . ." The parent interrupted to correct and confirm, "It was a lady. Yes, there was a scary lady, wasn't there, and she went, 'Aah.' " The child said, "Uh-huh, lady said, 'Aah.' Like this, lady 'Aah.' Like this." The child's 4-year-old sister joined in, echoing, "Lady 'Aah.' " The child repeated 4 times, "Lady 'Aah,' " and added, "Her said it. Lady 'Aah.' Her say, 'Aah.' " The child added 18 successive variations on these utterances as the parent interjected periodically, "We know that," and, "Okay, you said it enough times." The child held the floor for 13 more utterances before the parent finally succeeded in recapturing the floor and redirecting the conversation.

The data showed that during the 3 months before the decline in parent talk to the children, somewhat more than a third (34%–38%) of the child utterances to which the parents responded were restatements (repetitions, extensions, reductions) of what the child had just said. An increasing percentage (15%–23%) of what the children told their parents described what the children were doing, had just done, or were about to do, and an additional 12%–13% were demands that the parent attend ("Look") or respond ("Where is it?" "Give it here"). More and more often we saw parents engaged in conversations concerning something the parent had already heard about, something the parent had watched or was watching the child do, or something the parent was being directed to do.

The parents seemed to recognize that their children had learned to talk fluently enough, but the basis seemed to be less the maturity of the children's utterances and more the nature of their conversations. During the months of staying and playing, increased parent attention had encouraged the children to practice until most of what they said was adult-like in form and reference. Surprises, and challenges to discover what the children were trying to say, became ever fewer for their parents. At the same time, the months of emphasis on the children's contributions to conversations had encouraged the children to focus talk on topics of concern to a 2-year-old. The children's increasing insistence on independence seemed to co-occur with their parents' increasing interest in the shared conversations of adults.

Family Membership

After the children matched the amount of talk that went on in the family, they seemed to become similar to everyone else in the family, just other children. They began to assert their own ideas during interactions and correct their parents (see the Examples at the end of this chapter). They began to talk more and more with other children, beyond the presence of their parents. The amount of parent talk decreased markedly. The parental "tell me about it" became the child's "tell myself about it" as monologues accompanied play. The children averaged more talk than their parents in every observation hour from 28 to 36 months old (see Figure 7). The amount the children talked stabilized around an average of 400 utterances an hour, much like the amount of family talk the children had been exposed to from 11 to 18 months of age.

Contexts of Talk

The children began spending increasing amounts of time separate from their parents. Between 29 and 36 months old, the children produced an average of about 100 of their 400 average utterances per hour while their parents were not in the same room. The observers recorded extended monologues as children engaged in pretend play and described to themselves what they were doing (see the examples at the end of this chapter). Parents let the children play outside or in the basement, in the garage, or in another room with siblings or alone. They watched from a distance and came to check periodically, injecting a "How are you doing in here?" into an ongoing monologue.

Parents invited other children over to play, offering the children opportunities to converse with talkers less skilled than the parents. The number of utterances addressed to the children by other children doubled, from the average of 55 per hour of the prior months to an average of 128 utterances per hour when the children were 29–36 months old. But the children dominated the conversations, producing an average of 218 floorholding utterances per hour to other children's average of 62 per hour.

The parents left the children with relatives and sitters more often.[3] Before the children were 2 years old, we recorded 10 observations across six families when neither parent was at home; after the children were 2 years old, we recorded 18 observations across 9 of the 42 families when the parents were not at home. The children talked about the same amount when alone with relatives, and the adult relatives talked to the children (an average of 213 utterances per hour) about the same amount the parents had talked when present. When the parent was at home, though, other adults talked to the children less than half as much (an average of 34 utterances per hour) as they had when the children were 11–19 months old.

Responses

The parents, who had nearly always initiated talk less often than the children, decreased their initiations still further (to an average of 23 per hour), held the floor less often during conversations (see Figure 5), and responded to only 42% of the 365 utterances the children averaged in the parents' presence. Parent questions and repetitions of the children decreased to the levels seen when the children were 11–19 months old. But the 50:50 relationship between child–parent responses did not change. Once interaction began, parents were as responsive as ever. The change was in who held the floor. After showing that they could talk as much as an adult, the children held the floor as their parents had in prior months to explain and elaborate, and their parents listened and answered.

Increasingly often the children brought up the topics of talk. Increasing numbers of the different nouns and modifiers that the children used per hour were not recorded in the parents' data in that observation hour. During the period of staying and playing, an average of 62% of the different nouns and modifiers recorded for the children per hour were also recorded in use by the parents in the same hour. The parents introduced an average of 55% of them. During the period of practicing, the children introduced an average of 64% of the different nouns and modifiers that they were recorded using per hour. Only 44% also appeared in the parents' data within 10 utterances of the child's use of the word.

Although the numbers of different nouns and modifiers the children and their parents both used within 10 utterances of one another decreased during the period of practicing, the average number of new vocabulary words added per month to the children's dictionaries did not decrease. During 7 months of the period of staying and playing, when the children were 22–28 months old, an average of 44 words per month (range 40–49) were added to the average child dictionary. An average of 44 words (range 37–48) continued to be added each month during the period of practicing when the children were 29–36 months old.

From just the first 100 utterances of each observation when the children were 21–28 months old, an average of 21 new words were added per month to the average child dictionary. Of these 21 new words, an average of 13 were nouns and modifiers; an average of 57% of the 13 were also said by the child's parent within 10 utterances of the child's first use. During the period of practicing, when the children were 29–36 months old, an average of 14 new words were added per month to the average child dictionary from the 100-utterance subsamples. Of these 14 new words, an average of 12 were nouns and modifiers; an average of 39% of the 12 were also said by the child's parent within 10 utterances of the child's first use.

During the period of practicing, the children more often were addressing talk to people other than their parents and talking in the extended monologues of pretend play, exploring words they had doubtless heard but not had occasion to say during the period of staying and playing. The parents were more often acting as a receptive audience. Now, they seldom needed to confirm by repeating the child's topic or to insert a question to encourage the child to elaborate; they were more often answering only enough to show they were listening.

Although the average number of different words the children used per hour (see Table 7) continued to increase, the average number of different words the parents addressed to the children per hour decreased. When the children were 11–19 months old, their parents had addressed to them an average of 245 different words in an average of 345 utterances. During the months of staying and playing, the parents' average increased to 308 different words in an average of 379 utterances. During the period of practicing, the parents addressed to the children an average of 292 different words in an average of 301 utterances per hour. Although the parents said fewer different words to the children, their utterances became relatively richer after they stopped prompting, repeating, and recasting their own utterances in order to maintain conversation.

Function

We saw the results of the parents' focus on encouraging the children to tell them about things when we saw that during the period of practicing the children initiated most of the educational exchanges that we recorded. A 33-month-old child initiated to her mother, "Uh-oh, my moccasin tied out." Her mother asked, "Came untied?" The child said, "No," and the mother said, "Yes, that's untied." The child said, "Oh, not tied." The mother said, "When it's not tied, it's untied."

Parents seemed to wait for their children to show an interest before trying to educate them. A 34-month-old interrupted his mother's conversation with his older sister to ask, "Who makes food? Who makes food? Who makes the bread?" His mother said, "Well it starts with the farmer growing wheat." She paused, and the child asked, "What?" The mother did not respond. She seemed to wait for the child to contribute or elaborate and so display an interest in hearing more.

It seemed strange to hear parents state facts with "I think." When a 35-month-old child reached toward the knobs on the stereo and said, "That says, 'No,'" her mother corrected, "I think that says, 'On.'" Another 35-month-old gave his mother a book to read, saying, "I buyed those at the library." His mother answered, "I think we bought the book at the bookstore." Then we realized that these parents were taking care not to discourage their children from talking to them by suggesting the children needed to be right when they told their parents about things.

We noticed parents observing their children without interrupting when the children appeared to be solving a problem independently. A 32-month-old picked up a toy car and said, "That one opens up." He went toward the kitchen where his mother was washing dishes as he commented, "Maybe a knife will do it. I will get it. Go get a knife. Looking for one. I get a knife." He pried at the car as he continued, "This won't do it. This. See this kind of spoon? It'll work." After more prying, he reached for another spoon and commented, "Maybe this will do it. Get another one. Let me try it. I will do it. It's working. There. Got it." The parent said nothing; it seemed excusable that she might not want to encourage the child to tell her even more about what she was watching him do.

Mistakes

We saw parents actively encouraging their children to practice until the children gained skills and fluency. Then they let the children practice independently so that the children could gain flexibility. As though they were sure the children would not stray too far from the English spoken in the social group, the parents surrendered control of the topics and conversation and left the children free to vary what they said. The observers began to record the children's mistakes.

Almost all of the children, after regularly hearing their parents say, "Let me do it," began to say, "Me do it," as well as "I do it." Several children asked, "Can me do it?" No parent corrected the child; one parent said, "I think he says, 'Me' instead of 'I.' I never paid that much attention." Like a good listener, she focused on the sense of what the child was trying to say rather than on its form. When a parent asked a 32-month-old, "Where's dad?" the child said, "He's volley-balling." The mother said, "He's what?" and the child rephrased into English likely to make better sense to her mother, "See, he's . . . he's playing ball."

Some children began to talk as though there might be multiple past-tense forms, as though "go" and "went" might be different words rather than different forms, so that "goed" referred to one past action and "wented" referred to another. Children said, "He gets one," and (so), "He gots one," which seemed to lead naturally to trying out not only, "He got one," but, "He getted it," and, "He gotted it." When a 33-month-old's mother and sister were talking about delaying a trip due to flooding, the child interrupted to say, "All the buses are drunk." Her sister said, "Yeah, no cars or boat could go there." The child replied, "Cars will go there. But all the buses are dranked. Are drunked. Right?" No one answered.[4]

After talking with the parent about a fly buzzing around the living room, a 35-month-old child went to play in his bedroom. When he returned to the living room, he initiated, "Our flew went away." His mother said, "What went away?" The child said, "Our flew." His mother said, "You flew away? Are you a bird?" The child said, "No, that fly went away." As their parents intended them to, the children became increasingly flexible. They seemed willing to try to say anything, sometimes as though merely to see whether it would make sense to someone. And by the time the children were 34–36 months old, only 18% of what they said was recorded as nonword utterances that made no sense.

Talking at Age 3

When the children were 34–36 months old, in the last 3 months of our observations, they were producing an average of 413 utterances per hour plus 72 nonword utterances. They were initiating an average of 55 times per hour; 117 of their utterances were said when a parent was not in the same room, and 234 of their utterances were said as they held the floor, 45 as repetitions of their own immediately preceding utterance, 5 as self-corrections, and the remainder as elaborations of what they had just said. The average MLU in morphemes was 3.4, and the average longest utterance was 11 words. They said an average of 1,401 words in an hour or, in a 14-hour waking day, almost 20,000 words, comparable to averages reported in the literature.[5] They used an average of 232 different words per hour; although their speech was far less rich in different words than their parents', they were rapidly gaining on their parents' average of 309 different words per hour.

In comparison to their parents, more of the children's utterances were statements about what they had done or were doing (an average of 43%) and phrases (an average of 38%) such as "Hi" and "Not me," or answers to questions. Fewer of the children's utterances were questions and imperatives (an average of 10% for each)[6] in contrast to the average of 15% imperatives ("Do as I say") and 28% questions ("Why don't you?") in the speech their parents addressed to them.

The children were producing an average of 17 utterances containing future tenses such as "gonna," 19 containing a past tense, and 14 clause constructions per hour at 34–36 months old. They were well beyond restricting their talk to the "here and now." All of the children were telling readily about past events and happenings beyond the visible referents of home and the immediate surroundings and about connections between events. One 32-month-old child began by introducing the topic, "Do you remember thunder and lightning? It makes a loud bump." She then continued, "And it scared me, and then when thunders go loud booms I come into mom and dad's room and sleep with them."

A 34-month-old child first reported the most important events, "And we didn't call the police on my mom. And my mom too silly. And my mom just dropped the juice on the car." The child then filled in the complete story, continuing, "And my mom is got a car. She go work. And my mom drive. And hit the car. Call the police. And my mom lost the juice." A 36-month-old told a more cohesive narrative as she pointed to the patio doors, "A mouse come out of here. And comes right in the living room and the mouse—. Remember? And kittens wanna catch him. And I see one behind the chair, this chair. And kitten catch it and put it in his mouth. Remember? And dad throw it in the garbage can."

As they neared 36 months old, the children whom we had observed babbling contentedly to their toys at 9 months old had become highly talkative, eager to display and impress their parents, siblings, and observers with the skills they had gained. One child at 34 months old said as soon as the observer arrived, "I goed to the circus." Having recruited his audience, he said, "Then there was clowns, all different clowns that they changed clothes with. Then they changed their clothes again like their all kinds of shirts. Because they had all colored shirts that was on them and come on the elephants. There was a man. See, he shot that, that mans. And then it was funny. Then he shot out." His mother interceded to contribute, saying, "And he flew and landed on the net, didn't he?" The child said, "Yeah. Then the other man leaped up on the swings. Then the elephant and the rocket ship the man was in, on the elephant, and the clowns drove him, and then the other man got in shooting himself out."

The children had become fluent and flexible, but they still had much to learn from the social group about how topics are linked and narratives are constructed so as to improve their effectiveness and help listeners understand. The children's joy in just putting out words and sentences and the parents' continuing willingness to listen, however immature was what the children said and how the children said it, suggested that the parents were, as always, judging correctly that the children needed less conversation with their parents and more practice with other people such as relatives and friends who might be less accepting of talking just for the sake of telling about things.

The parents had seemed to tutor their children only in talking as a social partnership, a dance between speakers and listeners. We saw that rather than teach, parents arranged the practice necessary for their children to become fluent in telling about increasingly complicated and varied topics in more and more complex ways using more and more of the distinctions and nuances that English makes available to its speakers. When the children were talking as much as their parents and telling their parents while the parents were watching every action, "I just did that," "Now I'm doing this," "Next I'm gonna do that," we saw the children become just "other children" who gain flexibility by conversing with a variety of other people.

Examples: Family Membership

When the children began talking as much as everyone else in the family, they began to assert their own opinions during interactions and engage in monologues similar to those their parents had displayed.

Controlling Conversation

The following are examples of children who for months had been encouraged to tell their parents about things.

Byron, 32 months old, is sitting in the living room looking at a picture book; his mother and Antonio, the 32-month-old she is babysitting, are sitting beside him. Byron's mother addresses Antonio: "You went to Texas?" Antonio answers, "The moon's over there too." Byron interjects to Antonio, "No, that's my moon. That's my moon." The mother tells Byron, "It's everybody's moon." Byron insists, "That my moon," and, pointing to a black circular spot on a cow in the picture book he is holding, says to Antonio, "Look. This is your moon." Byron's mother says, "That's not a moon"; Byron answers, "He got a moon." Byron's mother turns back to Antonio.

◆◆◆◆

Vera, 35 months old, is sitting on the floor in her bedroom; she and her mother are drawing. Vera has asked her mother to draw her a puppy. Vera's mother begins to draw and then comments, "That doesn't look too good, does it?" Vera answers, "Yes it does." Her mother says, "Does it? Okay." Then Vera says, "Mom," and her mother answers, "Huh?" Looking at her mother's drawing of a cocker spaniel, Vera says, "It's not a dog." Her mother says, "You don't want him a floppy-eared dog? He does look like kind of an elephant, doesn't he?" Vera

134

says, "I don't want him a floppy dog." Her mother says, "Oh well, I don't. . . . I agree that's not too good of a dog. Should we start all over?" Vera's mother starts again, and Vera says, "Oh, you gotta make him legs." Her mother agrees, "Yeah, I gotta make him legs. You're right." Vera says, "You forgot, mom." Her mother says, "This dog is sitting down, but he kinda looks like a cross between Dumbo and. . . ." Vera says, "He's happy."

Dodging Test Questions

Once their children were talking as much as the family, most parents began to ask only for information they really wanted to know. The following, however, is an example of a parent who continued to prompt.

Liam, 33 months old, is talking to his older sister. When he says, "We're leaving," his mother initiates to imitate his pronunciation, saying, "No, you're not weaving." His sister says to their mother, "Weaving is crocheting." Their mother calls Liam to her and prompts him to say the *L* in "leaving." After trying twice Liam changes the topic, saying, "Weaving is crocheting."

Later in the hour when Liam's mother begins to ask him to name the people who are going with the family on vacation, Liam names six different people and then says, "Hey, I see Scooby Doo." His mother asks, "Hey, are you ignoring me?" and holds the floor to prompt again. Liam names two people and then says, "I have this many pillows." His mother responds, "Does how many pillows you have have anything to do with who is going with us?" Liam says, "This many pillows," and his mother does not answer.

After a while Liam's mother prompts him to repeat the alphabet. They get as far as *S* and then Liam says, "I don't hafta," and offers to put some trash in the wastebasket in the kitchen.

Practicing Alone

The following extracts from a single observation may suggest the flavor of children's monologues when pretending and even suggest why their parents busied themselves elsewhere rather than prompting and encouraging as they had done only months earlier.

Candice, 35 months old, has gone to her bedroom; as she sits three dolls on the floor with their backs leaning against her bed, she says, "I'm gonna read you this book. And I gonna sit some people up with people. You sit down. Sit down there my bed. Now there are . . . hmmm. First put my Alice. Sit there, Alice, and keep her company. Oh, right there. You can sit on the potty. No, you 3 years old. Now, Alice, you 3 years old. Now you 3 years old. You be 2 years old. Now you 3 years old. You still little tiny baby. Now her 3 years old, I guess. That book I gonna read."

Candice sits in front of the dolls and opens a picture book. She holds the book facing the dolls, saying, "Now you see this, guys? Cluck cluck. See this page? And this and this. The doggie going over here. I'm gonna show you the kitty. Oh, I need three. I forgot three. See, I have got three." Candice laughs and mutters something. Then she says, "Who can sit up? Here, somebody else can sit down. I find this. Oh, my bear can sit up. You can sit at my party." She adds the bear to the row of dolls, saying, "Want sit on here? There. Now who can sit up now? You and you. One two three. I need another one. Who can sit up? Here. They not sitting up. Hmmm. I put it one two three. Find another one. I need other one circle. And I'm finding one."

She gets another doll to add to the story circle, saying, "I'll sit this little tiny. Her hold him, okay? You hold her here. Her sit on your lap. Now I hold you. You sit right, and you lay down. Maybe that's all. Another one. Here bear. That my bear. And now that is enough, I guess. I guess." She again opens the book, saying, "Gonna read this book. Okay, listen here. Now kids, I'm gonna read this book today. I can't find the page. I just gonna find the yucky page and the yucky page. Here, that page. See? Look at this."

She takes one of the dolls from the circle, saying, "And now you, you poop in panties. You get in time-out." She lays the large doll in a small doll bed at the side of her room. She turns to the story group and says, "Now her in time-out." She returns to the doll in the doll bed, saying, "Now sit in there. Now you poop in your panties. You're in that little bed again. You sit like this and lay down. Now. You not poop in that bed. Now here, how about that? Time-out. Time-out for you, miss, right here. Sit in time-out. That's enough for you. And you's put in time-out. You sit."

She takes the doll from the doll bed and pats it, saying, "Okay, I'm sorry. Take you out. Take you out. I better find a bed in here, right in here. There there. You bed is right here." After pretending to change the doll's diaper, she sits in a chair and rocks the doll, singing, "Rockabye baby. Goodnight, don't wake up. Rockabye sweetie pie. Don't wake up. Don't wake up in the morning." Then she says, "Ah," puts the doll on the floor, and gets a tote bag of items.

As she dumps out the bag, she says, "Here I gonna get this out 'cause we going camping. Oh, maybe I just dump this out. So far I don't need this. Oh, cars. I found my cars right here in time. And I found this this this this and every stuff here. Oh, this too. I gonna put a coffee cup in here." She begins to refill the tote bag, saying, "Going camping today. Lots of toys and my horn and this and . . . going camping today. Like my car go camping. Oh, my barrettes. This, put in. And some gloves go with me and Alice and him and her and him. Every people can go along. Oh, me take kitty cat and my babies.

My babies and I hope Alice can come along. And I gonna put her in. And I gonna put her blanket in case her wants her blanket in the night. That's in. That's heavy to carry it."

She continues packing the bag, now full to the brim, saying, "Not ready to go yet. We get more stuff for camping. We get medicine and every stuff in my bag. I don't believe it. This put in there now. And getting full and full. No, don't need that. I'm getting this and those. I think that goes. Go camping. That's gonna be fun. Now we ready. Come on. Come on, everybody. Oh no, not ready yet. Put . . . . Getting fuller and fuller. Gonna tip over. Don't wanna tip it over. Maybe I do this. Maybe I put this to front door, okay?" She puts the chock-full bag just outside her bedroom door in the hall. Her mother comes to check, asking, "What's happening in here?"

Endnotes

1. For discussion of social learning theory and the importance of observational learning through watching what other people do, see Bandura & Walters (1963).

2. We examined each child's first 100 fully recognizable utterances in the three observations prior to the observation in which the child first said as many utterances per hour as the parent said to the child. To be fairly sure that the parent heard what the child said, we counted utterances only in the child turns when the parent answered.

   To examine the extent to which a child was telling about things without prompting, we counted the number of all of the different nouns and modifiers recorded for the child that were spontaneously introduced by the child (i.e., not a repetition within 10 utterances of a parent-introduced topic nor prompted by a preceding parent wh-question or request to say a word). To examine the extent to which a child was elaborating and clarifying what the child had just said, we counted the number of child floorholding utterances. To examine demands for action or attention, we counted the number of child imperatives and questions. To examine self-reference, we counted the number of child utterances containing "I," "me," "my," "mine," or the child's own name. To examine how informative a child was, we counted the number of utterances that repeated or recast what the child had said within 1–3 preceding utterances.

   Reliability of coding was assessed by having a second person independently code all 100 utterances in six observations, one from each of six randomly selected children. Intercoder percentage of agreement was 91 overall with a range from 86% to 98% on the individual categories coded.

3. In all months, the data for parents were averaged only for the number who were present during the observation.

The data for a relative acting as parent were always coded as Other Adult.

4. Listed at the end of Appendix A are all 61 of the overgeneralized past-tense verbs recorded for 29 of the 42 children. Only "throwed" was recorded in parent use.

5. Wagner (1985) reported 20,000 words said in a day by children 1½–14 years old. McCarthy (1954) cited reports of 11,000–15,000 words said in a day by children 40–52 months old.

6. Bloom et al. (1976) also found that questions and imperatives averaged about 10% of child utterances.

CHAPTER 8

The Range Among
Well-Functioning
Families

◆ ◆ ◆ ◆

W e have described patterns of interaction common to 42 well-functioning (see Table 1) families with 1- to 2-year-old children and how these patterns changed as the children learned to talk. The data have shown the average age at which the children's first words were recorded by the observers and repeated by the parents and the average age at which the children managed to put a word or words into half of all of the social/vocal behavior they produced in an hour. The data have shown the average age at which the children gained specific skills with word forms and sentence constructions and how their parents reacted when the children began to talk as much as their parents did in an hour.

The "average child" we have described resulted from dividing numbers in the data; none of the 42 children was actually average. We averaged the data to reduce the day-to-day variability of the interpersonal interactions we recorded and so to reveal patterns common to all of the families and changes in interactions as the children matured. We used averages deliberately to look beyond the remarkable, often alluring, differences we saw among 42 families all similarly socializing their children. Now we needed to address the range. Just how different were these well-functioning families in what they were doing with their children? Just how different from the average can a child be in learning to talk and still develop into a "normal," competent speaker of English at age 3?

Extremes in the Data

We describe the range among the 42 children by showing data for children who were at the extremes at the beginning of the study and for children who were at the extremes at the end of the study. We have labeled the four comparison groups in order to remind us of the extremes of the range. To the observers, though, the children in the comparison groups were not noticeably different from the rest of the children in the study. The children in the comparison groups all learned to talk very similarly to all of the other children, and all were speaking fluently, appropriately, and grammatically at age 3. Rather, their data represent the ends of the continuum that contributed to the average. We chose them to display the range in interaction patterns among children learning to talk and illustrate how changes in children's talk simultaneously prompt and react to changes in parent talk.

At the extremes in the beginning of the study were the children who began talking early and those who began late. The greatest difference among the children initially was seen in the number of months that intervened between saying the first words and becoming a talker who produced words in half or more of all speech per hour. The considerable range in the age when children attain developmental milestones (sitting up, walking, talking) is well-documented,[1] and no long-term effects on development have been attributed to attaining such milestones a few months earlier or later than average. But our data showed that one-to-one interactions increased markedly after the children became talkers. Thus, the initial range among the 42 children provides an opportunity to consider how patterns of interaction may be affected when children become talkers earlier or later than average.

At the end of the study, the greatest difference among the children was seen in how much they talked. Some were highly talkative; a periodic "Uh-huh" from a parent was enough to keep them describing in detail their every activity. Other children were taciturn, content to play silently for long periods between interactions with their parents. Talking a lot has been reported related to more rapid progress in learning to talk.[2] Our data showed a steep increase in the number of utterances the 42 children produced per hour during the months they and their parents were staying and playing, which suggests that their parents may have considered that practicing conversation might contribute to learning to talk. The range in talkativeness at the end of the study provides an opportunity to consider the course of learning to talk among the children who practiced more and less than average.

Early and Late Talkers

At the beginning of the study, we chose 4 of the 5 children who were youngest and 4 of the 5 children who were oldest when they became talkers who said identifiable words in half of all of their speech per hour. So that there would be no overlap of the groups, 2 children, both girls, who qualified for more than one of the extreme groups were removed from the selection. One child was both an early talker (at 16 months old) and highly talkative at age 3 (averaging 593 utterances per hour at 34–36 months old). The other child was a late talker (at 23 months old) and taciturn at age 3 (averaging 124 utterances per hour at 34–36 months old). The average child of the 42 became a talker at 19 months old, 8 months after the first recorded words at 11 months old. The 4 early talkers first produced identifiable words in half of all of their speech when they were an average of 17 months old (range 15–18), an average of 7 months (range 2–9) after their first recorded words. The 4 late talkers first produced identifiable words in half of all of their speech when they were an average of 25 months old (range 24–27), an average of 16 months (range 12–19) after their first words were recorded. Each group of 4 children contained 2 girls, at least 1 firstborn and 1 second-born child, and at least 1 child in a family whose occupation was classified as professional. In each group there were 2 children in working-class families and 1 African American child.

Talkative and Taciturn Children

We chose 4 of the 5 most and 4 of the 5 least talkative children at the end of the study. Averaged for the last three observations, at 34–36 months old, the average child produced 413 utterances per hour (range 124–687). The 4 most talkative children produced an average of 637 (range 582–687) utterances per hour at 34–36 months old. The 4 least talkative children produced an average of 206 (range 136–236) utterances per hour at 34–36 months old. Each group of 4 children contained 2 girls, at least 1 firstborn, 1 second-born, and 1 third-born child, and at least 1 child in a working-class family. Two of the most talkative children were in professional families; all were white. Three of the least talkative children were in families living on welfare; all were African American.

The Social World

In the sections that follow, we describe the range in the data in terms of the averages within each of the four groups of 4 children and their parents and compare them with the average for the 42 children during the successive periods of becoming partners, staying and playing, and practicing. We discuss first the similarities between the extreme groups and then the differences.

Similar Patterns of Interaction from 11 to 36 Months Old

For the children in the four groups at the extremes, family interaction patterns were similar to those in the average family. As in the average family, all of the parents of the children in the groups at the extremes both encouraged independence and demanded conformity. They let the children choose how to spend the day and what to receive at Christmas even as they prohibited dangerous explorations and required the proper use of a spoon and a toilet. Though the families differed considerably in lifestyle, nothing distinguished them for the observers from all of the other families nurturing and socializing their children. The data, not the families' daily activities, put these children at the ends of what was in fact a continuum across the 42 families.

The overall pattern of interaction described for the average describes equally well the pattern of interaction among the families of the children in the groups at the extremes. As did the average child, the children in the groups at the extremes initiated interaction more often than their parents did across the entire 2½ years of observations. Illustrated in the data from the children in the groups at the extremes is a relationship that held for nearly all of the families. Children who initiated interaction more often than the average tended to live with parents who initiated less often than the average, and vice versa, as though there were some "normal" frequency of parental attention that 1- to 2-year-old children need or get accustomed to receiving. An average of one to two child–parent contacts were made per minute when the children were 11–19 months old. Even when the children were 29–36 months old, exchanging as many as 200 responses per hour, child–parent contacts occurred more frequently than once per minute on average.

For the children in the groups at the extremes, as for the average child between 11 and 19 months old, almost half

(40%) of child–parent contacts were one sided. Before the children began talking, children and parents were equally likely to make contact without prompting an answering behavior. Also similar to the average child, the children in the groups at the extremes were consistently more responsive than their parents. But once an interaction started, the 50:50 ratio of child-to-parent responses was seen in all of the groups except the taciturn group, which was the only group in which more than the average number of the children's social behaviors took place when the parent was not in the same room. During the period of practicing (29–36 months old), the children in the groups at the extremes, again similar to the average child, held the floor more often than their parents.

Similar Patterns of Family Talk from 11 to 36 Months Old

In the families of the children in the groups at the extremes, as in the average family, the parents did most of the talking to the child over the entire 2½ years of observations. Other children and adults seldom talked to the children until after the children were talking. The remarkable consistency of the social environment of learning to talk (see Figure 4) is as apparent at the extremes as at the average. Despite the differences in the amounts of talk in the families representing the extremes in the data, in each group about half of the talk the children heard every hour was exchanged between the mature speakers whom the children would learn to be like.

When the children were 29–36 months old, the amount of ambient talk heard by the children in the groups at the extremes decreased, as it did for the average child. The children in the groups at the extremes, similar to the average child, were spending more of an observation hour playing where the observer's tape recorder did not pick up the talk going on between other people. The percentages of child utterances recorded when the parent was not in the room were similar to the average (22%) for the children in the late group and talkative group, somewhat less (12%) for the children in the early group, and proportionately more (37%) for the children in the taciturn group.

Different Families from 11 to 36 Months Old

We noted in Chapter 3 that the largest and most consistent difference among the families was in how often the families talked and interacted. The data from the families of the children in the groups at the extremes illustrate this statement. Families above (or below) the average in the period of becoming partners continued to be above (or below) the average throughout the periods of staying and playing and practicing. The children in the talkative group lived in families who consistently exchanged 200 utterances more per hour than the 800 utterances per hour of the average family. The children in the taciturn group lived in families who consistently exchanged 200 utterances less per hour than the average family. A child learning to talk did not change the amount of talk that went on in the family; rather, the child came to be similar to the family.

Our prior book, *Meaningful Differences in the Everyday Experience of Young American Children*,[3] described in detail the differences in everyday parenting that are related to differences in the amount of talking and interacting customary in a family. More talking involves more different words, more responses, and more floorholding to explain, to elaborate, or to persuade. We have noted the substantial relationship between the amount of parent talk and the amount of child talk. We saw this relationship illustrated in each successive period in the data from the groups at the extremes.

Developmental Change

The motor development and the daily lives of the children in the four groups at the extremes were similar to those

147

of the average child. Feeding, changing, and dressing were major activities, which gave way gradually to spending more time outdoors and playing with toys. The observers were surprised to see many of the same toys in almost every home (e.g., a See 'n Say) regardless of family income or years of parent education.

All of the children in the four groups at the extremes gained the fluency and flexibility that characterize a competent 3-year-old speaker of English. They all produced more and longer utterances so that at age 3 in each of the groups, the average utterance contained somewhat more than 3 words, similar to that of the average child and, again similar to the average, the longest utterance contained 9–12 words. At 34–36 months old, the children in all four groups at the extremes were producing clauses, past and future tenses, and the full range of auxiliary verbs. All were regularly using the full range of pragmatic functions. Similar to the average, one third to one half of their utterances were declarative statements (34%–52%); they gave orders as seldom as average (7%–13% of all utterances) and asked as few questions (6%–13% of all utterances). More than one third of what all of the children said continued to be phrases.

The children in all four groups at the extremes gained the skills categorized from the IPSyn[4] (see Table 5) in the same relative order as the average child. Only in three or fewer cases were particular skills (e.g., the first recorded use of the present progressive -*ing*) recorded earlier or later than for the average child, and these cases were as likely to be recorded earlier as to be recorded later. Gains in skill were recorded with equal regularity over successive months in all of the groups at the extremes.

A difference in gaining the skills categorized from the IPSyn was seen between the children in the early group and those in the late group. The relative order in which skills with morphemes and sentence structures were gained did not differ between the groups or from the average, nor did the age (20 months old) at which the first of the listed skills (see Table 5) was recorded. But the children in the early group had produced all 30 of the listed skills after 8 months of practice (by 28 months old), 5 months earlier than the average at 33 months old. The children in the late group had produced only 29 of the 30 listed skills at 36 months old, 3 months later than the average. When the children in the late group were 3 years old, the observers still had not recorded a wh-question containing a pre-posed auxiliary (e.g., "What are you doing?" rather than the more usual "What you doing?").

To our surprise, the talkative group and the taciturn group did not differ either in the timing or in the relative order the children gained skills with morphemes and sentence structures. Only when the children in each group were 36 months old had all 30 of the skills listed from the IPSyn been recorded, 2–3 months later than for the average child. The substantial differences between the two groups in the numbers of utterances the children produced and the numbers of parent prompts during conversation made no difference to how soon or in what order the children gained skill with the auxiliaries, morphemes, and sentence structures used by competent English speakers.

Becoming Partners

We labeled as a period of becoming partners the months from the children's first recorded word until they became talkers and half or more of their verbalizations during an hour of recording were utterances containing identifiable words. The average child said a first word at 11 months old and became a talker at 19 months old. At 11 months old the average child said 5 utterances containing identifiable words among a total of 132 verbalizations. At 19 months old the average child said 167 utterances containing identifiable words among a total of 305 verbalizations and used 57 different words drawn from a vocabulary that had grown from 1 word to 81.

Similar Patterns of Interaction

The pattern of increasing numbers of child and parent responses seen in the average family was also seen in each of the four groups at the extremes, and in each group, as in the average family, the children regularly responded slightly more often than their parents did. In all except the taciturn group, child and parent responses increased in amounts similar to the average, from about 100 per hour to 130–150 per hour within 6 months after the children said their first words. In those 6 months the children in each of the groups at the extremes increased their social/vocal behavior by 30–100 verbalizations per hour, similar to the average child.

Even as the amount of parent–child interaction increased and the children said increasing numbers of recognizable utterances, parent responsiveness remained unchanged. Similar to the average, the parents in each of the groups at the extremes did not respond to 20%–33% of their children's nonword utterances or to 15%–30% of the children's utterances containing identifiable words.

Like the average parent, the parents in each of the four groups at the extremes appeared more concerned with their children becoming partners than with increasing the number of recognizable utterances their children said. In none of the groups did the parents begin to ask more wh-questions for at least 5 months after the children said their first words. Except in the talkative group, the parents prompted imitation ("Say . . .") at most once per hour, and even when the children were saying 40 or more recognizable utterances per hour, the parents in the four groups at the extremes, similar to the average parent, confirmed by imitating fewer than one of three of the children's identifiable words. Similar to the average, though, in all except the taciturn group, the proportion of interactions in which the children responded only once steadily declined, and those interactions in which the children responded seven or more times increased, as though having a conversation of some kind was temporarily more important than producing words.

In each of the four groups at the extremes, as in the average, in the month the children first said 40–50 recognizable utterances per hour, the number of their imitations increased from a prior average of one to between four and seven per hour. Similar to the average child, the children in each of the four groups at the extremes were recorded reducing an utterance to one word at or before the month of becoming a talker half or more of whose verbalizations were utterances containing identifiable words.

Differences While Becoming Partners

When the children said their first words, the range among the children in the four groups at the extremes was at its narrowest. In all of the groups—even the taciturn group—the children averaged more social/vocal behavior per hour at 12 months old than the average child, and they differed in amount by less than 50 verbalizations per hour. The differences were more in how much talking and interacting typically went on in the families and less in how the parents responded when their children began saying words. In each group, interaction increased, but in the talkative group, child responses more than doubled (from 125 to 270 per hour) during the period of becoming partners, whereas in the taciturn group, child responses increased from 105 to 129 per hour, less than in the average family or in any of the other groups. When the children in the talkative and taciturn groups became talkers at 20–21 months old, the differences in amount of practice that put the groups at the extremes at age 3 were already evident.

Because we chose the early and late groups expressly to display differences between children who spend fewer and

151

more months than average between the month of saying the first words and producing an identifiable word in half or more of their utterances, the absence of initial differences between these two groups is worth remarking. Though the children in the late group took 7 months longer than the children in the early group to become talkers, when the children were 12–13 months old, neither the children's rates of speaking and responding nor their parents' rates of responding and asking questions differed markedly between the groups; in both groups they were slightly above the average.

The data from the late group differed from that of all of the other groups in the appearance of a 6-month-long plateau in the amount of the children's social/vocal behavior per hour (see Figure 8). For 6 months between the ages of 14 and 19 months old, the number of verbalizations recorded for the children in the late group varied only between 209 and 227 per hour. In these 6 months the children in the other groups had increased their numbers of verbalizations per hour by 100 or more, and the number of their recognizable utterances per hour had increased by 80 or more. The children in the late group had increased their recognizable utterances by 14 per hour in these 6 months. A parallel plateau appeared in the parents' data. During the same 6 months, no increases similar to those seen in the other groups appeared in the numbers of parent responses or questions recorded per hour. During these 6 months, though, the four families did not seem to the observers to be interacting differently than the other families, and the data did not indicate that they were other than within the normal range of ordinary families.

Staying and Playing

We labeled as a period of staying and playing the months of concentrated interaction during which parents encouraged their children to explore words and tell ever more elaborately about increasingly complex events. We separated the data at the month after half or more of the average child's verbalizations were utterances containing identifiable words. At that time the average child was 20 months old and produced 327 verbalizations per hour, of which 183 contained identifiable words.

Similar Patterns of Interaction

The pattern of steady month-by-month increase in interaction that characterized the period of staying and playing in the average family was also seen in each of the four groups at the extremes (see Figure 8). In each of the four groups, average child utterances increased more than average parent utterances. Between the ages of 20 and 28 months old, the children in each group, similar to the average child, doubled the number of recognizable utterances they produced per hour. Also similar to the average child, the greatest increase was seen in the number of floorholding utterances in which a child repeated, recast, amplified, or elaborated what the child had just said. In each of the four groups, as in the average, child initiations decreased slightly during the months of staying and playing, and in all except the early group, child responses also decreased slightly. The children in each of the four groups, similar to the average child, increased the number of floorholding utterances that held their parents' attention by between 75 (for the children in the taciturn group) and 310 (for the children in the talkative group) per hour.

As in the average family, the increase in amounts of parent talk was seen in the greater number of responses recorded as the parents answered increasing amounts of child talk. During the period of becoming partners, in the average family and in each of the four groups at the extremes, the largest percentage of parent utterances (from 47% in the taciturn group to 68% in the talkative group; 60% in the average family) were coded as floorholding utterances that prompted children to take a turn, that filled in when the children did not, or that merely entertained or maintained social closeness. Only 26%–41% (33% in the average family) of parent talk to their 11- to 19-month-old children was coded as responses to the children's behavior. During the period of staying and playing, 39%–47% of parent talk was coded as responses. Percentages of parent floorholding utterances decreased to between 40% in the taciturn group and 55% in the late group (46% in the average family). Between the ages of 24 and 30 months old, the children in all four groups at the extremes, similar to the average child, began producing more floorholding utterances per hour than their parents.

In each of the four groups at the extremes, as in the average family, the increased amount of parent talk during the period of staying and playing did not change the parents' style. Questions that prompted the children to practice increased in number in every family, but the proportion of questions in parent talk to the children remained much the same. In the average family, approximately 28% of all parent utterances were questions; the number of questions the average parent asked the child peaked at 118, 29% of the 402 utterances the parent addressed to the child at 25 months old. The number of questions asked of the children in the early group peaked at 194, 29% of the 669 utterances the parents addressed to the children at 23 months old.

The proportion of questions in the talk of the parents in the talkative group (approximately 32%) was slightly higher than the average, and the proportion of questions in the talk of the parents in the taciturn group (approximately 20%) was below the average. In neither group did the proportion change markedly or become average over the entire 2½ years of observations. These relative proportions resulted in recording the parents of the children in the talkative group asking their maximum number of questions, 232 per hour, when the parents addressed 639 utterances to their 21-month-old children. By contrast, the parents of the children in the taciturn group asked their maximum number of questions, 68, when the children were 19 months old and the parents addressed 322 utterances per hour to the children.

Also as in the average family, the parents in each of the four groups at the extremes regularly imitated an average of 1–7 times more often per hour than the children. In each of the four groups, child imitations peaked several months after the children became talkers and then dropped abruptly, as though the children had begun contributing their own complementary utterances rather than imitating their parents'. All of the parents, though, continued to confirm their children's responses by repeating them. Also, in each of the four groups at the extremes, as in the average family, the children appeared to be monitoring their own performance. They regularly recast and revised approximately 5% of their own utterances. Only the children in the taciturn group repeated verbatim a higher percentage of their own utterances than the average of 15% recorded for the other groups.

Differences While Staying and Playing

The timing of the period of staying and playing differed for the children in the late and taciturn groups. For the average child and for the children in the early and talkative groups, the increase in the amount of parent talk and in the numbers of parent questions and parent and child imitations peaked at approximately the same time, when the children were 22–24 months old.

For the children in the taciturn group, the peak in the amount of parent talk and in the numbers of parent questions and parent and child imitations appeared when the children were 18–20 months old, 4 months earlier than the average. At 20 months old, the children in the taciturn group said an average of 128 recognizable utterances, not yet half of the 286 verbalizations they produced in the hour. Their cumulative recorded vocabulary contained 88 words, and none of the skills categorized from the IPSyn had as yet been recorded. The peak number of the concentrated parent–child interactions that characterized the period of staying and playing in all of the groups occurred for the children in the taciturn group before half of what the children said during interaction was recognizable as English words. The parents may have been sure that vocabulary and grammar would develop with time and experience and so may have given priority to encouraging the children to practice conversing as much as was typical in the family.

For the children in the late group, the peak in parent and child imitations appeared when the children were 27 months old. For a full year after the children's first words at 11 months old, no upward trend was seen in the number of parent utterances, questions, or imitations. Amount of parent–child interaction changed little during the prolonged period when the majority of what the children in the late group said consisted of nonword utterances. The children were 24 months old, with a cumulative recorded vocabulary of 116 words, when they first produced 100 recognizable utterances in an hour of recording, and were 25 months old when half of all of their verbalizations were utterances containing identifiable words. The unusually late start of staying and playing impressed on us how crucial was a social partnership in taking up talking. In Chapter 5 we described one of the children in the late group and commented that when staying and playing began it was as though the parent and the child had finally decided to dance together.

Practicing

We labeled as the period of practicing the months after the children began to talk as much as they were talked to and their parents began to talk with them less and less. The period of practicing began when at 28 months old the average child produced 396 utterances in an hour to match the parent's 372 utterances. Child utterances averaged 394 per hour for the next 8 months; parent utterances averaged 301 per hour (78 fewer per hour than during the months of staying and playing and 44 fewer per hour than during the period of becoming partners).

Similar Patterns of Interaction

In each of the four groups at the extremes, we saw a similar pattern of steadily increasing amounts of talk that culminated in the children's matching the amount their parents typically talked to them. At 31 months old the children in the early group produced 386 utterances to match their parents' 391. At 26 months old the children in the talkative group produced 518 utterances to exceed their parents' 481. At 25 months old the children in the taciturn group at produced 212 utterances to exceed their parents' 170. At 29 months old the children in the late group produced 290 utterances to match their parents' 287.

The pattern of decreasing numbers of parent utterances in the 3 months prior to the month the average child matched the number of parent utterances was also seen in each of the four groups at the extremes, accompanied by evidence of the children's increasing fluency and independence. The children in all four groups at the extremes, similar to the average child, were telling about things spontaneously: 60%–70% of the mutual topics named by a noun or modifier were child chosen. In all four groups at the extremes, the children were holding the floor to amplify or clarify their own utterances, and increasingly often (25%–41% of the utterances their parents answered) they repeated or restated what they had just said. Similar to the average, 12%–13% of their utterances ordered the parent to act, and an increasing proportion (15%–30%) described something they were doing, had just done, or were about to do.

Also in all four groups at the extremes, a similar pattern of steadily decreasing amounts of parent talk with the children was seen following the month in which the children matched the amounts their parents talked to them, and, because parent styles did not change, parent questions decreased in each group to averages similar to those seen during the period of becoming partners. During the period of practicing, parent utterances ranged from 116 per hour in the taciturn group to 435 per hour in the talkative group, 114–139 fewer per hour than during the months of staying and playing and 60–90 fewer per hour than during the period of becoming partners.

In each of the groups at the extremes, as in the average, the numbers of child utterances recorded per hour during the period of practicing stabilized at averages within 90 utterances of the average number of parent utterances said to the child per hour during the period of becoming partners. Thus, during the period of practicing, child utterances ranged from 222 per hour in the taciturn group to 583 per hour in the talkative group. Though the children in the taciturn group, similar to all of the other children at age 3, presumably could have talked as much as the children in the talkative group, they seemed to settle at talking as much as was typical in their own families.

Differences While Practicing

In each of the four groups at the extremes, the children matched the amount of talk their parents addressed to them so that in the period of practicing, differences in amounts of parent talk became differences in the amount the children talked. The greater amount of talking that went on over the entire 2½ years of observation set the children in the early and talkative groups at the upper extreme. In both groups the parents prompted and responded more often than the average, and the children practiced more and used more different words than the average child.

Similar to the upper extreme, the lower extreme seemed in place from the start. The less than average amount of talking in the taciturn group put the children at the lower extreme over the 2½ years of observation. The children were exposed to fewer words, prompted, and responded to less often; they practiced less often than average, and used fewer different words. The children in the late group seemed to settle at the lower extreme by displacing to an older age the process of learning to talk. The data of the children in the late group would look quite similar to those of the average child if the 6 months of the plateau were omitted from their data and the two sets of data were aligned at the month the children became talkers.

At Age 3

In our previous book, *Meaningful Differences*, we grouped the parents by SES in order to examine the extremes among the families in material and educational advantages. Our analyses revealed that these advantages contributed far less to the number of different words that the children were using at age 3 than did the amount of language experience that the parents had provided the children before age 3. In this book we grouped the children in order to examine the extremes in the range that we observed among 42 children similarly learning to talk. Parent SES varied within each group of children. The data showed that the children who were using more different words at age 3 were children who had talked more and whose parents had provided more language experience before the children reached age 3. The link between the findings reported in this book and in our previous book is the social dance of family life, the reciprocity of everyday interactions that blends the amount of parent talk with the amount of child practice talking.

Examples: Talking at the Extremes

The following examples are from children whose data put them in the groups at the extremes of the 42. The examples were selected because they are more interesting than much of what those children said, although not atypical of the topics and skills recorded for the children.

A Child in the Early Group

Holly, 35 months old, is rolling a ball in the living room; her mother is watching while feeding Holly's baby brother. Holly rolls the ball and says, "Uh-oh, right into my Duplos"; as she picks the Duplos up, she says, "Shall I put them out and see what you or I could do with them? First, we need two lines to show you how to make a building. I'm gonna make a building. It's a type of building that's really hard. Because I'm gonna make it. Gotta do like two squares. Four squares. I poured them out. Now look at. See, this is how I make a building. First you need two sides and then you put two sides on them all and then. . . . And then you put two things. And then put all the squares. And then you know how you make a building. See? See the building? This is how you make a building."

Holly's mother responds, "Oh, that's gonna be a nice building. Are you gonna put a window in it?" Holly answers, "No, I think these are windows there." Her mother says, "Oh those are windows. That's fine." Holly puts some more blocks together and then says, "See, you always put these things all over so you can't touch. Because this, this building's very sharp. This building is very sharp." Her mother says, "It's sharp huh?" and Holly answers, "Uh-huh, it's sharp. You can't touch it." Her mother says, "I can't touch it. Okay."

A Child in the Late Group

For more than 27 minutes of the observation, the mother has been sitting in an armchair holding Ernest's baby sister and trying to persuade Ernest, 32 months old, to get dressed. He has changed his pajama top for a shirt and put both socks on. As he reaches for his shoes, his mother says, "Your overalls are up here, Bubby. Do you think you should put them on first?" Ernest says, "Uh-huh, when I put my shoes on." He pulls at the laces in the shoes and says, "Just gotta get these here. Where'd he get that? Where'd daddy get this tie out?" His mother says, "I don't know. Let me see. I can't see what you're doing." Ernest says, "Don't want," and his mother asks, "Well, are you trying to open them up so they go on your foot easier?" Ernest says, "Uh-huh," and gives his mother the shoe. His mother takes the shoe and loosens the laces, saying, "Well, we don't want to take it out. Just wanna open it up a little bit. See, the only time you have to open them up real wide is when you've got those high tops on them. Which I hate." Ernest says, "Those aren't high."

After Ernest gets one shoe on, he wraps the laces around one another. His mother says, "Are you tying? Going through the motions?" and Ernest asks, "How you gonna tie those?" His mother offers to show him how; when he puts his foot up on her lap, he asks, pointing, "What is that?" His mother says, "That's just an eyelet." Ernest says, "That's a eyelet?" and his mother says, "That's just where your shoestrings go through."

After his mother ties the shoe, Ernest pulls the bow loose. After he tries to retie it for a while, his mother asks, "Do you want me to tie it?" Ernest says, "I can tie it. I can do that. See, I did it." His mother says, "It's a little bit harder than you think. But you're trying, aren't you? I wish you'd put your overalls on. I'm afraid your legs are gonna get cold. Don't pull your laces. You might

161

break them." Ernest answers, "I won't break them," and after several more tries, declares, "Gonna chop them off. And put in some more." His mother says, "No, you don't wanna chop them off," and Ernest says, "With some pliers." His mother says, "No you don't need to chop them off with the pliers," and Ernest says, "Why?" His mother says, "Just because," and Ernest says, "Well I need to." His mother says, "Why? All you need to do is tie them and then they won't be so long."

Ernest takes off the shoe. As he starts putting it on again he says, "Let her watch me." His mother says, "Let her watch you?" She turns Ernest's baby sister on her lap so she is facing Ernest and says, "Okay, let's see if she's as impressed as I am. Let's see. She'd wanna see you put your overalls on, I know." Ernest says, "Put my shoes on here. Watch." His mother says, "Open it up real big now, like I showed you. Pull it apart. Pull the tongue up. This is what they call the tongue." Mother takes the shoe and shows Ernest, "See right there? Open it wide, and then pull the tongue up." Ernest takes the shoe saying, "Pull the tongue up." Mother says, "That's the shoe tongue. You didn't know a shoe had a tongue, did you?" Ernest says, "Uh-uh. Have a tongue."

As Ernest puts the shoe on, his mother speaks for the baby, saying, "Okay tell, say I wanna see you put on your overalls now." Ernest gets his overalls and gives them to his mother to undo the straps. His mother hands them back, asking, "Now where do your feet go?" Instead of taking the overalls, Ernest says, "I'm gonna do again." His mother says, "Oh brother, not the shoes again." Ernest says, "I just tie them," and his mother says, "Geezer."

At the end of the observation hour Ernest still did not have his overalls on.

A Child in the Taciturn Group

Boris, 35 months old, is in the living room with his sister, playing with a toy figure. He gets a stick and says,

"He-Man. I'ma whip you." He looks at the observer and says, "I ain't whipping you. Because you ain't bad." He turns to his sister, "I got whip you," and hits her with the stick. She says, "Ouch," and Boris says, "I hit you next time. So stop acting bad. You talking back?" His sister says a nonword, and Boris hits her with the stick and says, "Talking back again." She says, "Ow," and Boris says, "Get some say one time. One time. I'ma whip your butt," and hits her again. His sister says, "Ouch," and Boris says, "One more time. I'm whipping your butt." His sister says, "Shut up," and Boris says, "I'm whipping you if you talk no one time. I'm whip your butt." His sister says, "I'm whip your butt." Boris answers, "You don't run me," and hits her with the stick.

Boris's mother comes into the room and, taking the stick, says, "Why you hit your sister? Why you hit your sister? Huh? You know better. You don't suppose to be playing with this stick no way." Boris laughs, and his mother says, "It's not funny Boris." Boris does not answer.

A Child in the Talkative Group

Vivian, 35 months old, is in her bedroom with her brother Dennis, age 5. They are looking out the window their mother is covering with a plastic weatherproofing sheet. Dennis initiates, "I see a fat little birdie out there." As Vivian calls out, "Hi, fat little birdie," the mother asks Dennis, "What kind?" Dennis replies, "He's a blue jay." Vivian repeats, "He's a blue jay," and adds, "I like blue jays." The mother comments, "Probably got fat for the winter," as Vivian continues, "Because when I went to Sylvia's house there was a blue jay. There was a blue jay laying on Sylvia's grass, and he was dead." Dennis responds, "Oh, Vivian, wow!" The mother tells Dennis, "I think it kinda grossed her out, and that's why she remembers it." Vivian informs her mother, "He wasn't gross." Her mother confirms, "He was just dead," and Dennis suggests, "Maybe he died when he was flying. . . ." Vivian interrupts, "No," and the mother says, "I think the kitty probably helped him along." Vivian corrects her, "No, he just ate him all up. It wasn't. . . ."

Vivian changes the topic as she pulls a toothpick from her pocket and displays it for her mother, saying, "Mommy, I like toothpicks because something's stuck in my teeth." Her mother asks, "Oh, where'd you get that?" Vivian answers, "It was one of my dad's." Her mother takes the toothpick, saying, "Oh, don't get those toothpicks. You shouldn't play with them." Vivian says, "Oh, don't play with the toothpicks. Mommy, I stuck myself on . . . ." Dennis interrupts to return to a previous topic. He asks, "Vivian, who else is your friend besides Emmy and Izzy?" The mother adds, "Your imaginary friends." Vivian says, "They're not imaginary." She pronounces the word "imaniary," and her mother asks, "Can you say 'imaginary'?" Vivian says, "No."

Dennis reminds her, "Who else is your friend? Lanny?" Vivian answers, "Uh-huh, Lanny." Her mother says, "No. Lanny's a bear." Vivian says, "No, I like Lanny. He's not a bear. He's a Imogen bear." Her mother responds, "Oh, Imogen's the bear. You're right. Lanny was the nurse when you were born. Did you know that?" Dennis tells his mother, "Lanny, I thought it was Imogen," and his mother replies, "No, it was Lanny." Vivian interjects, "Lanny isn't that bear." Dennis responds to his mother, "But you called the bear Lanny," and his mother answers, "Yes, Vivian named it when she got it." Vivian continues, "Oh, Lanny is a name too, a doctor." Her mother says, "Oh, okay," and Dennis says, "You mean a nurse." The mother confirms, "A nurse," and Vivian disagrees, "No, a doctor. I mean a doctor." Her mother responds, "Well, it might be. I don't know all the doctors in the world." Vivian says, "All the doctors in the world. Not in the world."

Endnotes

1. See Carmichael (1954).
2. Landon & Sommers (1979); Nelson (1973). Menyuk, Liebergott, & Schultz (1995), however, did not find frequency of talking to be a good predictor of language development at age 3.
3. Hart & Risley (1995).
4. Scarborough (1990); see Chapter 4, endnote 3, in this book, for a description of how the IPSyn was used.

CHAPTER 9

Meaningful Differences

◆ ◆ ◆ ◆

*I*n our previous book, *Meaningful Differences in the Everyday Experience of Young American Children,*[1] we analyzed relationships between the parenting the 42 children had received before age 3 and the children's accomplishments at age 3 and at ages 9–10 when they were in third grade. We used three measures of accomplishment at age 3. As a measure of a child's rate of adding words to represent new concepts or to make distinctions among old words in a spoken vocabulary, we used the final parameter in the statistical description of that child's growth curve that Dr. David Thissen derived from a multilevel nonlinear analysis of the child's cumulative vocabulary over the years of observation.[2] As a measure reflecting a child's display of cognitive functioning during interactions, we used the average number of different words the child used at 34–36 months old. As an estimate of how much a child had learned in 36 months of life, we used the child's score on the Stanford-Binet Intelligence Scale,[3] which was administered to the child within a month after the last observation when the child was 3 years old.

When the children were 9–10 years old, in the spring semester of third grade, Dr. Dale Walker gave to each of the 29 children she recruited in a follow-up study[4] a test of receptive vocabulary, the Peabody Picture Vocabulary Test–Revised

(PPVT–R),[5] and a test of spoken language, the Test of Language Development–2 (TOLD–2).[6] Except for the correlation between IQ scores at age 3 and scores on the PPVT–R at ages 9–10, all of the correlations between the five measures of the children's accomplishments were highly significant ($r = .57$ or higher, $p < .001$).

The analyses reported in *Meaningful Differences*, like those reported in this book, were based on the corpus of more than 1,300 hours of in-home observations collected monthly for 2½ years in 42 families differing in size, race, and SES. The variables listed in Table 2 are those we used in aggregating the data in two separate computer runs. Preliminary assessments of the data for trends and reliability had shown us that the amount parents talked to their children was surprisingly consistent across the early years of life. The first aggregation of the data, then, produced parent-by-parent averages across the 2½ years so that we could examine what the parents were doing month after month that made a substantial difference to their children's accomplishments at age 3 and later.

The second aggregation of the data produced month-by-month averages across the 42 children and parents so that we could examine how interactions were changing as the children learned to talk. We grouped the children in this book in order to examine extremes in how early or late children begin to talk and in talkativeness and taciturnity. In *Meaningful Differences* we grouped the parents in order to examine extremes in material and educational advantage.

This book has shown that by age 3 all 42 children had learned to talk appropriately. The data in *Meaningful Differences* showed that all of the parents were talking appropriately to their 1- to 2-year-old children about much the same things in much the same ways. The data showed that when 13- to 36-month-old American children are awake and with their parents, they typically have an average of 340 utterances addressed to them per hour, of which 90 are questions,

62 are directives, and 105 are declarative statements. They have an average of 1,440 words addressed to them per hour. They are given affirmative feedback an average of 17 times per hour and a prohibition an average of 7 times per hour.

Differences in Parents

In addition to showing us the average amount of language experience young American children receive per hour from their parents, the data revealed staggering contrasts in the amount of interaction between parents and children, both at the extremes in advantage and within the middle class. In the 13 professional families, the parents addressed an average of 2,100 words per hour to their children. In the 23 working-class families, the parents addressed an average of 1,200 words per hour to their children. In the 6 welfare families, the parents addressed an average of 600 words per hour to their children. Simply in terms of words addressed to them, the children in the welfare families were getting half as much language experience as the children in the working-class families and less than one third as much as the children in the professional families.

In a typical hour, the parents in the 13 professional families spent nearly twice as much time interacting with their children as did the welfare parents. They gave their children affirmative feedback an average of more than 30 times per hour, twice as often as the working-class parents and 5 times as often as the welfare parents. The children in the welfare families heard a prohibition twice as often as they heard affirmative feedback.

These differences in the amount of early family experience translated into striking disparities in the children's accomplishments at age 3 in terms of predictors of success in school and the workplace, such as IQ scores, vocabulary growth rates, and vocabulary use. When we extrapolated the

169

amount of parent talk we had observed per hour to all of the children's waking hours before age 3, our estimates showed that by the time the children were 4 years old, the average child in a welfare family would have had 13 million fewer words of cumulative language experience than the average child in a working-class family. Some 4-year-old children would have heard more than 800,000 affirmatives from their parents, whereas others would have heard fewer than 80,000. The differences in the children's test scores on the PPVT–R and the TOLD—2 in third grade seemed to confirm the substance of these extrapolations.

The numerous in-depth analyses reported in *Meaningful Differences* revealed that a surprisingly simple dimension of family life is profoundly related to children's cognitive development: amount of parent–child interaction per hour. Most of the quality features of parent–child interactions studied in child development such as feedback tone, guidance style, responsiveness, and language diversity are automatic features of the "extra" parent–child interactions above and beyond those used to regulate the child's behavior. The longitudinal data showed that the parents in professional, working-class, and welfare families used similar numbers of initiations, imperatives, and prohibitions per hour to control their children. But the interactions in welfare families often concerned little else, whereas most of the extra talk in the professional families was about other topics (see the example of the talkative child at the end of Chapter 8). The extra talk of the parents in the professional families and that of the most talkative parents in the working-class families contained more of the varied vocabulary, complex ideas, subtle guidance, and positive feedback thought to be important to cognitive development.

The amount that the parents talked to their 1- to 2-year-old children was generally correlated with the parents' SES, with the welfare parents being taciturn and those in professional families quite talkative. Talkativeness varied greatly among the working-class parents, a group that included the most talkative of the 42 parents as well as the least talkative. The amount parents talked to their children, particularly the amount of extra talk beyond that needed to transact the everyday business of family life, was powerfully related to the children's cumulative vocabularies in use and to other measures of their verbal competence. The amount of language experience parents provided their children before the children were 3 years old accounted for all of the correlation between SES (and/or race) and the verbal-intellectual competence of the children.

Differences in Children

The similarity of the children's social worlds and of the developmental changes brought by maturation made the children at age 3 much more alike than different. All of the children were competent speakers at age 3; all had been socialized to behave acceptably in mainstream American society. Although the children varied in temperament, activity level, and interests, they all were participating members of their social groups. Although each child matured at an individual rate, differences in the timing of developmental milestones had little influence on subsequent progress. Despite major differences in amounts of experience with language and interaction, the children all lived in similar worlds of regulation, conversation, and active engagement with materials. Although there were differences in the timing, duration, and intensity of the periods of becoming partners, staying and playing, and practicing, learning to talk followed the same pattern.

The important differences appeared less in the characteristics of the children and more in the amount of their experience. We noted in Chapter 3 that differences in the ongoing family culture that made a place for the child seemed more important than the birth order or gender that accompanied the child. The differences seen among the children at age 3 seemed related primarily to differences among the families in the amount of talking customary in the family because, to our surprise, when the children began to talk as much as other family members, the amount they talked leveled off. The 4 children in the taciturn group presumably could have talked as much as the children in the talkative group, but they talked only as much as their own parents.

At age 3, in comparison to the children in the taciturn group, the children in the talkative group were averaging 3 times as many utterances per hour containing an average of more than twice as many different words drawn from an average recorded vocabulary twice as large as the average for the children in the taciturn group. The larger numbers of unique words in the vocabularies recorded for the more talkative children came from the larger number of different words the children used when they produced more utterances in an hour. At 34–36 months old the 4 children in the talkative group used an average of 332 different words in an average of 637 utterances per hour; the 4 children in the taciturn group used an average of 129 different words in an average of 206 utterances per hour. The difference remained even when the children in the 2 groups at the extremes were equated for amount of talk in the 100-utterance subsamples at 34–36 months. An average of 107 different words were recorded in the 100 utterances of the 4 children in the talkative group, and an average of 76 different words were recorded in the 100 utterances of the 4 children in the taciturn group. The differences in the amount of interaction the parents of the children in the talkative and taciturn groups had devoted to encouraging their children to talk as much as others in the family seemed to have contributed something to the differences in the children's performance at age 3 beyond mere differences in talkativeness. The outcomes reported in *Meaningful Differences* suggested that the trajectories of vocabulary growth of the children were influenced by amounts of talking, especially in the conversational interactions of staying and playing.

Differences in Interactions

In *Meaningful Differences* we noted that children's early experience with words accumulates as a dictionary of meanings and that new experiences are noticed and categorized because they evoke associations with remembered experiences. Children's early interactions set up a general approach to words as symbols for experience and lead to dispositions to seek new experiences and explore them through talking with other people. The data of the children in the talkative and taciturn groups illustrate that the sizable and lasting differences in amount of experience with words reported in *Meaningful Differences* were accumulating month by month during the years when the children were depending on interaction with adults for virtually all of their understandings of words and the world.

In *Meaningful Differences* we noted that when parents talk to their children just to be sociable, letting immediate circumstances determine the words they use, their children hear vocabulary in reference to the many different objects, places, and events of daily activities. When parents talk casually with their children, they naturally adapt what they say to the immediate responses of the children so that what the children say determines much of what the parents say. Without planning, as parents engage maturing children in more complex activities, they increase the complexity of what is said.

In this book we have noted that in roughly half of all of the contacts we recorded between parents and children, only one party spoke, usually only as much as needed to satisfy the immediate wants of the person who initiated and usually in familiar words without distracting elaborations. The parents initiated interactions with 11- to 36-month-old children an average of 33 times per hour, and the rates the parents of the children in the talkative and taciturn groups initiated interactions both were similar to the average. The average child initiated interactions an average of 59 times per hour. Between the ages of 11 and 36 months old, though, the 4 children in the taciturn group initiated interaction an average of 68 times per hour, 19 more times per hour than the average of the 4 children in the talkative group. Fewer initiations were recorded for the children in the talkative group because in that half of all of the contacts in which both parties spoke, interaction tended to be prolonged and to become occasions for the extra conversational talk characterized by affirmative feedback, gentle guidance, mutual responsiveness, and language diversity.

The data of the 4 children in the taciturn group make clear that substantial amounts of one-to-one interaction are not needed in order to learn to talk. The more extended interactions of the 4 children in the talkative group, though, exposed the children to a greater number of different words presented in association with more subtle variations in ongoing experience. More interaction involved more questions, more confirming repetitions, more responses to the children's topics and actions, more appreciation of the children as important and interesting dance partners, more noticing, distinguishing, expressing, and explaining, more displays of skill by the children to draw challenge and information from their parents—more of everything potentially beneficial to learning about words, symbolic relations, and self-competence.

Meaningful Differences showed the importance of amount of language experience to cognitive development. This book shows the importance of the social dance as the context of that experience.

Differences in Cultures

In *Meaningful Differences* we reported our comparisons that showed that at 34–36 months old the children were behaving like their parents in language and interaction styles. Affirmative feedback predominated in the talk of children who were given predominantly affirmative feedback when they were 13–18 months old, and negative feedback predominated in the talk of children who were given mostly negative feedback. In this book we note that an average of 86% of the words listed in any individual child's recorded dictionary were also listed in the dictionary of the parent words addressed to that child. Yet of the 15,000 words in the dictionary recorded for all speakers in all 42 families over the 2½ years of data collection, only 859 words were listed in the recorded dictionaries of more than 10 parents, and only 94 words were listed in the recorded dictionaries of all 42 parents and children. These numbers suggest the diversity of the family cultures in which ordinary American parents are raising children to enter the mainstream of school and workplace.

In *Meaningful Differences* we contrasted American family cultures in terms of extremes in the material and educational advantages of the parents. In this book we have contrasted the extremes in the relative talkativeness of the children and have seen the amount the children talked becoming similar over time to the amount their parents talked. In both books the data make clear that talkativeness characterizes families rather than socioeconomic or ethnic groups. In all of the families we observed, the parents and children talked primarily about whatever they happened to be doing together at the moment. But some parents spent twice as much time interacting with their children as other parents did. In many of these families the parents and the children seemed to be talking just because they enjoyed being together and because talking was the culturally prescribed mode for maintaining social closeness.

Observers of children learning to talk in non-Western cultures[7] have suggested that an increased frequency of parent questions, repetitions, and recasts may be a middle-class American style of interacting with toddlers. In other cultures,[8] adults apparently almost never ask children "training" questions designed to elicit information in a systematic way. In America, though, performance on test questions is critical to educational and career advancement. We recorded most of the parents asking their children training questions such as "How old are you?" but only a few parents engaged their children in prolonged or frequent rehearsals of answers to questions about colors, names, or numbers. Once the children were spontaneously naming pictures, we seldom recorded interactions devoted to training questions in the professional-class families. Rather, such interactions seemed to contribute to the talkativeness and to the increased amount of interaction we saw in those working-class families who seemed most intent on preparing their children for professional-class membership.

The data of the children in the taciturn group remind us that in some American cultures[9] conversation between adults and little children is considered pointless or inappropriate. Children are expected to learn from listening to the ambient talk that surrounds them.[10] They are expected to speak primarily when spoken to so that what they say will be relevant and socially acceptable. Taciturn cultures produce fluent storytellers and often draw children back from the chaotic verbosity of much of American society into the community of a shared culture.[11] For the children in the taciturn group, we could foresee difficulties not with a taciturn culture but with transition to a talkative one, difficulties similar to those that the children at the extreme in talkativeness might face on entering the more taciturn culture of public school.

The differences in family cultures that we observed were in fact small differences. All 42 families were well-functioning families whose members had been participating in mainstream urban American culture for several generations. We would need to collect another corpus of longitudinal data before we ventured statements about the applicability of the findings from our data to cultures outside America, or inside America to the cultures of families that are not well-functioning, that are caring for someone with a disability, that are recent immigrants or that are living in conditions of extreme poverty or wealth.

Differences in Reality

In most research, reality is variability. Time, statistics, and exploratory analyses are devoted to finding ways to discover regularities within that variability. Laboratory research is designed to control variability by arranging that people interact in highly similar contexts. The design of our longitudinal study, however, expressly invited variability by asking parents to do just what they usually did when at home with the child and then recording for 2½ years as the child developed within an everchanging individual family culture. Our choice was to obtain many observations so that much of the variability might be averaged out and we could use split-half reliability to verify the consistency of the behaviors we recorded. In *Meaningful Differences* we averaged the data to reveal the differences in language and interaction that contributed most significantly to differences in children's accomplishments at age 3 and later. Here we averaged the data to reveal the pattern of learning to talk.

In both books the variability in the month-by-month data is evident across the parents' data, as shown in Appendix B of *Meaningful Differences,* and across the children's data, as shown in the ranges and standard deviations in Tables 4–6 of this book. But the books complement each other in the convergence of the findings from the differing aggregations of the data. In *Meaningful Differences* the number of words the parents addressed to their children per hour over the months the children were 13–36 months old were averaged for each of the three SES groups. The split-half reliability of the data averaged for each group is shown in Figure 7 in *Meaningful Differences*. In that figure, in each of the groups, in each half of the data, may be seen the pattern we have described in this book: an increase in amounts of parent talk until the children were 28 months old followed by a decrease in the average number of words addressed to the children per hour.

In this book we averaged the data of the children whose data lay at the extremes of the database: the children who were earliest and latest to become talkers half of whose verbalizations were utterances containing recognizable words and the children for whom the most and the fewest utterances per hour were recorded in the 34- to 36-month observations. The families in each group varied in SES, yet the relationships between the amount the children were talking at 34–36 months old and the average amount their parents talked to them per hour in the prior 3 years illustrate the differences among the families that produced the highly significant correlations reported in *Meaningful Differences*.

We set out to discover, within the incredible variability that makes everyday life so interesting, the aspects of American children's early experience that remain after removing the pervasive and powerful influence of individual personalities, family culture, material and educational resources, and changes in mood, health, and levels of stress. The magnitude of the relationship we found between measures of children's early experience and their accomplishments at age 3 and still at ages 9–10, regardless of SES or race, gives us confidence that the amount of language experience parents provide their children before age 3 is important. That the pattern of learning to talk revealed in data averaged for 42 children was also seen in data averaged for each of 4 groups of as few as 4 children gives us confidence that the pattern is lawful.

Cumulative Language Experience

In order to show the effects of cumulative language experience on children's accomplishments at age 3 and later, *Meaningful Differences* focused on amount of exposure. In order to show the pattern of learning to talk, this book focused on practice. We separated exposure and practice in order to examine in detail, longitudinally, these two aspects of children's experience. Our observations have shown us, though, that most important was a third aspect, the social dance that is conversational interaction. The reciprocity of conversation made an extra contribution to learning to talk because during conversation, what the child said governed what the parent said in response, and the parent's response came increasingly often to govern what the child said next. Conversation exposed the child to what might be said in the language and at the same time prompted the child to practice selecting what could be said appropriately in the immediate circumstances. Parents were seen responding spontaneously rather than planning what they said during conversations. As the children gained fluency and flexibility, their parents' focus seemed to be on maintaining interaction, letting the reciprocity of the dance guide the process of learning to talk.

Together the children and the parents changed the content of interactions because the complexity of the children's display determined the complexity of the parents' responses. The limiting condition was the availability of the parent and thus the "extra" conversational interactions that did not concern daily routines. Brief spontaneous moments of dancing inserted into ongoing activities were occasions for elaborating talk beyond an exchange of necessary instructions, for sharing

179

ideas, and for solidifying a social relationship. Practice and exposure often occurred outside of interaction. Children talked to their toys while their parents talked on the telephone. Our data suggest, though, that it was primarily through conversation, dancing together, that children and parents came to talk similar amounts about similar things, as indicated by the shared vocabulary in their recorded dictionaries.

In *Meaningful Differences* we addressed the cumulative amount of children's exposure to language; we can now address children's cumulative experience by adding practice to exposure. We extrapolated from the averages in the observational data to a 100-hour week of roughly 14-hour waking days. The amount of exposure ranged from an average of 3 million words per year (600 per hour) in the welfare families to an average of 11 million words per year (2,100 per hour) in the professional families. The average for the 42 families was 6 million words per year (1,400 per hour). In the first year of life, then, the children had been exposed to an average of 6 million words that were addressed to them; they had produced an average of 8,000 words. In the 7 months of becoming partners, until the children were 19 months old and half or more of their utterances contained recognizable words, the children produced an average of 300,000 words to the average of 4 million words their parents said to them. During the 9-month period of staying and playing, the children said an average of almost 3 million words to the average of somewhat more than 6 million words their parents said to them. During the 8-month period of practicing, the children said an average of 4½ million words to the average of 5 million words their parents said to them.

Practice added very little to exposure for the 9 months after the children said their first words. The children's practice had contributed one tenth of a percent to their cumulative experience with language when the children were 12 months old and had added only 2% to the 10 million words accumulated from exposure by the time the children were 19 months old. During the 9-month period of staying and playing, the children's practice increased tenfold from 300,000 to 3 million words so that the children's cumulative experience with words doubled from 10 million when the children were 19 months old to 20 million when the children were 28 months old. During the 8-month period of practicing, the children's practice began to contribute as much to accumulating language experience as did exposure to the parents' talk. From this point on, children and parents would probably continue to contribute equally to the children's cumulative experience with language.

In *Meaningful Differences* when we grouped the families by SES, we discovered that the most important difference among families was not the relative advantages conferred by education and income but the amount of talking the parents did with their children. In this book we have examined the amount of talking the children did and have compared children at the extremes in the data in terms of the amount they talked. Because all of the children at age 3 were talking approximately as much as was customary among family members, the data from the children in the talkative and taciturn groups presents an opportunity to examine both the amount that children's practice adds to the amount of cumulative language experience provided by their parents and the extremes in recorded amounts of talk irrespective of SES.

Adding the children's practice to exposure (see Figure 9) revealed trends in both the talkative and taciturn groups similar to the trend seen in the average family. Before the children were 19 months old, practice contributed very little (less than 5% of the words added to exposure). In the final months of the period of practicing, similar to the average child, the children in the talkative and taciturn groups were contributing approximately as much as their parents to their cumulative language experience. The amount of exposure of the average child and the children in both groups at the extremes was slightly above the averages for the three SES groups as described in *Meaningful Differences*. The average amount of exposure for all 42 families was 1,400 words per hour; the range was from 700 words per hour for the parents of the 4 children in the taciturn group to 2,200 words per hour for the parents of the 4 children in the talkative group.

The differences in the amount of the children's cumulative language experience are very similar to those reported in *Meaningful Differences*. By 19 months old the 4 children in the talkative group had had 16 million words of cumulative language experience, 6 million more than the average child and 9 million more than the 4 children in the taciturn group. After the children's practice began to be added to exposure during the 9-month period of staying and playing, the children in the talkative group at 28 months old had had 31 million words of cumulative language experience, 11 million more than the average child, and 20 million more than the children in the taciturn group. At age 3, when practice was adding as much as exposure to accumulating language experience, the children in the talkative group had accumulated 46 million words of language experience, 17 million more than the average child and 31 million more than the children in the taciturn group. At 36 months old the average cumulative language experience of the 4 children in the taciturn group was 14.5 million words, half as much as the 29 million words of the average child.

The trajectory of accumulating language experience (see Figure 9) may be seen to be determined largely by the amount of experience parents provide before children are 2 years old. The amount of language experience accumulated from the first 2 years of exposure is added into cumulative experience forever and so serves to maintain relative inequalities in children's amounts of cumulative language experience. The customary amount of talk in the family not only sets the initial trajectory of accumulating language experience but influences the amount the child practices in subsequent years when the child is drawing talk from a more varied audience outside the home.

The amount of child practice compounds the effects of the amount of exposure documented in *Meaningful Differences* and makes even greater the impact of amount of early language experience on the magnitude of children's accomplishments at age 3 and later. In the casual interactions of children's daily lives, reciprocity blends practice and exposure to increase the complexity of the dance and amplify its contribution to cumulative experience with words and ideas. The data presented here converge with those presented in *Meaningful Differences* to demonstrate the significance of the amount of dancing that parents and children do during the childrens' first 3 years of life.

Endnotes

1. Hart & Risley (1995).
2. See Chapter 4, endnote 5, for a description of Dr. Thissen's multilevel model of vocabulary growth.
3. Terman & Merrill (1960).
4. Walker, Greenwood, Hart, & Carta (1994).
5. Dunn & Dunn (1981).
6. Hammill & Newcomer (1988).
7. Schieffelin & Ochs (1983).
8. Goody (1978); Schieffelin & Ochs (1983).
9. Chisholm (1981); Heath (1989).
10. Schieffelin & Eisenberg (1984); Ward (1971).
11. Erikson (1950); Gazaway (1969).

CHAPTER 10

Talking as a Social Dance

◆◆◆◆

W e have described the data from 2½ years of observing children's and parents' unstructured interactions at home during the months the children were learning to talk. Now we want to summarize the lawful pattern of changing interactions the data revealed and put our observations in the broader context of the study of language development.

Learning to Talk

The observational data of 42 children learning to talk revealed a lawful pattern of developmental change that gradually shifted the social world of an infant into that of a family of speakers. We saw the social world of an infant to be replete with nurturing, parentese, and play provided by parents who were largely uninformed about the steady gains the infants were making in the discrimination and production of speech sounds. Rather than attending to their infants' sounds, parents emphasized the context of learning to talk: face-to-face interaction, affection, and engagement with people. As the children began saying words, showing they were listening, their parents began attending to vocalizations and inviting the children to join in talking as a social dance in which what each partner does governs what the other does. Becoming partners gradually shifted the social world of an infant into that of an apprentice to conversation. Parents automatically made effective the children's utterances that made sense, tolerated the mistakes of a novice, modeled and demonstrated the skills to be learned, and continuously prompted and encouraged practice. Parents and children stayed and played at conversation until the children were talking as much as everyone else in the family and so entered the social world of practicing speakers.

Becoming Partners

We called the early months of learning to talk a period of becoming partners because the data showed a gradual shift in parent–child talk from parallel to reciprocal. The data showed the 7- to 10-month-old children vocalizing some 100 times per hour whether unengaged, engaged with objects, or interacting with people. The data showed their parents speaking some 300 times per hour to the children, holding the floor to talk at length regardless of whether the children happened to be vocalizing. Parents asked questions and prompted their children to speak without waiting for the answering words the children never produced. Then when the children began to say words at an average age of 11 months old, parent–child interactions began to change. Conversations, reciprocal responses, and utterances increased month after month. Parents responded more and more often as though the children's vocalizations might be words. Children began to answer more and more often with recognizable words, and reciprocal imitation increased.

Staying and Playing

We described as a period of staying and playing the months after recognizable words were recorded in half or more

186

of the 200 or more verbalizations the average child said in an hour at 19 months old. The data showed a continuing, steady increase in parent–child responses as parents encouraged their children to practice talking about the increasingly varied activities they and their parents were doing together. Interactions increased markedly as the parents talked more and more, asking ever more questions and prompting ever more elaborate answers from the children. As the children talked more and more, they used ever more different words from their growing vocabularies and produced ever longer utterances, including in them auxiliary verbs and markers for tense and number. More and more often the children held the floor to add a comment or prompt a response from their parents.

Practicing

We called practicing the period after the children, at an average age of 28 months old, began talking as much as their parents talked to them and parent utterances to the children began a steady decline in number. In a reversal of the period of becoming partners, the children began to hold the floor more often than their parents. They began to talk more when alone or with other children. They used increasing numbers of different words per hour, and clauses began to appear in the data as the children practiced independently.

Lawfulness

The lawfulness of the pattern of learning to talk was revealed when we tested it using the data from the four groups at the extremes of the 42 children. Two groups of 4 children each were at the extremes at the beginning of the study: the children who spent the most and the fewest months between saying a first word and saying words in half of all of their utterances. Two other groups of 4 children each were at the extremes at the end of the study: the children who talked most and least in an hour when they were 34–36 months old.

187

In each of the 4 groups, the pattern of changing interactions was similar to the pattern revealed by averaging the data of all 42 children, despite differences in the amounts the parents and children talked and in the timing of events such as matching the family amount of talk. In each of the 4 groups, child and parent responses increased as the children's utterances contained more and more identifiable words. In each group a period of staying and playing was similarly characterized by reciprocal imitation and by increasing numbers (but not proportions) of parent questions of the children. In each group when the children began to talk as much as their parents talked to them in an hour, parent utterances began a steady decline in number.

Watching Children Learning to Talk

The data revealed a lawful pattern of changing interactions, but over the years of our observations of children learning to talk, we saw only a seamless development of the relationship between an individual child and family. We saw activities and interactions familiar from descriptions in the literature, and we saw all the children develop language just as our textbooks had led us to expect. However, we saw two major characteristics of interactions we had not expected. First, we saw that parents did not seem to do anything deliberate to encourage language development. This did not particularly surprise us because children in non-Western cultures are reported to learn to talk without their parents doing anything special.[1] Second, we saw how actively the children were influencing what happened to them and how important to learning to talk were the utterances the children displayed to their parents. This did surprise us, given the emphasis in much of the literature on the meanings, structures, and functions of language children are learning and what parents are contributing to that learning. Watching children learning to talk brought us a new perspective on some of our old ideas about what was happening between parents and children.

As soon as we began observing children's everyday lives, we were struck by the absence of any need or pressure to learn to talk. Everything the children needed was delivered, often before the children communicated that they were hungry or uncomfortable. Parents prompted the children to say words but almost always gave the children objects or continued talking as though they did not expect an answer. Although parents engaged in bouts of exchanging noises with their children, they imitated the children's vocalizations as rarely as the children imitated those of their parents. We never saw a parent try to shape sounds into words as is done in language remediation.[2] We saw parents present food and affection immediately after children vocalized, but it never looked planned to be contingent or occurred consistently. We were surprised at how seldom parents responded to or even seemed to notice their children's vocalizations. Many of the children's vocalizations, though, were produced as the children were exploring toys, so it seemed natural that the parents often paid no attention.

Then, in the absence of any need, training, or programmed consequences, the children began saying words anyway. Surprisingly, their parents did not suddenly seem to start listening for an occasional word to be produced instead of or among the children's usual vocalizations. When the parents recognized a word, they repeated it or answered it, but they appeared less concerned with encouraging the children to accumulate vocabulary than with making conversation out of the few words the children had. They began, as the children did, to respond more often, but their relative responsiveness did not change. As in prior months, on more than one third of the occasions when the children spoke, no one answered. We saw children begin responding to their parents with recognizable utterances that could sound autistic because they were so unrelated in content to what the parents had just said. We realized that learning to talk could not really begin until the children began to answer what their parents said instead of simply responding as usual.

We saw parents begin predisposing their children to answer by asking the children to name the familiar objects with which the children were engaged and offering the children opportunities to imitate by themselves naming the objects. Parents asked the children to say words but chiefly, it seemed, to test whether the children would imitate, for the parents always appeared willing to continue interacting as long as the children appeared to be listening, whether the children responded with a word or a vocalization. The children began saying more words and adding gestures to vocalizations, demanding a response from their parents. For months, though, parent–child interactions seemed to change very little, and then, almost abruptly, the children began imitating spontaneously as well as when prompted. They began reducing their utterances to single words enunciated with exaggerated care and began answering, "Yes," as soon as the parent paused. We began to see conversations devoted to dancing, the parents leading with questions and, if need be, the answers, and the children following with answers and, if need be, imitations.

The parents seemed to act much as they had when the children took their first steps. They encouraged the children to practice and show off, but they did not change their styles of interacting. We recorded more parent questions because the parents talked more; proportions of questions did not change. The parents responded more often but became relatively less responsive as the children began to hold the floor and elaborate without being prompted. We were surprised at how seldom we saw teaching of the kinds described in the literature[3] and disappointed to see even the most highly educated parents direct their children to pictures more often than to natural science. We saw children being asked to distinguish alligators from xylophones and squares from triangles but not elms from evergreens or solids from liquids.

Then we realized that the parents were doing what the observers were doing: enjoying the experience of returning from a goal-directed, custom-bound adult world to share the surprises and discoveries made by children exploring a new world of words. The difference was that the parents had to act as the partner that socially appropriate conversation requires. But if the majority of what we saw parents doing was done simply to keep the children practicing and exploring, it would explain for us why the parents asked so many questions to which they (and increasingly often the children) already knew the answers, why they recast the children's utterances instead of elaborating on them, and why they never corrected the children's grammar or made obtaining a material contingent on a child labeling it.

When the children were speaking fluently and grammatically and started talking as much in an hour as their parents did, the observers, and the parents too, it often seemed, began to find listening to them less entertaining. The children were still limited in vocabulary and experience, such that they could be as talkative but not as interesting as the adults who were temporarily choosing to talk with them. The children made it increasingly clear that they no longer needed encouragement to practice; parents' "Uh-huh" seemed more of an interruption than confirmation that the parents were focused as usual on what the children were saying. Increasingly often the children were asserting their independence, controlling the times and topics of conversation, and engaging in monologues. The children began to act and sound just like their siblings and began to be treated similarly, relieved of close monitoring, attentive care, and encouraging prompts.

191

Throughout the 2½ years of observations, we were impressed by the casual spontaneity of the parents' talk to their children. The parents never seemed to plan or monitor what they said. As soon as the children began to answer as conversational partners, the parents seemed always to respond automatically just as they did to anyone else who talked. When what the children said was clear enough to be recognized as words, the parents responded unhesitatingly with an answer customary in the culture. When what the children said was not clear in its articulation or relevance, the parents asked for clarification. When the children stumbled, the parents waited or supplied a missing word. When what the children said was not true or when they held the floor too long, the parents corrected or interrupted. They modeled mature utterance forms because that was how they naturally spoke.

We saw why the parents seemed to deal as casually with learning to talk as they did with the other aspects of socializing their children. As members of the culture, the parents were well-rehearsed as conversational partners and so needed no special training. They showed us that in every society once children's answers are governed by what mature speakers in the culture say to the children, any practicing member can act as the social partner needed for learning to talk. The customary practices of a social group place powerful constraints on what members can learn to do and say.

Implications for Parents

The data we have presented in this book indicate that what parents ordinarily do is enough for their children to learn to talk. As members of mainstream culture, parents automatically socialize talking just as they do the other behaviors necessary for group membership. Our observations are in accordance with observations of non-Western cultures that show that no special ways of speaking are needed for children to learn to talk. Exposure to words and practice producing them are cultural universals.

The data have shown that the most important aspect of parent talk is its amount. Parents who just talk as they go about their daily activities expose their children to more than 1,000 words (in some families 2,000) every hour, words that are presented alone, in phrases and sentences, in reference to all the everyday objects, events, and relationships about which the children need to learn. The parents we observed rarely appeared to think before they spoke, as though they knew that whatever they said would expose their children to words that could be added to a vocabulary that was starting from zero.

Something special happens, though, when this amount of talk is embedded in conversation. Beyond encouraging practice and providing language experience, conversation contributes to a parent–child relationship. Parents learn about their children, and children learn about themselves. What is important to the parent becomes important to the child. The relationship is expressed naturally in quality features such as the responsiveness, gentle guidance, positive affect, and language diversity that characterize the extra interactions undertaken by close friends.

The data imply that the important concern for parents is the amount of dancing. The data show that the first 3 years of experience put in place a trajectory of vocabulary growth and the foundations of analytic and symbolic competencies that will make a lasting difference to how children perform in later years. During these first 3 years, children are almost entirely dependent on adults for dance partners. With their rudimentary skills, 2-year-olds have less need for language experts than for willing dance partners. What children need from adults is time, not tricks.

Parents can rely on their natural responses to provide their children with all of the support needed to learn to talk as much and as well as other people in their social group. Parents who talk a lot and have large vocabularies will naturally transmit those aspects to their children. In the case of parents who want their children to talk more and use a larger vocabulary than the family typically does, our data suggest that the most important consideration is amount of practice conversing. Our data showed that children who practiced more in conversation with their parents used more different words and had larger vocabularies. But talkativeness, amount of practice in itself, did not lead the children we observed to display at earlier ages the grammatical categories listed on the IPSyn.[4] This suggests that, as studies of physical maturation have shown,[5] practice may have little influence on a genetically endowed rate of development.

Conversation, though, is a social dance that involves not just talking but also speaking and listening in partnership with another person. Parents can use books from the library, catalogs, or even advertisements as occasions for many bouts of conversation during a day. Children who become adept as social partners and really enjoy conversing are likely to be invited to dance by other people who can present all of the fancy footwork the parent has not learned.

Implications for Speech-Language Intervention

If a goal in intervention is that children learn to talk like everyone else in their social group, such that parents and others respond naturally to them, then it becomes important to consider how parents naturally respond. Our observations impressed us with a primary characteristic that made parent behavior appear natural: an absence of planning. Parents did not seem to do anything deliberately. They responded to children learning to talk just as they responded to anyone who spoke to them. In accordance with the rules of conversation, they tried to make sense of what was said even when it was not readily apparent. With other people, they did not naturally wait, delay a prompt, or withhold objects during conversation, and they did not do so with their children either.

There were differences in the forms and frequencies of the particular behaviors that parents addressed to children versus adults because the parents were responding naturally to how recognizable and sophisticated was the speech addressed to them. At first, parents imitated frequently in order to confirm children's words; as the children's pronunciation improved, imitation was increasingly often embedded in an utterance that confirmed a mutual topic. Expansions, extensions, and recasts were more frequent when the children were beginning to talk, but they never seemed planned. Parents seemed to expand children's utterances chiefly because omitting articles and copulas was not their natural way of speaking. Extensions and recasts seemed naturally responsive to the children's talk about simple things in simple ways. The closer conversation came to that between equals, the fewer parent recasts became.

When the children were beginning to talk, parents often needed to ask questions to clarify the sense of what was said ("You did what?"), but even then they were more likely to keep conversation going with a yes/no question ("Is that right?") that permitted an easy answer. We were surprised at how rarely we saw incidental teaching before the children were 28 months old; then we remembered that we had designed incidental teaching[6] for elaborating the repertoires of children who were already fluent. We saw the procedures commonly used in speech-language interventions[7] used by parents with greater or lesser frequency depending on the frequency with which the child's behavior called the procedures automatically from a parent's repertoire. The parents seemed always to present the child with the "real world" conditions that had shaped the parents and everyone else in the social group naturally into socially appropriate speakers.

There was only one procedure we saw parents use with children that they never used with other people: prompts for imitation. When a child vocalized while looking at an object, the parent named the object ("Car") as though that had been the sense of the child's vocalization; then the parent prompted an imitation ("Say 'car'"). We saw parents using in natural settings a procedure developed in unnatural clinical settings for training imitation.[8] The imitation training trials conducted by parents, embedded in varied everyday activities, nearly always in response to a child vocalization relative to an object, and conversation invariably continued whether the child imitated or not. As soon as the children began imitating spontaneously and reliably, their parents began doing what they did with everyone else. They condemned imitation ("Don't mock me"). Even "Say 'please'" soon became "What's the magic word?"

We saw parents using naturally a procedure of "overwhelming importance" in a therapeutic technology for operant language development[9] and using it for the same purpose: to get talking started. Parents targeted imitation because it showed them that the children were attending to what the parents were saying. Conversation required that what each partner said be automatically controlled by what the other partner said, and until such control was established, "real-world" conditions could not begin to operate on the child's practice. Dance instruction could not begin until the children were paying attention to what the dance partner was doing. The primary implication of our research for intervention lies in the importance of getting the dance started so that the responses natural to a social partnership can take over learning to talk.

Implications for Research

Talking is important because researchers, parents, and teachers must rely on children to tell them about language development. All of the literature and every theory is based on what children say, and what children actually say depends as much on what they can say and who is asking as on what they know. The early months of learning to talk are described as a "one-word" stage when most of what children say is limited to single words because 1) their parents ask them for single words ("What's that?"), 2) their knowledge is limited to basic concepts, 3) they have difficulty articulating more than single words, 4) their parents have difficulty understanding more than one word at a time, or 5) all of the above. A major challenge in studying language development lies in getting children to reveal to investigators what they "really" know about language. To the extent that the literature is based on records of what children say, research on language development cannot be usefully isolated from research on learning to talk.

The scarcity of research on learning to talk may be due largely to methodology. Transcribing and analyzing data by hand promotes theory-based selection from small samples recorded for a few months, for a few children, cross-sectionally, from parent report, or from brief laboratory sessions. Historically, analysis has focused at the utterance level, on writing the taxonomies necessary for classifying specimens into semantic, syntactic, functional, or speech act categories. The need for a scientific description of the nature and growth of classes of trees necessarily delays examining the forest. But an additional reason for delay may be seen in the years of concentrated effort that were required for us to record longitudinally what was actually happening between only 42 children and their parents during only the first 3 years of their casual interactions at home.

The importance of context and culture to language development has long been acknowledged, but their pervasive influence is difficult to capture at the level of the utterance, so research has often described epiphenomena, isolated aspects of what children and parents do that affects the numbers and kinds of trees that grow. The truths revealed by this research can be neither ignored nor denigrated. Parentese, consequences, and imitation are real parts—but only parts—of the natural world in which children learn to talk.

Adults address parentese—high-pitched, slowed, stressed speech—to infants, pets, hospital patients, and others whom a social group views as unable to talk.[10] Our data showed that as soon as the children began saying words, the parentese that marked the social world of infancy was replaced by patterns of speech similar to those the parents used with everyone else. The contribution of parentese to language development may lie less in exposure to words and more in arranging the context of learning to talk, fostering attention and engagement with people.

Consequences for talking have been considered crucial (reinforcement), reported helpful (recasts), or declared nonexistent (correction of grammar). Our data showed that verbal behavior that specified (and got) its reinforcer ("Stop") was learned early and easily but required a limited repertoire practiced primarily in conditions of deprivation, which occurred relatively seldom in the nurturing families we observed. Our data showed that parent recasts and child practice increased in tandem until the children were 23 months old. After that the children recast their own utterances more often than they heard parent recasts, as though the children had picked up both the forms their parents modeled and the techniques their parents were using to maintain interaction. Our 1,300 hours of data contained only a single instance of adult correction of grammar, but the social world seemed to provide the children a basis for self-correction. Several months after the children began saying, "Goed," they stopped. If they were listening both to themselves and to other people, then they had more than a few opportunities to conclude that "Goed" was not "wrong" or "silly" as was so much that they tried but that it was just another of the unspecified things apparently not done in the culture.

Imitation has been assigned variously a pivotal or a peripheral role in learning to talk and has been defined to range from immediate to delayed and from rote to observational learning. Imitation—doing what other people do—is the core of culture, practiced in songs, ceremonies, and child-rearing. There are specified circumstances in which imitation is absolutely required (rituals), usually permitted (routines), and largely condemned (conversation). In the first years of life, imitation not only makes learning easy, it ensures socialization. It assures that children pay attention to what other people are saying and doing. Parents encourage imitation while children are learning to act in partnership with adults; then they criticize it because imitation impedes conversation.

Learning to talk is about becoming a partner in a culture's dances. Imitation, modeling, prompting, and consequences are each a small part of learning to dance, of learning to perform socially approved steps (words) in culturally determined sequences (utterances, sentences). Practice can then make performance more perfect and fluent. The hard part is learning how to dance, how to regulate actions so that they correspond to the actions of a partner. Once children have learned how to dance, they can be freed to do what children seem to have been designed to do: explore and elaborate. They can be relied on to recruit more and more of the repertoire their parents use with other people so that the partnership can advance effortlessly from a two-step to a *pas de deux*, from ritual greetings to repartee.

We propose that language development is governed by the same natural laws as motor, social, and cognitive development. Biology (developmental change) interacts with opportunity (a social world) to determine the everyday experience of young children. Everyday experience is influenced by parenting (cultural customs) and childing (temperament, energy level, sensibility). What children and parents are doing together in their casual interactions concentrates in children's practicing and parents' providing the experience that supports practice. Differences in how children grow up are differences in the amounts of these.

Endnotes

1. Ochs (1988); Pye (1986).
2. Lovaas, Berberich, Perloff, & Schaeffer (1966).
3. Moerk (1992).
4. Scarborough (1990).
5. Gesell & Thompson (1934).
6. Hart & Risley (1975).
7. Hepting & Goldstein (1996).
8. Risley & Wolf (1967).
9. Risley, Hart, & Doke (1971).
10. Hirsh-Pasek & Treiman (1982).

References

◆ ◆ ◆ ◆

Baldwin, A.L., Kalhorn, J., & Breese, F.H. (1945). Patterns of parent behavior. *Psychological Monographs, 58*(3).

Baltaxe, C.A.M., & Simmons, J.Q. (1977). Bedtime soliloquies and linguistic competence in autism. *Journal of Speech and Hearing Disorders, 42,* 376–393.

Bandura, A., & Walters, R.H. (1963). *Social learning and personality development.* Austin, TX: Holt, Rinehart & Winston.

Barton, M.E., & Tomasello, M. (1991). Joint attention and conversation in mother–infant–sibling triads. *Child Development, 62,* 517–529.

Bates, E. (1976). *Language and context.* San Diego: Academic Press.

Bates, E., Bretherton, I., & Snyder, L. (1988). *From first words to grammar: Individual differences and dissociable mechanisms.* New York: Cambridge University Press.

Bayley, N., & Schaefer, E.S. (1964). Correlations of maternal and child behaviors with the development of mental abilities: Data from the Berkeley Growth Study. *Monographs of the Society for Research in Child Development, 29*(6, Serial No. 97).

Bee, H. (1975). *The developing child.* New York: HarperCollins.

Belsky, J., Gilstrap, B., & Rovine, M. (1984). The Pennsylvania Infant and Family Development Project: I. Stability and change in mother–infant and father–infant interaction in a family setting at one, three, and nine months. *Child Development, 55,* 692–705.

Bloom, L. (1970). *Language development: Form and function in emerging grammars.* Cambridge, MA: The MIT Press.

Bloom, L. (1991). *Language development from two to three.* New York: Cambridge University Press.

Bloom, L. (1993). *The transition from infancy to language: Acquiring the power of expression.* New York: Cambridge University Press.

Bloom, L., & Lahey, M. (1978). *Language development and language disorders.* New York: John Wiley & Sons.

Bloom, L., Margulis, C., Tinker, E., & Fujita, N. (1996). Early conversations and word learning: Contributions from child and adult. *Child Development, 67,* 3154–3175.

Bloom, L., Rocissano, L., & Hood, L. (1976). Adult–child discourse: Developmental interaction between information processing and linguistic knowledge. *Cognitive Psychology, 8*, 521–552.

Braine, M.D.S. (1976). Children's first word combinations. *Monographs of the Society for Research in Child Development, 41*(1, Serial No. 164).

Brown, R. (1973). *A first language: The early stages.* Cambridge, MA: Harvard University Press.

Brown, R., & Hanlon, C. (1970). Derivational complexity and the order of acquisition in child speech. In J.R. Hayes (Ed.), *Cognition and the development of language* (pp. 155–207). New York: John Wiley & Sons.

Brown, P., & Levinson, S. (1978). Universals in language usage: Politeness phenomena. In E.N. Goody (Ed.), *Questions and politeness* (pp. 56–324). New York: Cambridge University Press.

Bruner, J.S. (1975). The ontogenesis of speech acts. *Journal of Child Language, 2*, 1–19.

Bullowa, M. (Ed.). (1979). *Before speech.* New York: Cambridge University Press.

Carmichael, L. (Ed.). (1954). *Manual of child psychology.* New York: John Wiley & Sons.

Chase-Lansdale, P.L., Mott, F.L., Brooks-Gunn, J., & Phillips, D.A. (1991). Children of the National Longitudinal Survey of Youth: A unique research opportunity. *Developmental Psychology, 27*, 918–931.

Chisholm, J.S. (1981). Residence patterns and the environment of mother–infant interaction among the Navajo. In T.M. Field, A.M. Sostek, P. Vietze, & P.H. Leiderman (Eds.), *Culture and early interactions* (pp. 3–19). Mahwah, NJ: Lawrence Erlbaum Associates.

Chomsky, N. (1957). *Syntactic structures.* The Hague, Netherlands: Mouton.

Coulthard, R.M. (1977). *An introduction to discourse analysis.* London: Longman.

Cross, T.G. (1977). Mother's speech adjustments: The contribution of selected child listener variables. In C.E. Snow & C.A. Ferguson (Eds.), *Talking to children: Language input and acquisition* (pp. 151–188). New York: Cambridge University Press.

de Saussure, F. (1959). *Course in general linguistics* (W. Baskin, trans.). New York: Philosophical Library. (Original work published 1916)

de Villiers, J.G., & de Villiers, P.A. (1973). A cross-sectional study of the acquisition of grammatical morphemes. *Journal of Psycholinguistic Research, 2*, 267–278.

Dore, J. (1977). Children's illocutionary acts. In R.O. Freedle (Ed.), *Discourse production and comprehension* (pp. 227–244). Greenwich, CT: Ablex Publishing Corp.

Dromi, E. (1987). *Early lexical development.* New York: Cambridge University Press.

Dunn, L.W., & Dunn, L.M. (1981). *Peabody Picture Vocabulary Test–Revised* (Forms L and M). Circle Pines, MN: American Guidance Service.

Durkin, K. (1987). Minds and language: Social cognition, social interaction, and the acquisition of language. *Mind and Language, 2,* 105–140.

Ellis, R., & Wells, G. (1980). Enabling factors in adult–child discourse. *First Language, 1,* 46–62.

Elman, J.L., Bates, E.A., Johnson, M.H., Karmiloff-Smith, A., Parisi, D., & Plunkett, K. (1996). *Rethinking innateness: A connectionist perspective on development.* Cambridge, MA: The MIT Press.

Erikson, E.H. (1950). *Childhood and society.* New York: W.W. Norton.

Ervin-Tripp, S. (1971). Social backgrounds and verbal skills. In R. Huxley & E. Ingram (Eds.), *Language acquisition: Models and methods* (pp. 29–37). San Diego: Academic Press.

Fenson, L., Dale, P., Reznick, J.S., Thal, D., Bates, E., Hartung, J., Pethick, S., & Reilly, J. (1992). *MacArthur Communicative Development Inventories (CDI).* Baltimore: Paul H. Brookes Publishing Co.

Field, T.M., & Widmayer, S.M. (1981). Mother–infant interactions among lower SES Black, Cuban, Puerto Rican and South American immigrants. In T.M. Field, A.M. Sostek, P. Vietze, & P.H. Leiderman (Eds.), *Culture and early interactions* (pp. 41–62). Mahwah, NJ: Lawrence Erlbaum Associates.

Furstenberg, F.F., Jr. (1985). Sociological ventures in child development. *Child Development, 56,* 281–288.

Gardner, R. (1984). Discourse analysis: Implications for language teaching with special reference to casual conversation. *Language Teaching, 17,* 102–117.

Gazaway, R. (1969). *The longest mile.* New York: Bantam Doubleday Dell.

Gesell, A. (1928). *Infancy and human growth.* New York: Macmillan.

Gesell, A., & Thompson, H. (1934). *Infant behavior: Its genesis and growth.* New York: McGraw-Hill.

Gleason, J.B. (1975). Fathers and other strangers. In D.P. Dato (Ed.), *Developmental psycholinguistics: Theory and applications* (pp. 289–297). Washington, DC: Georgetown University Press.

Gleason, J.B. (1988). Language and socialization. In F.S. Kessel (Ed.), *The development of language and language researchers: Essays in honor of Roger Brown* (pp. 269–280). Mahwah, NJ: Lawrence Erlbaum Associates.

Gleitman, L.R., & Wanner, E. (1982). Language acquisition: The state of the state of the art. In E. Wanner & L.R. Gleitman (Eds.), *Language acquisition: The state of the art* (pp. 3–48). New York: Cambridge University Press.

Goffman, E. (1971). *Relations in public.* New York: HarperCollins.

Golinkoff, R.M., & Gordon, L. (1983). In the beginning was the word: A history of the study of language acquisition. In R.M. Golinkoff (Ed.), *The transition from prelinguistic to linguistic communication* (pp. 1–25). Mahwah, NJ: Lawrence Erlbaum Associates.

Goody, E.N. (1978). Towards a theory of questions. In E.N. Goody (Ed.), *Questions and politeness: Strategies in social interaction* (pp. 17–43). New York: Cambridge University Press.

Gottfried, A.W. (1984). Home environment and early cognitive development: Integration, meta-analyses, and conclusions. In A.W. Gottfried (Ed.), *Home environment and early cognitive development: Longitudinal research* (pp. 329–342). San Diego: Academic Press.

Green, G.M. (1989). *Pragmatics and natural language understanding.* Mahwah, NJ: Lawrence Erlbaum Associates.

Green, J.A., Gustafson, G.E., & West, M.J. (1980). Effects of infant development on mother–infant interactions. *Child Development, 51,* 199–207.

Grice, H.P. (1975). Logic and conversation. In P. Cole & J.L. Morgan (Eds.), *Syntax and semantics: Vol. 3. Speech acts* (pp. 41–58). San Diego: Academic Press.

Grigsby, O.J. (1932). An experimental study of the development of concepts of relationship in preschool children as evidenced by their expressive ability. *Journal of Experimental Education, 1,* 144–162.

Hall, W.S., Nagy, W.E., & Linn, R. (1984). *Spoken words: Effects of situation and social group on oral word usage and frequency.* Mahwah, NJ: Lawrence Erlbaum Associates.

Halliday, M.A.K. (1975). *Learning how to mean.* New York: Elsevier/North Holland.

Hammill, D.D., & Newcomer, P.L. (1988). *Test of Language Development–2 (TOLD–2): Intermediate* (2nd ed.). Austin, TX: PRO-ED.

Harris, M. (1992). *Language experience and early language development: From input to uptake.* Mahwah, NJ: Lawrence Erlbaum Associates.

Harris, M., & Davies, M. (1987). Learning and triggering in child language: A reply to Atkinson. *First Language, 7,* 31–39.

Hart, B., & Risley, T.R. (1975). Incidental teaching of language in the preschool. *Journal of Applied Behavior Analysis, 8,* 411–420.

Hart, B., & Risley, T.R. (1990). The longitudinal study of interactive systems. *Education and Treatment of Children, 12,* 347–358.

Hart, B., & Risley, T.R. (1995). *Meaningful differences in the everyday experience of young American children.* Baltimore: Paul H. Brookes Publishing Co.

Heath, S.B. (1989). Oral and literate traditions among Black Americans living in poverty. *American Psychologist, 44,* 367–373.

Hepting, N.H., & Goldstein, H. (1996). What's natural about naturalistic language intervention? *Journal of Early Intervention, 20,* 249–265.

Hirsh-Pasek, K., & Treiman, R. (1982). Doggerel: Motherese in a new context. *Journal of Child Language, 9,* 229–237.

Hoff-Ginsberg, E. (1991). Mother–child conversation in different social classes and communicative settings. *Child Development, 62,* 782–796.

Hymes, D. (1972). Models of the interaction of language and social life. In J.J. Gumperz & D. Hymes (Eds.), *Directions in sociolinguistics: The ethnography of communication* (pp. 35–71). Austin, TX: Holt, Rinehart & Winston.

Jenkins, J.J. (1991). Summary of the conference: Speech is special. In I.G. Mattingly & M. Studdert-Kennedy (Eds.), *Modularity and the motor theory of speech perception: Proceedings of a conference to honor Alvin M. Liberman* (pp. 431–442). Mahwah, NJ: Lawrence Erlbaum Associates.

Kaye, K. (1979). The social context of infant development. Final report to the Spencer Foundation. (Quoted in Golinkoff & Gordon, 1983, p. 19).

Keenan, E.O. (1974). Conversational competence in children. *Journal of Child Language, 1,* 163–183.

Lakoff, R. (1977). What you can do with words: Politeness, pragmatics, and performatives. In A. Rogers, B. Wall, & J.P. Murphy (Eds.), *Proceedings of the Texas conference on performatives, presuppositions, and implicatures* (pp. 79–105). Arlington, VA: Center for Applied Linguistics.

Landon, S.J., & Sommers, R.K. (1979). Talkativeness and children's linguistic abilities. *Language and Speech, 22,* 269–275.

Lenneberg, E.H. (1967). *Biological foundations of language.* New York: John Wiley & Sons.

Locke, J.L. (1988). The sound shape of early lexical representations. In M.D. Smith & J.L. Locke (Eds.), *The emergent lexicon: The child's development of a linguistic vocabulary* (pp. 3–22). San Diego: Academic Press.

Lovaas, O.I., Berberich, J.P., Perloff, B.F., & Schaeffer, B. (1966). Aquisition of imitative speech by schizophrenic children. *Science, 151,* 705–707.

Lyon, G.R., & Rumsey, J.M. (Eds.). (1996). *Neuroimaging: A window to the neurological foundations of learning and behavior in children.* Baltimore: Paul H. Brookes Publishing Co.

Lyons, J. (1968). *Introduction to theoretical linguistics.* New York: Cambridge University Press.

Lytton, H. (1973). Three approaches to the study of parent–child interaction: Ethological, interview, and experimental. *Journal of Child Psychology and Psychiatry, 14,* 1–17.

Maccoby, E.E. (1984). Socialization and developmental change. *Child Development, 55,* 317–328.

McCarthy, D. (1954). Language development in children. In L. Carmichael (Ed.), *Manual of child psychology* (pp. 492–630). New York: John Wiley & Sons.

McFarlane, M. (1994). *Nonlinear multilevel modeling of growth.* Unpublished doctoral dissertation, University of North Carolina at Chapel Hill.

McNeill, D. (1970). *The acquisition of language.* New York: HarperCollins.

Menyuk, P., Liebergott, J.W., & Schultz, M.C. (1995). *Early language development in full-term and premature infants.* Mahwah, NJ: Lawrence Erlbaum Associates.

Moerk, E.L. (1992). *A first language taught and learned.* Baltimore: Paul H. Brookes Publishing Co.

Mowrer, O.H. (1954). The psychologist looks at language. *American Journal of Psychology, 9,* 660–694.

Mussen, P.H., Conger, J.J., & Kagan, J. (1974). *Child development and personality.* New York: HarperCollins.

Nelson, K. (1973). Structure and strategy in learning to talk. *Monographs of the Society for Research in Child Development, 38*(1–2, Serial No. 149).

Nelson, K.E. (1989). Strategies for first language teaching. In M.L. Rice & R.L. Schiefelbusch (Eds.), *The teachability of language* (pp. 263–310). Baltimore: Paul H. Brookes Publishing Co.

Newport, E.L., Gleitman, H., & Gleitman, L.R. (1977). Mother, I'd rather do it myself: Some effects and non-effects of maternal speech style. In C.E. Snow & C.A. Ferguson (Eds.), *Talking to children: Language input and acquisition* (pp. 109–149). New York: Cambridge University Press.

Nichols, R.C. (1981). Origins, nature, and determinants of intellectual development. In M.J. Begab, H.C. Haywood, & H.L. Garber (Eds.), *Psychosocial influences on retarded performance: Vol. 1.*

Issues and theories in development (pp. 127–154). Baltimore: University Park Press.

O'Brien, M., & Nagle, K.J. (1987). Parents' speech to toddlers: The effect of play context. *Journal of Child Language, 14,* 269–279.

Ochs, E. (1986). Introduction. In B.B. Schieffelin & E. Ochs (Eds.), *Language socialization across cultures* (pp. 1–13). New York: Cambridge University Press.

Ochs, E. (1988). *Culture and language development.* New York: Cambridge University Press.

Peters, A.M. (1986). Early syntax. In P. Fletcher & M. Garman (Eds.), *Language acquisition: Studies in first language development* (pp. 307–325). New York: Cambridge University Press.

Piaget, J. (1970). *Genetic epistemology.* New York: W.W. Norton.

Pinker, S. (1988). Learnability theory and the acquisition of a first language. In F.S. Kessel (Ed.), *The development of language and language researchers: Essays in honor of Roger Brown* (pp. 97–119). Mahwah, NJ: Lawrence Erlbaum Associates.

Pinker, S. (1994). *The language instinct: How the mind creates language.* New York: William Morrow.

Pye, C. (1986). Quiché Mayan speech to children. *Journal of Child Language, 13,* 85–100.

Risley, T.R., Hart, B., & Doke, L.A. (1971). Operant language development: The outline of a therapeutic technology. In R.L. Schiefelbusch (Ed.), *Language of the mentally retarded* (pp. 107–123). Baltimore: University Park Press.

Risley, T.R., & Wolf, M.M. (1967). Establishing functional speech in echolalic children. *Behavior Research and Therapy, 5,* 73–88.

Ryan, J. (1974). Early language development: Towards a communicational analysis. In M.P.M. Richards (Ed.), *The integration of a child into a social world* (pp. 185–213). New York: Cambridge University Press.

Scarborough, H.S. (1990). Index of Productive Syntax. *Applied Psycholinguistics, 11,* 1–22.

Schaffer, H.R. (Ed.). (1977). *Studies in mother–infant interaction.* San Diego: Academic Press.

Schieffelin, B.B. (1990). *The give and take of everyday life.* New York: Cambridge University Press.

Schieffelin, B.B., & Eisenberg, A.R. (1984). Cultural variation in children's conversations. In R.L. Schiefelbusch & J. Pikar (Eds.), *The acquisition of communicative competence* (pp. 377–420). Baltimore: University Park Press.

Schieffelin, B.B., & Ochs, E. (1983). A cultural perspective on the transition from prelinguistic to linguistic communication. In R.M. Golinkoff (Ed.), *The transition from prelinguistic to linguistic communication* (pp. 115–131). Mahwah, NJ: Lawrence Erlbaum Associates.

Searle, J.R. (1969). *Speech acts: An essay in the philosophy of language.* New York: Cambridge University Press.

Seidenberg, M.S. (1997). Language acquisition and use: Learning and applying probabilistic constraints. *Science, 275,* 1599–1603.

Smith, M.E. (1926). An investigation of the development of the sentence and the extent of vocabulary in young children. *University of Iowa Studies in Child Welfare, 3*(5).

Smolucha, F. (1992). Social origins of private speech in pretend play. In R.M. Diaz & L.E. Berk (Eds.), *Private speech: From social interaction to self-regulation* (pp. 123–141). Mahwah, NJ: Lawrence Erlbaum Associates.

Snow, C.E. (1977). The development of conversation between mothers and babies. *Journal of Child Language, 4,* 1–22.

Snow, C.E. (1981). The uses of imitation. *Journal of Child Language, 8,* 205–212.

Snow, C.E. (1986). Conversations with children. In P. Fletcher & M. Garman (Eds.), *Language acquisition: Studies in first language development* (pp. 69–89). New York: Cambridge University Press.

Snow, C.E. (1988). The last word: Questions about the emerging lexicon. In M.D. Smith & J.L. Locke (Eds.), *The emergent lexicon: The child's development of a linguistic vocabulary* (pp. 341–353). San Diego: Academic Press.

Speidel, G.E., & Nelson, K.E. (Eds.). (1989). *The many faces of imitation in language learning.* New York: Springer-Verlag.

Stevenson, H.W. (1972). *Children's learning.* New York: Appleton-Century-Crofts.

Stone, L.J., & Church, J. (1957). *Childhood and adolescence.* New York: Random House.

Streeck, J. (1980). Speech acts in interaction: A critique of Searle. *Discourse Processes, 3,* 133–154.

Terman, L.M., & Merrill, M.A. (1960). *Stanford-Binet Intelligence Scale: Manual for the Third Revision Form L-M.* Boston: Houghton Mifflin.

Thal, D., Tobias, S., & Morrison, D. (1991). Language and gesture in late talkers: A one-year follow-up. *Journal of Speech and Hearing Research, 34,* 604–612.

Thissen, D., & Bock, R.D. (1990). Linear and nonlinear curve fitting. In A. von Eye (Ed.), *Statistical methods in longitudinal research: Vol. II. Time series and categorical longitudinal data* (pp. 289–318). San Diego: Academic Press.

Tomasello, M. (1992). *First verbs: A case study in early grammatical development.* New York: Cambridge University Press.

Veneziano, E. (1988). Vocal-verbal interaction and the construction of early lexical knowledge. In M.D. Smith & J.L. Locke (Eds.), *The emergent lexicon: The child's development of a linguistic vocabulary* (pp. 109–147). San Diego: Academic Press.

Vihman, M.M., & Miller, R. (1988). Words and babble at the threshold of language acquisition. In M.D. Smith & J.L. Locke (Eds.), *The emergent lexicon: The child's development of a linguistic vocabulary* (pp. 151–183). San Diego: Academic Press.

Wachs, T.D. (1984). Proximal experience and early cognitive-intellectual development: The social environment. In A.W. Gottfried (Ed.), *Home environment and early cognitive development: Longitudinal research* (pp. 273–328). San Diego: Academic Press.

Wagner, K.R. (1985). How much do children say in a day? *Journal of Child Language, 12*, 475–487.

Walker, D., Greenwood, C., Hart, B., & Carta, J. (1994). Prediction of school outcomes based on early language production and socioeconomic factors. *Child Development, 65*, 606–621.

Ward, M.C. (1971). *Them children: A study in language learning.* Austin, TX: Holt, Rinehart & Winston.

Weir, R. (1962). *Language in the crib.* The Hague, Netherlands: Mouton.

Wells, G. (1974). Learning to code experience through language. *Journal of Child Language, 1*, 243–269.

Wells, G. (1985). *Language development in the preschool years.* New York: Cambridge University Press.

Wells, G. (1986). Variation in child language. In P. Fletcher & M. Garman (Eds.), *Language acquisition: Studies in first language development* (pp. 109–139). New York: Cambridge University Press.

Wilhite, M. (1983). Children's acquisition of language routines: The end-of-meal routine in Cakchiquel. *Language in Society, 12*, 47–64.

Wilkinson, L.C., & Rembold, K. (1982). The communicative context of early language development. In S.A. Kuczaj (Ed.), *Language development: Vol. 2. Language, thought, and culture* (pp. 113–129). Mahwah, NJ: Lawrence Erlbaum Associates.

Zaslow, M., & Rogoff, B. (1981). The cross-cultural study of early interaction: Implications from research in culture and cognition. In T.M. Field, A.M. Sostek, P. Vietze, & P.H. Leiderman (Eds.), *Culture and early interactions* (pp. 237–256). Mahwah, NJ: Lawrence Erlbaum Associates.

Zegiob, L., Arnold, S., & Forehand, R. (1975). An examination of observer effects in parent–child interactions. *Child Development, 46*, 509–512.

Appendix A

Child Vocabulary in 100 Utterances, 19–36 Months Old

◆ ◆ ◆ ◆

Appendix A lists all of the vocabulary words recorded in the first 100 utterances in each hour of observation for 42 children between the ages of 19 and 36 months.

Category

The words are listed using the categories from the CDI (Fenson et al., 1992), plus some added categories. Words listed on the CDI are preceded by a bullet.

Word

The words are listed in root form; inflected forms recorded are subsumed under the root form. Proper nouns, animal sounds, and words recorded only as imitations are not included.

Period

Because sampling resulted in considerable range in child age at the recording of any particular word, the words listed within each category are grouped in periods indicating when the word was first recorded for half or more of the children who used it. The periods are:

- 11–24 months old, when most of the children were adding words rapidly to a vocabulary in use, especially by naming pictures, objects, and states
- 25–30 months old, when children were staying and playing and parents were encouraging their children to explore words and tell them about things
- 31–36 months old, when the children were often practicing alone in monologues, introducing the topics for talk, and controlling the course of interactions with their parents and other people.

Because the sizes of the child dictionaries that contributed to the lists differed considerably, the periods indicate less about the age at which particular words came into use than about the children's cumulative experience using words. The final size of a child's recorded dictionary depended on how early the first words were recorded and how much the child talked thereafter. The child with the smallest recorded vocabulary at 36 months old (253 words) had 4 words listed in her dictionary at 12 months old. By contrast, the child with the largest recorded vocabulary at 36 months old (1,644 words) had 7 words listed in her dictionary at 12 months old; when this child was 18 months old, 235 words were listed in her dictionary. In 6 months, this child had almost as many words in her dictionary as were accumulated for the child with the smallest dictionary in 2 years of sampling. Yet across these 2 years of sampling, one word ("dangerous") that was listed as recorded for only one child came from the 253 words listed in the smallest of the recorded vocabularies.

The word lists in this appendix thus suggest what the children were talking about as they added new words to a vocabulary in use and elaborated familiar words, rather than the age at which the children actually learned the words they were recorded saying during sampling.

Number of Children and Parents

Before each word is listed the number of children and parents for whom the word was recorded.

The number of children (C) is the number for whom the word was recorded within the first 100 fully recognizable utterances during each hour-long observation from 19 through 36 months of age. (All of the words recorded for the children between 11 and 18 months old also appeared after the children were 19 months old.) When the count was based on all child utterances in each hour-long observation rather than on the 100-utterance subsample, the number of children was greater for 40% of the listed words; those cases are indicated by a plus sign (+) after the number of children (because of space limitations, the numbers based on all child utterances are not listed). The absence of a number preceding a word indicates that across all of the 100-utterance subsamples, the word was recorded for only one child. We based the child counts on 100 utterances to facilitate comparisons across databases.

The number of parents (P) is listed only for those words recorded for 10 or more of the parents and is based on all parent utterances addressed to the child in all 2½ years of hour-long observations. The absence of a number in the P column indicates that across all of the hour-long observations, the word was recorded for fewer than 10 of the parents. We based the parent counts on all utterances to see how relatively often the children had been exposed to the words.

Use

For each child word that was also recorded for 10 or more of the parents, the relative frequency of use per hour by those children and parents is listed in one of eight categories indicating how often the word was recorded. The codes indicating relative frequency of use are listed below.

Frequency of use

Code	Total times recorded in 28 average hours of observation	Times recorded per month of observation	Times recorded per hour in one or more of 42 families per month of observation
A	1–280	1–10	
B	281–840	11–30	Up to 1 time every 2 hours
C	841–1,680	31–60	Up to 1 time per hour
D	1,681–3,360	61–120	1–2 times per hour
E	3,361–8,400	121–300	2–5 times per hour
F	8,401–16,800	301–600	5–10 times per hour
G	16,801–33,600	601–1,200	10–20 times per hour
H	33,601 or more	1,201 or more	20 times or more per hour

There were major differences among the 42 families in how much they talked per hour. Hence, the frequencies listed give no indication of the actual number of times that any one parent or child used a word or during which or how many ob-

servations the word was recorded. Rather, the frequencies indicate which words are more or less likely to be recorded during naturalistic samples of parent–child interaction and suggest characteristics of everyday language use, such as the
frequency of the closed classes of functors in comparison to
the variety of the open classes of contentive words.

It is not surprising that words listed in the third period
(31–36 months old) were recorded 10 times or fewer for the
children. More interesting is the number of words that were
recorded only 10 times or fewer across all of the hour-long observations of parents talking to their children. An average of
48% of the nouns and modifiers added to a child's vocabulary
recorded in the first 100 utterances in each sample (and thus
listed in Appendix A) were also recorded for that child's parent within 10 utterances of the child's first recorded use; this
suggests that many of the words were recorded for both parent
and child within the same interaction.

The relative frequencies suggest characteristics of interactions and differences in topics of concern to parents and
children. Examples are the relative frequency of the question
words in parent and child talk, and of "I" versus "you."

"I" was recorded more than 50 times per hour for the 42
children across all of the months of observations; the actual
number was 40,177 times. "I" was one of only four words
recorded more often for the children than for the parents; the
others were "mine," "my," and "mom." "Mine" was recorded
for the 42 children almost twice per hour; the actual number
was 2,711 times.

"I" was recorded for the parents more than 20 times per
hour across all of the hour-long observations; the actual number was 30,183 times. Only 34 parents were recorded saying
"mine" to their children; for those who did so, "mine" was
recorded less than once every other hour; the actual number
was 413 times.

By contrast, "you" was recorded for the parents more
than 50 times per hour across all of the hour-long observa-

tions; the actual number was 100,793 times (3,600 times per hour, more than 85 times per parent per hour).

Further contrast may be seen for a word such as "careful," which was recorded for 12 children fewer than 10 times (44 times total) in the 12 hours of observation between the months when the children were 25 and 36 months old. "Careful" was recorded for 1 or more of 34 of the parents almost once per hour over all of the hour-long observations (916 times total).

Appendix A is most impressive, though, in its display of the immense variability in what ordinary American families, all similarly engaged in child rearing, say to children during their daily activities when no structure is provided and they are asked just to do what they usually do when at home. Only 94 words were common across all of the parents and their children. Only 36% of the words recorded for the children within their first 100 utterances per hour were also recorded for 10 or more of the parents, and 39% of those words were recorded 10 or fewer times for both children and parents during more than 2½ years and 1,300 hours of sampling.

Category: Animals

11–24 months old				25–30 months old				31–36 months old			
Number of		Use by		Number of		Use by		Number of		Use by	
C	P	C-P	Word	C	P	C-P	Word	C	P	C-P	Word
31	32	B-B	•bear	12			•alligator	3			dragon
19			•bee	22	34	A-A	•animal	5			fly
35	43	B-B	•bird	8			•ant	10			•goose
35	27	B-A	•bug	25	33	A-B	•bunny	2			hippo
3			camel	23			•butterfly	2			mosquito
24			•cow	38	39	B-C	•cat	2			parrot
42	42	D-D	•dog	3			chick	4			•penguin
28	30	B-B	•duck	20	31	A-A	•chicken	3			snail
3			fox	7			•deer	13			•turkey
5			goat	3			dinosaur	10			•wolf
2			gorilla	7			•donkey	6			•zebra
35	36	B-B	•horse	23	30	A-A	•elephant				
6			kangaroo	29	31	A-B	•fish				_One child_
36	34	C-C	•kitty	25			•frog	bat			hummingbird
2			lobster	5			giraffe	bluebird			neon
11			•owl	9			•hen	buzzard			partridge
2			pet	14			•lamb	flamingo			puffin
25	29	A-B	•pig	20			•lion	gerbil			starling
16	31	A-A	rabbit	28	31	B-B	•monkey	hog			toucan

220

				2		•moose
2		rat		27		•mouse
5		reindeer		19		•pony
3		rhinoceros		2		potato bug
2		robin		28	27 B-B	•puppy
7		•sheep		5		•rooster
6		snake		9		spider
9		worm		5		•squirrel
	One child			22		•teddy bear
				20		•tiger
ape		fleabag		15		•turtle
buffalo		magpie			*One child*	
crab		octopus				
cuckoo		ostrich		bull		mole
				caterpillar		panther
				catfish		pigeon
				chipmunk		raccoon
				eagle		shark
				lizard		woodpecker

Category: Vehicles

28	30	A-A	•airplane	25	24	A-A	•boat	3	bulldozer
38	27	B-B	•bicycle	2			camper	3	diesel
4			bigwheel	4			cart	3	•fire truck

C, children; P, parents; + number greater when based on all child utterances in hour-long observations; • word on CDI.

221

Category: Vehicles (continued)

11–24 months old

| Number of | | Use by | |
C	P	C-P	Word
24	24	A-A	•bus
41	39	D-C	•car
13			choo-choo
2			dump truck
2			school bus
11			•tractor
7			•tricycle
35	34	B-B	•truck
9			wagon

One child

baby carriage   scooter
police car

25–30 months old

| Number of | | Use by | |
C	P	C-P	Word
2			engine
18			•motorcycle
4			•sled
28	27	A-B	•train
2			van

One child

buggy   glider
cab   hot rod
caboose   trailer

31–36 months old

| Number of | | Use by | |
C	P	C-P	Word
2			•helicopter
2			jet
8			•stroller
2			tow truck

One child

ambulance   road grader
crane   taxi
motorboat

Category: Toys

11–24 months old

C	P	C-P	Word
7			ABCs
41	40	D-C	•ball
29	34	A-B	•balloon
8			baseball

25–30 months old

C	P	C-P	Word
17			•bat
16+	26	A-A	card
6			cartoon
11			•chalk

31–36 months old

C	P	C-P	Word
3			goal
3			•glue
3			marble
3			mask

Count	Code	Word
11		basketball
23	29 A-B	•block
41	40 C-D	•book
25		•bubbles
3	31 A-A	coloring book
32	36 B-B	•doll
2		•dough
2		globe
2		hoop
5		horn
3		marker
2		paintbrush
2		piggy bank
2		playing card
2		railroad
3		roller skate
4		somersault
4		teapot
3		tower
37	39 B-C	•toy
4		toybox

One child
ark — playhouse
pattern — touchdown

Count	Code	Word
4		chalkboard
2		clubhouse
21		•crayon
10		football
30	31 A-A	•game
10		gun
3		kite
3+	23 A-A	letters
6+	27 A-A	numbers
9+	29 A-A	page
7		paint
26	32 A-A	•pen
26	29 A-A	•pencil
18		puzzle
2		soccer
10		sticker
8	27 A-A	•story
2		tea party
2		tennis ball
3		track
2		trampoline
2		whistle

One child
racetrack

Count	Word
2	nursery rhyme
12	•present
2	puppet
3	rattle
5	robot
2	stethoscope

One child

boxing glove	jump rope
cash register	machine gun
collage	peg
darts	rocket
dice	rocket ship
dominoes	score
drum	shuttle
homework	storybook
jacks	sword

C, children; P, parents; + number greater when based on all child utterances in hour-long observations; • word on CDI.

Category: Toys (continued)

11–24 months old				25–30 months old				31–36 months old			
Number of		Use by		Number of		Use by		Number of		Use by	
C	P	C-P	Word	C	P	C-P	Word	C	P	C-P	Word
						One child					
							compass				
							construction paper				
							paste				
							saber set[+]				

Category: Food and Drink

11–24 months old				25–30 months old				31–36 months old			
Number of		Use by		Number of		Use by		Number of		Use by	
C	P	C-P	Word	C	P	C-P	Word	C	P	C-P	Word
33	35	B-B	•apple	4			•applesauce	2			cinnamon
24	28	A-A	•banana	2			bacon	2			cupcake
16			•beans	23	33	A-A	•bread	11			•french fries
3			beer	2			brownie	6			•lollipop
11			bubblegum	18			•butter	5			•melon
36	33	A-B	•cake	17			•carrot	5			•noodles
36	34	B-B	•candy	24	32	A-B	•cereal	2			oatmeal
6			candy bar	2			cherry	2			pineapple
3			candy cane	21			•chocolate	12			•popsicle
3			catsup	20			•coffee	14			potato
30	35	B-B	•cheese	12			•corn	4			•pretzel
4			cocoa	2			crust	3			roll
36	36	B-C	•cookie	11			•doughnut	5			salad

Word	C	P	Code
•cracker	25		
•drink	28	29	A-B
•egg	31	32	B-B
fruit	5		
ham	2		
honey	7+	35	A-C
hot dog	6		
•juice	36	38	B-C
macaroni	2		
•milk	39	40	B-C
peach	3		
peanut	4		
•pop	33		
•pumpkin	14	28	A-A
sugar	6	26	A-B
tea	7		
•water	41	42	C-C

One child

beef	jam
celery	mustard
corn flakes	olive
deviled egg	peel
fritter	

Word	C	P	Code
•food	38	38	A-B
frosting	2		
•grape	17		
•gum	34		
•hamburger	19		
•ice	23	24	A-A
•ice cream	33	29	A-A
ice cream cone	2		
•jell-o	7		
•jelly	17	27	A-A
•meat	11	22	A-A
nugget	2		
•orange	26	37	A-A
•pancake	11		
•peanut butter	22		
pear	2		
•peas	13		
pepper	2		
•pickle	9		
pie	5		
•pizza	20		
•popcorn	22		
•potato chip	24		
•pudding	3		
•raisin	13		

Word	C
•salt	6
tomato	3
•tuna	2

One child

artichoke	lettuce
banana split	meatball
beet	•nuts
blueberry	peppermint
chili	pork chop
cider	sausage
cone	soufflé
egg roll	taco
flour	vegetable
gingerbread	watermelon

C, children; P, parents; + number greater when based on all child utterances in hour-long observations; • word on CDI.

225

Category: Food and Drink *(continued)*

11–24 months old				25–30 months old				31–36 months old			
Number of		Use by		Number of		Use by		Number of		Use by	
C	P	C-P	Word	C	P	C-P	Word	C	P	C-P	Word
				2			rice				
				19	25	A-A	•sandwich				
				7			•sauce				
				12			•soup				
				9			•spaghetti				
				18			•strawberry				
				2			syrup				
				19	25	A-A	•toast				
				2			•vanilla				
				10			•vitamin				
				3			wheat				
				3			•yogurt				

One child

apricot	cottage cheese
bologna	currant
bun	cough drop
cabbage	graham cracker
cashew	iced tea
cobbler	onion
cornbread	

226

Category: Clothing

C	P	Type	Word
3			bracelet
21+	40	A-B	clothes
19	35	A-B	•diaper
6			earring
40	36	B-B	•hat
3			jewelry
5			•mittens
10+	30	A-A	pocket
5			rubber
42	41	C-D	•shoe
4			sleeve
2			snap
38	38	B-B	•sock
3			stocking
2			sweatshirt
2			underwear
4			•zipper

One child

britches	shoelace
hanky	thong

C	P	Type	Word
7			barrette
11			•beads
18	25	A-A	•belt
11			•bib
24	24	A-A	•boots
2			bow
22	29	A-A	•button
3			cap
29	34	A-A	•coat
25	29	A-A	•dress
15			gloves
15			•jeans
6			•necklace
16			•pajamas
4			panties
35	40	A-B	•pants
3			ribbon
5			rubber band
2			sandal
3			•scarf
3+	36	A-B	•shirt
10			•shorts
14			•slipper

C	P	Type	Word
2			clip
19	26	A-A	•jacket
2			suspenders
5			•underpants

One child

blouse	robe
bootie	strap
cologne	swimsuit
perfume	

C, children; P, parents; + number greater when based on all child utterances in hour-long observations; • word on CDI.

Category: Clothing (continued)

11–24 months old				25–30 months old				31–36 months old			
Number of		**Use by**		**Number of**		**Use by**		**Number of**		**Use by**	
C	P	C-P	Word	C	P	C-P	Word	C	P	C-P	Word
				10			•sweater				
				19	18	A-A	•tennis shoe				
				3			•tights				
				3			tee-shirt				

One child (25–30 months old):

ballet suit	pantyhose
bra	skirt
cape	shoehorn
hood	•snowsuit
overalls	

Category: Body Parts

11–24 months old				25–30 months old				31–36 months old			
Number of		**Use by**		**Number of**		**Use by**		**Number of**		**Use by**	
C	P	C-P	Word	C	P	C-P	Word	C	P	C-P	Word
19+	37	A-B	back	4+	34	A-B	•arm	2			blood
8			belly	3			ass				pressure
7			•belly button	2			beak	2+	25	A-A	cold
5			bone	3+	17	A-A	body	3			fingernail
2			booger (snot)	30	34	A-A	•bottom/butt	3			germ
4			elbow	7			•cheek	2			haircut
37	39	B-C	•eye	3			chickenpox	6			•shoulder

C	P		Word
39	40	B-C	•feet
40	40	B-D	•hand
7+	21	A-A	heart
8+	30	A-A	lap
6+	29	A-A	neck
38	42	A-C	•nose
12		B-C	•ouchy
10		B-C	poopy
			thumb
31	34	A-B	•toe

One child

eyebrow	paw
eyelash	stomachache
hiccups	

C	P		Word
10			•chin
34	35	A-B	•ear
31	40	A-B	•face
30	36	A-B	•finger
6+	33	A-A	front
2			fur
40	39	B-C	•hair
41	40	B-C	•head
23			•knee
30	38	A-B	•leg
13			•lips
38	40	A-C	•mouth
4			pee
6			•penis
4			self
2			sore
4+	25	A-A	tail
5+	38	A-B	•teeth
14	30	A-A	•tongue
29	19	A-A	•tummy

One child

breast	ponytail
navel	privates
pinky	wart

C		Word
2		throat
3		wing
2		wool

One child

bangs	muscle
breath	mustache
flu	skeleton
headache	slobber
hump	smile
jaw	tiptoes

C, children; P, parents; + number greater when based on all child utterances in hour-long observations; • word on CDI.

Category: Household Items

11–24 months old

Number of C	P	Use by C-P	Word
8+	33	A-A	bag
10	22	A-A	battery
8			bell
25	29	A-B	•blanket
7			board
31	38	B-B	•bottle
5			candle
2			change
28	23	A-A	•clock
35	38	B-B	•cup
10+	15	A-A	dollar
4			fan
2			grease
13			•hammer
28	30	A-A	•key
3			lid
40	36	B-B	•light
3			makeup
6			•mop

25–30 months old

Number of C	P	Use by C-P	Word
2			aspirin
2			backpack
21	30	A-A	•basket
30	35	A-A	•bowl
36	39	A-B	•box
9			•broom
20	30	A-A	•brush
13	27	A-A	•can
2			channel
23	26	A-A	•comb
2			coupon
9			cover
18	33	A-A	•dish
19			•fork
3			garbage
22	34	A-A	•glass
21	27	A-A	•glasses
4+	18	A-A	groceries
2			junk

31–36 months old

Number of C	P	Use by C-P	Word
19			•bucket
7			•camera
3			flashlight
6			•jar
2			nipple
2			pedal
2			pill
4			quarter
5			record player
2			remote control
2			saxophone
10			•scissors
2			sponge
2			ticket
8			wheel

One child

alarm clock	hanger
ashtray	holder
alcohol	hook

Word			
paddle	2		
pan	3+	24	A-A
pin	6		
pipe	2		
plug	3		
pot	8		
powder	2		
•purse	34	30	A-B
•radio	27	28	A-A
rag	4		
saw	2		
shampoo	3		
sheet	5		
stuff	16+	40	A-C
sunglasses	3		
switch	4		
thing	37+	40	C-C
umbrella	3		
•knife	16		
•lamp	8		
lipstick	5		
lotion	6		
mail	2+	20	A-A
•medicine	19	30	A-A
mirror	6		
•money	35	36	B-B
•nail	10		
•napkin	8		
newspaper	2		
nickel	2		
pacifier	2		
pad	3		
•paper	36	42	B-B
•penny	19		
•phone	39	39	A-B
phone book	2		
•picture	34	37	A-B
•pillow	30	33	A-A
pillowcase	2		
•plant	12		
•plate	25	28	A-A
pliers	2		
pocketbook	2		
polish	3		

One child

can opener	poison	bill	keyring
crystal	stopper	blow dryer	lead
dime	violin	calculator	light bulb
hairbrush	wreath	calendar	mat
iron	xylophone	cent	microphone
magazine	yarn	check	mobile
ornament		chopsticks	napkin ring
		cigarette	needle
		cloth	note
		cotton	nut
		cross	silver
		curtain	stereo
		file	tick-tock
		flute	toolbox
		garbage can	trombone
		guitar	tuba

C, children; P, parents; + number greater when based on all child utterances in hour-long observations; • word on CDI.

231

Category: Household Items *(continued)*

| 11–24 months old | | | | 25–30 months old | | | | 31–36 months old | | | |
| Number of | | Use by | | Number of | | Use by | | Number of | | Use by | |
C	P	C-P	Word	C	P	C-P	Word	C	P	C-P	Word
				8			record				
				2			roller				
				2			rope				
				6			sack				
				4			screw				
				2			screwdriver				
				2			shade				
				24	25	A-A	•soap				
				28	32	A-B	•spoon				
				3			straw				
				8+	26	A-A	string				
				3			suitcase				
				26	32	A-A	•tape				
				4			tape recorder				
				5			•tissue				
				2			toilet paper				
				4			tools				
				13			•toothbrush				
				2			toothpick				

27	26	A-A	•towel
33	38	A-B	•trash
3			trash can
4			•tray
2			trunk
9			•vacuum cleaner
2			•walker
2			washcloth
15			•watch

One child

bubble bath	pail
chart	sweeper
checkbook	toaster
chimes	toothpaste
cord	wallet
cuckoo clock	wrench
ink	

Category: Furniture and Rooms

42	40	B-C	•bed	10	22	A-A	•basement	9	23	A-A	•bathtub
38	40	B-C	•chair	29	40	A-B	•bathroom	2			booster chair
3+	26	A-A	corner	21	25	A-A	•bedroom	2			carpet
41	40	B-C	•door	3			•bench	3			cradle

C, children; P, parents; + number greater when based on all child utterances in hour-long observations; • word on CDI.

233

Category: Furniture and Rooms (*continued*)

11–24 months old

Number of		Use by	Word
C	P	C-P	
20	40	A-C	floor
2			gate
5			motor
3			•playpen
3			playroom
29+	36	A-B	•potty
7+	30	A-A	seat
12+	23	A-A	•stairs
9+	26	A-A	steps
37	40	B-B	•TV
8	32	A-A	wall

One child

drain   hamper

hall

25–30 months old

Number of		Use by	Word
C	P	C-P	
3			bookcase
3			ceiling
16	28	A-A	•closet
26	33	A-A	•couch
3			computer
4			counter
5			•crib
19	30	A-A	•drawer
3			dresser
5			•dryer
22			•garage
8			•highchair
25	36	A-B	•kitchen
16	24	A-A	•living room
10	26	A-A	•oven
4			piano
7			•porch
17	27	A-A	•refrigerator
8			•rocking chair

31–36 months old

Number of		Use by	Word
C	P	C-P	
2			front room
3			furniture
7			•stove
11			•washing machine
2			water bed

One child

air conditioner   mantel

attic   mattress

buffet   organ

fireplace   patio

footstool   railing

freezer   rec room

humidifier   shutter

234

C	P		Word
34	39	B-C	•room
7+	24	A-A	rug
2			shelf
5			•shower
11	25	A-A	•sink
3			•sofa
3			stool
38	40	A-B	•table
23	33	A-B	•window

One child

cabinet	nursery
cellar	pallet
compressor	potty chair
davenport	toilet
dining room	

Category: Outside Things

C	P		Word		C	P		Word		C	P		Word
12+	28	A-A	dirt		5+	29	A-A	air		5			bridge
12+	29	A-A	fire		10			•backyard		2			feather
5			•flag		2			brick		2			fishing pole
33	27	A-B	•flower		4			building		2+	24	A-A	ground
7			hill		2			cage		3			jingle bell

C, children; P, parents; + number greater when based on all child utterances in hour-long observations; • word on CDI.

Category: Outside Things (*continued*)

11–24 months old

Number of C	P	Use by C-P	Word
14+	32	A-A	hole
2			lake
2			lawn
11			•lawn mower
5			leaf
6			mud
21	24	A-A	•swing
2			swing set
29	33	A-B	•tree

One child

base
driveway
jack
poison ivy
pole
sandpile
seed
shell
tunnel
weed

25–30 months old

Number of C	P	Use by C-P	Word
2			chainsaw
6			•cloud
2			doghouse
3			•garden
9+	19	A-A	gas
19	27	A-A	•grass
2			heaven
5			•hose
11			•ladder
3			mailbox
2			net
22	23	A-A	•rain
2			road
24			•rock
4			sand
11			•sandbox
2			siren
20			•sky
15			•slide

31–36 months old

Number of C	P	Use by C-P	Word
15			•moon
5			nest
17			•pool
3			rainbow
9			•roof
14			•shovel
2			•sidewalk
3			smoke
2			temperature
2			trap

One child

acorn	patch
chain	petunia
dandelion	shadow
firecracker	space
license plate	stable
moonbeam	suntan
oar	traffic light
oil	weather

21	25	A-A	•snow
12			•snowman
24	24	A-A	•star
30	32	A-A	•stick
3			•stone
21	29	A-A	•street
22	25	A-A	•sun
8			teeter-totter
2			tire
2			treasure
16	20	A-A	•wind
3			wood
3[+]	19	A-A	world

One child

barn	scarecrow
crocus	shed
dune	tent
fence	thunder
horseshoe	water wings
maple	wheelbarrow
pinecone	woodpile
raft	

C, children; P, parents; [+] number greater when based on all child utterances in hour-long observations; • word on CDI.

237

Category: Places to Go

11–24 months old

Number of C	P	Use by C-P	Word
6			bank
17+	32	A-B	downstairs
41	39	B-B	•home
12+	33	A-B	inside
4+	31	A-B	job
5			outdoors
41	41	B-C	•outside
8+	34	A-A	place
3+	20	A-A	town

One child

city   depot   office

25–30 months old

Number of C	P	Use by C-P	Word
4+	23	A-A	anywhere
2			carnival
4			castle
18	17	A-A	•church
2	25	A-A	everywhere
8			•farm
5+	17	A-A	hospital
41	40	B-C	•house
2			jail
2			nowhere
13			•park
16	27	A-A	•party
7			picnic
30	35	A-B	•school
8+	33	A-A	somewhere
29	36	A-A	•store
2			trip
13+	30	A-B	upstairs
32	36	A-B	•work

31–36 months old

Number of C	P	Use by C-P	Word
4			•beach
2			•camping
6			•circus
2			•downtown
2			library
15			•movie
2			restaurant
3			shop
3+	19	A-A	show
2			someplace
3			•woods
16	25	A-A	•yard
11			•zoo

One child

ball game	market
dance	post office
elevator	sale
exhibition	sea
•gas station	surgery
inn	

Category: People

2			angel
42	42	E-E	•baby
2			batter
41	42	B-D	•boy
4			buddy
3+	20	A-A	•child
4+	18	A-A	company
42	42	E-E	•dad
38	38	B-C	•grandma
27	33	B-B	•grandpa
17+	27	A-B	guy
15+	32	A-B	kid
34	36	B-A	•lady
41	38	B-B	•man
42	41	G-E	•mom

armory barbershop

22	23	A-A	•aunt
2			boogieman
23			•clown
5			crybaby
25	24	A-A	•doctor
2			dummy
13			•fireman
23	23	A-A	•friend
7			ghost
38	40	B-D	•girl
2			jumper
14			•mailman
2			meanie
13+	27	A-A	mother
23	33	A-B	•people

One child
•country village

6			•babysitter
3			baker
20	33	A-B	•brother
12			•cowboy
2			driver
2			dude
2			king
4			•nurse
7	20	A-A	•person
16			•police
11			•teacher

One child

bobber	painter
copycat	passenger
cutter	prince
dentist	prizefighter
elf	pumper

C, children; P, parents; + number greater when based on all child utterances in hour-long observations; • word on CDI.

239

Category: People (continued)

11–24 months old

Number of C	P	Use by C-P	Word
15			monster
2			player
5			witch

One child

	Word
helper	pilot
infant	queen
nudnik	team
parent	waiter

25–30 months old

Number of C	P	Use by C-P	Word
4			punk
26	29	A-B	•sister
15	26	A-A	•uncle

One child

	Word
boyfriend	neighbor
caveman	pusher
chopper	showoff
devil	stinkpot
farmer	striper
grouch	sweetie
idiot	woman

31–36 months old

One child

Number of C	P	Use by C-P	Word
fathead			robber
fatty			scout
fixer			shooter
fool			sissy
freak			stamper
giant			stinker
grownup			waitress
innkeeper			wife
knucklehead			wizard
maker			

Category: Games and Routines

11–24 months old

Number of C	P	Use by C-P	Word
32+	42	B-D	all right
20+	34	B-B	birthday
42	42	D-D	•bye
3			giddyup
32	35	A-B	•hello
40+	42	C-D	hey

25–30 months old

Number of C	P	Use by C-P	Word
6			amen
22	36	A-A	•bath
19	34	A-B	•breakfast
4+	28	A-A	good-bye
18	32	A-B	•lunch
18	35	A-B	•nap

31–36 months old

Number of C	P	Use by C-P	Word
18	27	A-A	•dinner
2			treat
2			merry (Christmas)

One child

	Word
blessing	prayer
grace	present (here)

42	C-C	•hi			sir	2
4		ma'am			•snack	7
42	F-F	•no			supper	3
42	F-G	oh			surprise	3
42	E-F	okay				
41	B-B	•ouch			*One child*	
10		•pat-a-cake			praises (grace)	
20		•peekaboo				
40	B-C	•please				
21+	B-C	ready				
42	E-E	right				
15		ring				
2		rockabye				
8		rosey				
9		set				
5		shoot				
10	A-A	thanks				
42	F-F	uh-huh				
41	C-C	•uh-oh				
42	E-D	uh-uh				
7+	A-A	welcome				
22+	A-C	whoops				
42	F-F	•yes				
11+	A-B	yuk				

C, children; P, parents; + number greater when based on all child utterances in hour-long observations; • word on CDI.

Category: Other Nouns

11–24 months old

Number of C	P	Use by C-P	Word
12			circle
15+	31	A-B	color
8+	28	A-A	end
8+	36	A-B	fun
16+	36	A-B	kind
12+	39	A-B	mess
6+	33	A-A	music
30+	39	B-C	name
9+	35	A-A	noise
2			power
9+	35	A-B	side
7+	34	A-A	trouble
33+	39	B-C	way
4			whipping

One child

beam	patience
favor	payment
goo	pity
goodness	polka dot
habit	scribbles
jive	

25–30 months old

Number of C	P	Use by C-P	Word
7+	16	A-A	line
4+	39	A-B	matter
2			program
4			shot
9+	33	A-A	song
2			spot
4			square
4			triangle
7+	29	A-A	word

One child

action	racket
brake	ray
diamond	rectangle
gold	trigger
joy	type
luck	

31–36 months old

Number of C	P	Use by C-P	Word
2+	13	A-A	course
4			dot
5			middle

One child

age	list
chance	lullaby
collection	magic
danger	melody
death	mistake
degree	navy
design	poetry
energy	scripture
form	slot
fortune	style
grade	verse

Category: Verbal Nouns

C	P		
3			break
6+	30	A-A	help
3+	31	A-B	hug
7+	38	A-B	kiss
2			race
2+	29	A-A	ride
14+	27	B-A	turn

One child

blow shake walk

C	P		
3			bump
4+	25	A-A	care
2			exercise
2			jump
6			mark
2			trick

One child

catch hit march rhyme snuggle spin wrap

C		
2		fight
3		love

One child

burn clap crack flash flip hold kick pay sleep strike touch

Category: Action Words

C	P		
6+	39	A-B	ask
42	42	G-H	be
19+	30	A-B	beat
6			bend
36	38	B-B	•bite
3			bless
33	39	A-B	•blow

C	P		
5			bake
3			bark
4			belong
2			bleed
35	38	A-B	•break
33	41	A-C	•bring
18			•build

C	P		
5	30	A-A	act
3+	25	A-A	believe
5+	35	A-B	bet
2			born
7			•clap
17	25	A-A	•cover
2			dream

C, children; P, parents; + number greater when based on all child utterances in hour-long observations; • word on CDI.

Category: Action Words *(continued)*

11–24 months old

Number of C	P	Use by C-P	Word
6+	19	A-A	bother
4			bounce
13+	33	A-B	brush
7			burn
4			burp
18+	37	B-B	•call
9+	35	A-B	change
3+	31	A-A	check
12			color
7+	33	A-B	comb
42	42	E-F	come
4			crawl
3			dig
42	42	E-G	do
42	42	D-E	•eat
15+	37	A-B	excuse
41	41	C-C	•fall
3			fill
41	38	C-D	•find

25–30 months old

Number of C	P	Use by C-P	Word
32	28	A-A	•bump
5			bust
4			button
37	34	B-B	•buy
4+	33	A-A	care
27	32	A-A	•carry
36	32	B-B	•catch
2			charge
8			•chase
5+	31	A-A	chew
2			choke
26	38	A-B	•clean
22	34	A-A	•climb
34	39	A-B	•close
26	29	A-A	•cook
2			cool
7+	26	A-A	count
4			crack
6			crash

31–36 months old

Number of C	P	Use by C-P	Word
3			fire
2			gobble
15	16	A-A	•hate
3			hop
8			•hug
2			jack
2			marry
16			•paint
2			pat
3			plug
2			pump
2			raise
3			•rip
13			shoot
11			•skate
5+	35	A-A	smell
4			•smile
2			smoke
2+	26	A-A	sound

10⁺	38	A-A	forget
42	42	F-G	•get
42	42	D-E	•give
42	42	F-G	•go
42	41	E-E	got (have)
5⁺	37	A-B	guess
7			hand
10⁺	30	A-A	hang
9⁺	31	A-B	happen
41	41	D-E	•have
40	37	B-C	•help
40	40	B-C	•hit
40	42	B-C	•hold
3⁺	33	A-A	hope
3			itch
13⁺	41	A-B	keep
8			kill
38⁺	41	C-E	know
12⁺	39	A-B	lay
25⁺	42	A-D	leave
2			lift
11	23	A-A	lock
42	42	E-E	•look
40	41	C-E	•make
3			march

36	35	A-B	•cry
36	39	B-B	•cut
23	32	A-B	•dance
2			dial
5			die
22	26	A-A	•draw
3⁺	24	A-A	dress
37	40	A-C	•drink
35	26	A-A	•drive
32	33	A-B	•drop
12	26	A-A	•dry
23			•dump
3			exercise
3			fart
22	32	A-A	•feed
9⁺	40	A-B	feel
10⁺	24	A-A	fight
23	41	A-B	•finish
			fish
27	30	A-B	•fit
38	40	B-C	•fix
12	22	A-A	fly
6⁺	26	A-A	fold
7⁺	16	A-A	follow
2			freeze

5			•splash
5			stink
2			stomp
3			suck
2⁺	29	A-A	swallow
2			tape
2			train
3⁺	31	A-A	wonder

One child

ache	puff
argue	puke
blink	rob
borrow	rollerskate
break dance	scat
butter	send⁺
cost	serve
curse	sharpen
dribble	shovel
erase	slam
excite	slap
flash	sneak
glow	sniff
grab⁺	snuggle
hammer	spit⁺
hook	split

C, children; P, parents; ⁺ number greater when based on all child utterances in hour-long observations; • word on CDI.

Category: Action Words *(continued)*

11–24 months old

Number of C	P	Use by C-P	Word
6+	40	A-B	mean
30+	42	B-C	move
42	42	B-C	•open
4+	17	A-A	pay
21+	26	A-A	pee
3			peek
5			pinch
42	42	D-E	•play
14			poop
9+	24	A-A	pop
38	40	B-C	•pull
42	42	E-F	•put
15+	36	A-C	quit
6			race
12+	26	A-A	reach
31	34	C-C	•read
40	38	B-B	•ride
7			ring
15+	30	A-A	rock

25–30 months old

Number of C	P	Use by C-P	Word
4+	22	A-A	grow
34	40	A-C	•hear
31	29	A-B	•hide
17	34	A-B	•hurry
9			hush
39	32	B-B	•jump
31	36	B-B	•kick
21	34	A-A	•kiss
22	35	A-A	•knock
17			•lick
3			lie
41	40	A-D	•like
18	38	A-B	•listen
5+	27	A-A	live
16+	33	A-B	lose
21	38	A-B	•love
5			match
2			meddle
10+	30	A-B	mess

31–36 months old

Number of C	P	Use by C-P	Word	One child
			iron	squash
			laugh+	squeak
			lean	squirt
			leap	stab
			line (up)	stub
			loan	thrash
			manage	thrill
			mark	unbuckle
			meet	unsnap
			munch	visit
			park	wreck
			peck	wrestle
			praise	

C	P	Code	Word
22+	33	B-B	roll
40	42	C-F	•say
42	42	E-F	•see
5	29	A-A	set
15+	37	B-B	shut
13			shut up
42	42	C-D	•sit
3			slip
13+	40	A-B	start
8+	36	A-B	stick
4			stir
41	42	C-D	•stop
42	42	D-E	•take
32+	42	B-E	tell
41	42	B-D	•thank
42	41	C-D	•throw
14+	28	A-A	tie
3			trip
16+	41	B-C	try
42	42	C-D	•turn
11+	40	A-C	use
42	42	B-C	•wait
42	42	F-F	want
20+	34	A-B	wear
9			whip

C	P	Code	Word
11	36	A-A	miss
3			mix
5			mow
5			name
41	40	C-D	need
2			pedal
4			peel
2			phone
40	42	B-C	•pick
2			pound
26	21	A-A	•pour
3			pray
2			press
12			•pretend
3			punch
41	38	B-C	•push
14+	25	A-A	rain
12+	33	A-C	remember
5			rest
35	37	B-B	•run
3	28	A-A	save
14+	24	A-A	scare
7+	26	A-A	scoot
7			scratch
2	22	A-A	scream

C, children; P, parents; + number greater when based on all child utterances in hour-long observations; • word on CDI.

247

Category: Action Words *(continued)*

11–24 months old

C	P	C-P	Word
			bid
			bowl
			box
			buckle
			cough
			crowd
			dust
			earn
			flop
			flush
			fuel
			wind

One child

Word
heat
mop
pet
smash
snap
snatch
stumble
tumble
waggle
water

25–30 months old

C	P	C-P	Word
3			sew
15	30	A-A	•shake
13	30	A-A	•share
5			shine
10	20	A-A	•shopping
35	42	B-C	•show
24	38	A-B	•sing
36	38	B-B	•sleep
22	19	A-A	•slide
2			smack
2			sneeze
2			snore
2			snow
4+	28	A-A	spank
4			spell
3+	15	A-A	spend
23	31	A-A	•spill
3			spray
2			squeeze

31–36 months old

C	P	C-P	Word

31	41	A-C	•stand
38	42	B-C	•stay
9+	28	A-A	step
2			straighten
10			•sweep
23			•swim
27			•swing
36	40	A-C	•talk
24	35	A-A	•taste
30	32	A-B	•tear
4			tease
34	40	B-E	•think
26	30	A-B	•tickle
4			tip
28	37	A-B	•touch
3			trick
2			unlock
2			vacuum
2			wade
25	30	A-A	•wake
32	39	A-B	•walk
35	40	A-C	•wash
4			waste
40+	42	C-C	•watch
2			wave

C, children; P, parents; + number greater when based on all child utterances in hour-long observations; • word on CDI.

Category: Action Words *(continued)*

| 11–24 months old | | | | 25–30 months old | | | | 31–36 months old | | | |
| Number of | | Use by | | Number of | | Use by | | Number of | | Use by | |
C	P	C-P	Word	C	P	C-P	Word	C	P	C-P	Word
				2			weep				
				2			wet				
				6			win				
				24	38	A-B	•wipe				
				11	30	A-A	•wish				
				34	35	B-B	•work				
				3			wrap				
				38	37	B-B	•write				
				7			zip				

One child

back	rub
bat	screw
chain	settle
cheat	sic (the dog on)
chop	skip
cross	sock
crush	speed
disappear	spin

One child

dive
dunk
fasten
fool
hem
learn[+]
milk
pin
punish
rewind
rhyme
roar
spread
stack
stretch
teach
tick
tighten
treat
untangle
untie
unwrap
whisper
wink

Category: Descriptive Words

C	P	Code	Word	C	P	Code	Word	C	P	Code	Word
7[+]	35	A-B	almost	8[+]	30	A-A	apart	7			•awake
14[+]	39	A-B	alone	10	28	A-A	•asleep	2[+]	26	A-A	best
3			angry	2[+]	22	A-A	awful	24	32	A-A	•clean
42		C-D	•big	4[+]	28	A-A	backward	24	25	A-A	•dark
31		B-B	•blue	37	40	B-B	•bad	7			dead
38		B-B	•cold	6			bald	3	22	A-A	early
4[+]	22	A-A	dear	25[+]	38	A-B	•better	3[+]	24	A-A	easy
33	38	B-B	•dirty	2			bitty	2[+]	19	A-A	hardly
4			fair	29	27	A-A	•black	20	40	A-B	•last

C, children; P, parents; [+] number greater when based on all child utterances in hour-long observations; • word on CDI.

Category: Descriptive Words *(continued)*

11–24 months old

C	P	Use by C-P	Word
6+	30	A-A	fat
4+	29	A-A	favorite
16+	37	A-B	funny
3			fuzzy
42	39	B-C	•gone
41	42	B-E	•good
6+	24	A-A	great
32	27	B-B	•green
28	34	A-B	•happy
40	40	B-C	•hot
41	41	B-C	•hurt
4+	32	A-B	kinda
41	42	C-E	•little
5+	25	A-A	messy
2			naked
5			nasty
2			near

25–30 months old

C	P	Use by C-P	Word
2			bright
21	28	A-A	•broken
21	24	A-A	•brown
12	34	A-C	•careful
3			chilly
5+	29	A-A	close
3+	26	A-A	crazy
11	26	A-A	•cute
12	30	A-A	•dry
3	26	A-A	•empty
5+	39	A-B	even
30	37	A-B	•fast
23	29	A-A	•fine
33	41	A-B	•first
4			flat
22	35	A-A	•full
2			funky

31–36 months old

C	P	Use by C-P	Word
12	23	A-A	•loud
2			low
2			nosy
9	35	A-A	only
26	28	A-A	•orange
4			scary
15	38	A-B	•sleepy
4			•slow
11			•soft
3			sore
8+	28	A-A	•sticky
6			•thirsty
13			•tiny
2			ugly
4+	26	A-A	upside down

One child

anyway+	loose+
barefoot	mighty
calico	open face

4+	25	A-A	neat
2+	22	A-A	o'clock
12+	37	A-A	own
35	40	A-C	•pretty
16			purple
15+	37	A-B	real
35	31	B-B	•red
21+	41	B-E	right
2			round
14+	36	A-D	silly
3+	22	A-A	small
16+	39	A-C	sorry
19+	40	A-C	still
9+	30	A-A	tight
6+	36	A-B	together
7+	30	A-C	very
18+	30	C-D	way
22+	41	A-E	well
14+	39	A-B	yet

One child

dumb	rainy
•gentle	sudden
icky	truly
raggedy	•windy

2			gently
2			gray
29	40	A-B	•hard
22	33	A-A	•heavy
29	30	A-A	•high
22	35	A-B	•hungry
32+	41	C-E	just
4+	37	A-B	late
20	38	A-B	•long
22	37	A-B	•mad
14+	38	A-B	maybe
4+	25	A-A	mean
5			•naughty
31	36	A-B	•new
31	35	A-C	•nice
8			•noisy
36	41	A-C	•old
11			pink
2			plastic
10	34	A-A	•poor
4+	36	A-B	probably
4+	32	A-A	quick
17	36	A-A	•quiet
9+	39	A-B	really
2			regular

One child

clever	rather+
crunchy	rotten
dangerous	sharp
extra+	slowly
false	smart+
fantastic	super
floppy	sweet
foul	teeny weeny
frontward	terrible
furry	ticklish
grand	weird
grumpy	wonderful
ignorant	woolly

C, children; P, parents; + number greater when based on all child utterances in hour-long observations; • word on CDI.

Category: Descriptive Words *(continued)*

11–24 months old				25–30 months old				31–36 months old			
Number of		Use by	Word	Number of		Use by	Word	Number of		Use by	Word
C	P	C-P		C	P	C-P		C	P	C-P	
				9			•sad				
				31	31	A-A	•scared				
				2+	25	A-A	short				
				25	34	A-A	•sick				
				4+	28	A-A	stinky				
				3+	27	A-A	straight				
				6+	24	A-A	strong				
				29	37	A-B	•stuck				
				7			stupid				
				8+	40	A-B	sure				
				9			tall				
				26	40	A-B	•tired				
				2			tough				
				7+	28	A-A	warm				
				35	38	A-B	•wet				
				29	28	A-A	•white				
				11+	41	A-B	wrong				
				32	28	B-B	•yellow				
				18			•yucky				
				2			yummy				

254

One child

able⁺	haunted
ahead⁺	jealous
bare	lonely
beautiful	piggyback
brand new	proud
capital	salty
cool	smooth
cozy	special⁺
crooked	true⁺
delicious	upper
dizzy	usually⁺
electric	weak
filthy	wide
grouchy	wild
grown	

Category: Words About Time

C	P	Code	Word	C	P	Code	Word	C	P	Code	Word
33⁺	42	B-C	again	5⁺	38	A-A	always	27	38	A-B	•after
9⁺	40	A-B	already	30	38	A-B	•day	22	40	A-B	•before
12⁺	40	A-D	minute	2⁺	30	A-A	ever	20	37	A-B	•morning
33	40	B-C	•night	25			•later	4⁺	37	A-B	never
42	42	D-E	•now	4⁺	33	A-A	once	22	36	A-A	•tomorrow
9⁺	28	A-A	sometime	37	42	B-C	•time	12	29	A-A	•tonight

C, children; P, parents; ⁺ number greater when based on all child utterances in hour-long observations; • word on CDI.

255

Category: Words About Time (continued)

11–24 months old				25–30 months old				31–36 months old			
Number of		**Use by**	**Word**	**Number of**		**Use by**	**Word**	**Number of**		**Use by**	**Word**
C	P	C-P		C	P	C-P		C	P	C-P	
3+	28	A-A	year	28	39	A-C	•today	14	30	A-A	•yesterday
				2+	28	A-A	week				
		One child	bedtime			*One child*	someday			*One child*	weekend+
								afternoon+			a while+
								lunchtime			

Category: Pronouns

11–24 months old				25–30 months old				31–36 months old			
Number of		**Use by**	**Word**	**Number of**		**Use by**	**Word**	**Number of**		**Use by**	**Word**
C	P	C-P		C	P	C-P		C	P	C-P	
42	41	D-E	•he	7+	28	A-A	everybody	2+	27	A-A	anybody
42	42	D-E	•her	41	42	C-D	•him	15	22	A-A	•hers
42	42	H-G	•I	37	40	B-D	•his	13	40	A-B	•yourself
42	42	G-H	•it	32	22	A-A	•myself	anyone		*One child*	ours
42	42	F-F	•me	9+	34	A-A	nobody	himself+			theirs
42	34	D-B	•mine	37	33	B-B	•our	itself			whatever+
42	42	F-E	•my	42	42	C-E	•she				
42	42	G-H	•that	7+	40	A-B	somebody				
42	42	D-E	•them	2+	19	A-A	someone				
42	40	C-D	•these	17	26	A-B	•their				
42	41	C-E	•they	26	35	A-B	•us				
42	42	F-F	•this	40	42	D-F	•we				

C	P		
40	40	C-D	•those
42	42	E-H	•you
12			you all
42	42	D-G	•your
25+	41	B-B	yours
2+	35	A-A	whose
		One child	whichever
18	35	A-B	•which

Category: Question Words

C	P			C	P		
40+	42	E-F	huh	39	42	B-E	•how
42	42	E-G	•what	33	42	B-D	•when
42	42	E-F	•where	25+	42	B-D	•why
41	42	B-E	•who				

Category: Connecting Words

C	P			C	P			C	P		
42	42	E-G	•and	4+	40	A-B	as	3+	37	A-A	than
				38	42	B-D	•because	5+	36	A-B	while
				35	41	B-D	•but				
				15+	39	A-B	either				
				30	41	A-D	•if				
				5+	16	A-A	neither				
				14+	41	A-D	or				
				41	42	B-E	•so				
				36	42	B-D	•then				
				2+	34	A-B	though				

C, children; P, parents; + number greater when based on all child utterances in hour-long observations; • word on CDI.

Category: Connecting Words (continued)

25–30 months old

Number of C	P	Use by C-P	Word
2	24	A-A	unless
2+	40	A-B	until

Category: Prepositions and Locations

11–24 months old

Number of C	P	Use by C-P	Word
42	41	D-E	•at
39	40	B-C	•away
42	42	D-E	•back
42	42	D-E	•down
42	42	D-E	•for
3			forth
24+	40	A-C	from
42	42	F-G	•here
42	42	F-G	•in
38+	42	C-E	like
42	40	D-E	•of
42	41	D-E	•off
42	42	F-G	•on
42	41	D-E	•out

25–30 months old

Number of C	P	Use by C-P	Word
33	41	A-D	•about
3+	24	A-A	along
38	40	B-C	•around
22+	37	A-A	•behind
6			•beside
40	40	B-B	•by
21	38	A-B	•next to
3			onto
2			past
29	38	A-B	•top
30+	38	A-B	•under
3+	31	A-A	without

One child underneath

31–36 months old

Number of C	P	Use by C-P	Word
2			•above
2+	25	A-A	across
17	36	A-B	•into

One child upon

C	P	Category	Word
42	41	C-E	•over
42	42	F-G	•there
19+	41	A-B	through
41	41	D-E	•to
42	41	E-F	•up
41	42	D-E	•with

Category: Quantifiers and Articles

C	P	Category	Word
42	42	F-G	•a
42	42	D-E	•all
18+	34	A-B	a bite
10+	39	A-C	else
13+	40	A-B	enough
7+	32	A-B	many
42	42	D-E	•more
42	42	D-E	•not
17+	42	A-B	nothing
24+	38	A-B	piece
42	42	E-E	•some
23+	41	B-C	something
42	42	F-H	•the
41	41	D-E	•too
2	29	A-B	also
22	40	C-C	•an
38	40	A-C	•another
32	35	A-B	•any
9+	39	A-A	a bit
11+	23	A-A	both
6+	28	A-A	a bunch
4+	28	A-A	a couple
4+	24	A-A	different
2	36	A-A	•each
15	36	A-B	•every
5+	34	A-A	everything
2+	34	A-A	few
4+	34	A-A	half
31	37	A-B	•a lot
23	26	A-A	•none
6+	36	A-B	anything
20	40	A-B	•much
2			a pack
2+	18	A-A	pair
11+	31	A-A	•same

One child

plenty

a drop, most+, a pile, single, a stack

C, children; P, parents; + number greater when based on all child utterances in hour-long observations; • word on CDI.

Category: Quantifiers and Articles *(continued)*

25–30 months old

Number of C	P	Use by C-P	Word
40	40	B-D	•other
12+	33	A-A	part
4+	35	A-A	rest
10+	36	A-A	whole
		One child	
		double	

31–36 months old

Number of C	P	Use by C-P	Word

Category: Number Words

11–24 months old

Number of C	P	Use by C-P	Word
42	42	E-F	one
41+	40	D-D	two
33	39	C-C	three
25+	37	B-B	four
25+	40	B-B	five
14+	28	A-A	eight
15+	30	A-A	nine
12+	31	A-A	ten

25–30 months old

Number of C	P	Use by C-P	Word
19+	32	A-A	six
12+	28	A-A	seven
4+	17	A-A	eleven
3+	16	A-A	twelve
3			thirteen
3			fourteen
3+	12	A-A	fifteen
2			sixteen
2			nineteen
3+	23	A-A	twenty

31–36 months old

Number of C	P	Use by C-P	Word
2+	19	A-A	thirty
2			sixty
2			fifth
		One child	
forty		third	
fourth		sixth	

Category: Overgeneralized Verbs

One child

			One child				
feeled		rided					
finded		wetted					

Verb	*seventeen eighteen*	Verb	*One child hundred*
bringed	2	blowed	7
broked	8	breaked	2
doed	6	builded	2
felled	5	buyed	9
getted	2	camed	3
gived	4	catched	3
goed	2	comed	2
gotted	2	drawed	2
hitted	2	falled	11
sleeped	2	flied	2
teared	10	hurted	3
throwed	13	maked	5
		runned	5
		sawed	3
		sticked	2
		taked	6
		tooked	2
		tored	2

One child

beated		standed	3
heared		stucked	2
pusheded		telled	6
putted			

C, children; P, parents; ⁺ number greater when based on all child utterances in hour-long observations; • word on CDI.

Category: Overgeneralized Verbs *(continued)*

11–24 months old				25–30 months old				31–36 months old			
Number of		Use by		Number of		Use by		Number of		Use by	
C	P	C-P	Word	C	P	C-P	Word	C	P	C-P	Word
								2			waked
								2			weared
								3			winned
								One child			
								bited			ranned
								blewed			seed
								dranked			shutted
								drinked			singed
								drunked			swinged
								eated			wented
								growed			woked
								keeped			writed
								leaved			

C, children; P, parents; + number greater when based on all child utterances in hour-long observations; • word on CDI.

262

Appendix B

Steps in
Describing the Social Dance

◆ ◆ ◆

The Families

The 42 families who participated in the study for the full 2½ years represented a broad spectrum of society. They were not a random sample, however, and were all well-functioning families. None were severely stressed financially or emotionally, none were addicted or abusive, and none had a family member with a disability. Also, the parents who welcomed an observer into their homes were probably more confident than average in their child-rearing practices. Priority was given to recruiting families who owned their homes, an indication that they were likely to remain in the area for the 2½ years of the study. Of the eight families who missed enough observations that their data could not be included in the group analyses, one was a professional family, two were working-class families, and five were families on welfare. For further information, see Hart and Risley (1990, 1995).

Table 1. Averages and (ranges) in family characteristics by socioeconomic status (SES) group

Characteristic	SES group		
	Professional	Working-class	Welfare
Number of families	13	23	6
Number of African American children	1	10	6
Number of girls	8	12	3
Number of observations	28 (27–30)	28 (23–30)	29 (28–30)
Child's age in months at first observation	9 (7–11)	9 (7–12)	8 (7–9)
Number of siblings	1 (0–2)	2 (0–5)	2 (1–4)
Mother's age[a]	30 (22–35)	27 (18–36)	21 (19–24)
Father's age[a]	34 (26–46)	30 (20–45)	25 (21–31)
Mother working[b]	5	14	0
Mother's education[c]	16 (12–18)	13 (11–18)	12 (11–12)
Father's education[c]	18 (16–24)	13 (11–18)	12 (11–14)
Family income[d]	43 (25–68)	28 (9–64)	5 (4–6)

[a]Parent-reported age at the time the observed child was born.
[b]Mother was regularly employed full or parttime during the period of the study.
[c]Number of years reported.
[d]Reported annual family income in thousands of dollars.

The Observations

We collected data by putting a noninteractive observer in each of the 42 homes. The observer audiotaped for an hour everything said by, to, and around the child while noting what the child was doing, where, and with whom. The observer transcribed the tape, meshing utterances and actions noted in the home. Codes for aspects of language, context, and interaction were added to the transcription.

Figure 1 shows a page of coded data ready for computer processing. The page contains interactions recorded when the parent was cleaning up after dinner and talking with her son (22 months old) and daughter (3 years old) who were playing in an adjacent alcove. The boy was bouncing vigorously on a spring-set rocking horse; when he got off, he began trying to turn on the kitchen radio.

The corpus of longitudinal data consists of 30,000 similarly coded pages. The codes on the utterances are among those listed in Table 2. See Chapter 2 for a description of the reliability assessments made at each step in recording, transcribing, and coding the data. The line numbers to the left of the utterances were used in editing and verifying the data and in the line-by-line reliability assessment of the data coding. Reliability between independent raters for each instance of each code averaged .93. Split-half reliability between the amounts of each code on odd and even observation months averaged .96.

```
1100 OB,50,90,0,64,70/CAN I HAVE SOME MORE/VFVFF
1102 PB,50,91,94,60/BUT YOU TOLD ME YOU DIDNT WANT ANY MORE/FFVFF\
1104 OB,50,90,0,64,70/ARE WE GOING TO GRANDMAS NOW/VFVFNM
1106 PB,51/IN A FEW MINUTES/FFMN
1108 P3,50,90,0,60/WE NEED TOCHANGE YOUR SHEET/FVVFN
1110 FB,56,60/AND GET THE BAG READY TOGO/FVFNFV
1112 IA,33,P/S
1114·C1,56,61/LOOK AT ME MOM/VFFN
1116 C3,56,61,71/LOOK AT ME/VFF
1118 F2,56,61/YEAH YOU BE CAREFUL/FFVM
1120 C2,11//
1122 PB,50,90,0,60/AND I VE GOTTA CHANGE MY CLOTHES/FFVVVFN
1124 P,31//
1126 PB,50,90,0,60/UHUH UHUH THAT GOES TO GRANDMAS HOUSE/FFFVFNN
1128 PB,56,61,84/PLEASE DONT TOUCH THAT/FVVF
1130 OB,50,90,63,94/WHY DID YOU PUT/FVFV
1132 FB,50,60,91,95/BECAUSE SHE S GONNA PUT IT IN HER GARAGE SALE
1134 IA,33,P/S
1136 OC1,50,90,0,63/WHY ARE YOU WEARING THAT SHIRT TODAY/FVFVFNM
1138 OC3,50,64,70,94,90/DID YOUR OLD ONE HURT YOU/VFMFVF
1140 C2,54/YEAH/F
1142 OC2,54/OH/F
1144 C2,50,90,94,60,80/OTHER ONE HURT ME/FFVF
1146 F1,50,90,94,64,73/THE OTHER ONE HURT YOU/FFFVF
1148 P3,50,90,60,94/OH GEE YOU ALMOST FELL/FJFMV
1150 C3,54/GEE/J
1152 C2,50,90,0,60/I WANT/FV
1154 C3,50,90,0,61/HELP ME MOM/VFN
1156 C3,71,50,90,0,61/HELP ME/VF
1158 F2,56,64,72/HELP YOU/VF
1160 F3,56,63,82/HELP YOU WHAT/VFF
1162 C2,56,60/I OFF/FF
1164 F2,56,60/THANK YOU/VF
1166 C2,50,90,0,60/I GO MOM/FVN
1168 F2,56,61/LET GO/VV
1170 F3,71,50,90,0,61/LET GO/VV
1172 C2,56,60/I OFF/FF
1174 F2,50,0,64,70,91/IS THAT WHAT YOU WANTED/VFFFV
1176 C2,50,90,0,60/NO I REACH HERE/FFVF
1178 C3,62,50,90,0,60/I REACH/FV
1180 F2,56,61/OKAY JUST BE CAREFUL/FMVM
1182 F3,50,90,60,95/MOM S GONNA GO CHANGE REAL QUICK/NVVVVMM
1184 C,31//
1186 IA,33,P/S
1188·C1,17,50,90,0,60/THAT ONE DONT WORK/FFVV
1190 C3,82,50,90,0,60/ONE DONT WORK MOM/FVVN
1192 F2,50,0,60,91/WELL THAT S BECAUSE IT S NOT PLUGGED IN/MFVFFVF
1194 C2,92,50,90,0,60/ONE DONT WORK NOW/FVVM
1196 F2,50,0,60,91/NO IT DOESNT WORK BECAUSE IT S NOT PLUGGED IN/F
1198 C2,50,90,0,60/I WANT GO/FVV
1200 C3,50,90,0,60/I WANT GO WORK NOW/FVVVM
1202 F2,50,64,70,95,90/ARE YOU GONNA MAKE IT WORK FOR ME/VFVVFVFF
1204 OB,50,90,0,60/I M/FV
1206 OB,71,50,90,0,60/I M/FV
1208 OB,71,50,90,0,60/I M/FV
```

Figure 1.   The observations.

267

The Data Codes

For each line of the 1,300 observation files, we used interactive computer programs to assign codes to the aspects of language and interaction we were interested in analyzing. For each observation file, computer processing produced frequency counts of each code by speaker and context. Another computer program compiled a dictionary for each speaker; output were counts for each speaker of total and different words by part of speech for each observation and cumulative counts of words used. Additional computer programs were used to compute MLU in morphemes, to remove family-identifying information as required by the informed consent form the parents had signed, and to find particular utterance types of interest for further analysis. For example, each parent auxiliary-fronted yes/no question could be found by asking for the code combination of P with 64 and 70.

A copy of the definitions of the codes is available from the authors on request.

Table 2. Codes applied to each transcript in the longitudinal data

Nonverbal behaviors

16	Point
17	Reach
18	Touch
19	Give, offer
20	Take
24	Hit
25	Pick up/put down child
31	No response within 5 seconds

Speakers

C	Child
P	Parent
OC	Other child
OA	Other adult
P8	Parent to others
O8	Others to others

Contexts

RC	Routine care
MP	Games and books
IA	Unstructured activity

Adjacency

1	Initiation
2	Response
3	Floorholding

Proximity

33	Parent in same room
34	Parent not in the room

Use

78	Rule statement
79	Evaluation
80	Report of feelings
81	Explanation
83	Positive feedback
84	Negative feedback
85	Attentional

Words

N	Noun
V	Verb
M	Adjective, adverb
F	Functor
P	Proper noun—person
L	Proper noun—location
T	Proper noun—other
J	Nondictionary word

Utterances

	11	Babble, gibberish, nonword
Types:	50	Sentence
	56, 60	Sentence of 50, 90, 00
	51	Contentive phrase
	54	Noncontentive phrase
	53	Unanalyzable
Clauses:	90	One
	91	Two
	92	Three
	94	Four or more
Tenses:	00	Present
	94	Past
	95	Future
Functions:	60	Declarative
	61	Imperative
	63	Wh-question
	64	Yes/no question
	65	Other question
	70	Auxiliary-fronted

Repetition

71	Of self
72	Of other
73	Expansion
74	Extension
75	Reduction
82	With one substitution

Comparing New Data with Known Facts

All 42 of the children we observed were normal. We saw in each child all of the developmental changes the literature had led us to expect. Skill gains appeared in the longitudinal data in the order reported in other normative research. Replicating known facts prepared us to add new information about the social world in which the developmental changes occurred.

Table 3 shows the median chronological age of the 42 children in the longitudinal study at the month when skills were first recorded and the average and ranges reported in prior studies (Bloom, 1991, 1993; Brown, 1973; Carmichael, 1954; de Villiers & de Villiers, 1973; Gesell & Thompson, 1934; Grigsby, 1932; Hall, Nagy, & Linn, 1984; Nelson, 1973; Smith, 1926; Stone & Church, 1957).

The ages are those recorded for typically developing children. Ages, especially the range in ages, can differ greatly for children with disabilities. The ranges in age and the standard deviations for the 42 children are shown in Tables 4–6.

Table 3. Sequential skill development in learning to talk

Child age in months			
Present study	Prior studies		
Median	Average	Range	Skill
		0–3	Vocal play: cry, coo, gurgle, grunt
		3–	Babble: undifferentiated sounds
		6–10	Babble: canonical/reduplicated syllables
11		9–	Imitation
11	13	8–18	First words
11		13–15	Expressive jargon, intonational sentences
14	15	13–19	10-word vocabulary
18	19	14–24	50-word vocabulary
	17	13–27	Single-word stage + a few sentences
19	21		Two- to three-word combinations
20	20		Articles: a/the
21	21		Plural: -s
23		23–24	Present progressive: -ing
23		23–25	Irregular past: went
25	24		Modal + verb: can/will
23	24		28- to 436-word vocabulary
23	24		93–265 utterances per hour
27		25–27	Regular past: -ed
26	26		Auxiliary "be": -'m, -'s
26		23–26	Third-person singular: -s
36	36		896- to 1,507-word vocabulary
36	36		1,500–1,700 words per hour

Gains in Auxiliary Verbs in Everyday Use

Learning auxiliary verbs enabled the children to talk about aspects of experience that seemed important to asserting their independence ("I don't want one," "I can/can't do it myself") and to talking about the future. All except five of the children, however, were recorded using an irregular past-tense verb ("I did it," "I made one") earlier than a future auxiliary ("I'll do it," "I'm gonna make one").

Table 4 shows the median and range in chronological age at which each listed auxiliary or modal verb was first recorded when a 100-utterance subsample was examined for each child at each child age. Examined were only utterances in which all of the words were recognizable. Use was recorded only when the auxiliary or modal verb was followed by a main verb.

The number of children for whom each item was recorded is shown in the left-most column. For those children for whom an item was recorded, the next column shows the range in age at which that item was first recorded among those children. A blank at the lower range indicates that the criterion of three different uses of the item was met in the data of one or more of the children within the first 100-utterance subsample examined (when the median age was 19 months); that is, the item may have been recorded in a sample in which a child younger than 19 months old produced fewer than 100 utterances containing recognizable words in the hour.

Table 4. Gains in auxiliary verbs in everyday use

n	Range	20	21	22	23	24	25	26	27	28	29	30	31	32	33	34	35	36
7	26–36														would			
11	24–36														could			
19	21–35														are			
12	22–35														am			
7	23–35													doesn't				
12	27–36													might				
28	23–35												won't					
29	–36												do					
20	20–36											was						
28	20–36											better						
22	23–36											hafta						
37	–36											gotta						
20	–35											is						
29	22–36										didn't							
20	–35										ain't							
17	23–35										're							
35	–36										's							
23	20–36									did								
30	21–35									will								
37	–36								'll									
41	–36							gonna										
41	–36							'm										
41	–34							can't										
40	–33						can											
42	–29				don't													
41	–35			wanna														

		20	21	22	23	24	25	26	27	28	29	30	31	32	33	34	35	36
n	Range											Age of child in months						

Gains in Grammatical
Structures in Everyday Use

The average MLU calculated in the data (see Table 6) increased as the children gained skills in adding articles, prepositions, and auxiliaries to utterances, in attaching morphemes to words to indicate tense and number, and in combining sentences or turning them into questions. The cumulative gains in grammatical structures indicate the increasing sophistication of the utterances to which the children's parents were responding during conversations.

Table 5 shows the median and range in chronological age at which grammatical categories listed on the IPSyn (Scarborough, 1990) were first recorded in the 100-utterance subsamples examined for each child at each child age. Listed are only those grammatical categories found in the data of half or more of the 42 children. An example of each grammatical category is given, and the specific skill gain is underlined (unless a word or word combination, as a prepositional phrase). See Chapter 4, endnote 3, for a description of the IPSyn and how it was used in the present study.

The number of children and the ranges are shown as in Table 4.

Table 5. Gains in grammatical structures in everyday use

n	Range	Age of child in months (20–36) / Structure
21	24–36	I got one_I like
23	–35	what are you playing
27	22–36	a car and a truck
28	21–36	I want you to play
34	21–35	look what I'm playing
34	–36	I just play
35	20–36	I got me a car
37	–35	I'm not playing
33	23–36	I know_I can play
34	22–36	because
37	21–35	you sit and I drive
34	20–35	I did play
35	21–36	I like to play
37	–35	car's big
37	–36	I played
39	–36	a car drives
40	–36	a big car
41	–34	can I play
32	–36	he plays
41	20–36	I'm playing
41	–36	let me play
41	–30	I can play
39	–35	very big
42	–31	playing
41	–34	now
41	–36	I wanna play
42	–30	in a car
42	–28	get a car
42	–32	cars
42	–27	a car

20 21 22 23 24 25 26 27 28 29 30 31 32 33 34 35 36

n   Range   Age of child in months

Talking and Interaction in Everyday Life

The frequency counts of each coded behavior in each family were aggregated for analysis first across families and second across months. In Hart and Risley (1995) each parent's utterances were averaged over the 2½ years of observation in order to examine the relative amount of talk the parents regularly addressed to their children. In this book all 42 parents' utterances to the children were averaged each month in order to examine changes in amounts of talk as the children began contributing words to interactions. Quantifying the longitudinal data revealed the children gradually adding more and more utterances that contained recognizable words until at an average age of 19 months old, word utterances exceeded the frequency per hour of nonword utterances and the children could be termed talkers. Also revealed was the acceleration of the children's word utterances until at an age of 28 months old, they reached the frequency per hour of their parents' utterances and the children could be termed speakers in their family cultures.

Nonword utterances include babble, gibberish, jargon, and intonational sentences. Word utterances include only those containing recognizable words. MLU is mean length in morphemes of the first 100 word utterances. All verbalizations include all child speech whether containing recognizable words, nonwords, babble, or gibberish. An initiation indicates the first utterance after 5 seconds or more of no interaction. A response indicates the first utterance in a speaker's turn during an interaction. Floorholding indicates an utterance that adds more to what the speaker just said before the speaker pauses for a response from the listener.

Table 6. Average and (standard deviations) for child and parent behaviors per hour

Child										Parent	
Age in months	Nonword utterances	(SD)	Word utterances	(SD)	MLU	All verbalizations	Initiations	Responses	Floorholding	Utterances	(SD)
11	127	(43)	5	(13)	1.1	132	53	90	4	311	(191)
12	132	(42)	8	(15)	1.1	140	56	101	4	316	(190)
13	148	(47)	15	(30)	1.2	164	59	113	7	333	(211)
14	153	(53)	21	(42)	1.2	174	57	127	10	353	(235)
15	153	(49)	34	(43)	1.2	187	63	127	18	348	(203)
16	152	(45)	54	(51)	1.3	206	58	139	29	369	(223)
17	158	(52)	84	(96)	1.3	242	58	154	48	332	(195)
18	141	(49)	103	(99)	1.4	244	56	150	58	368	(228)
19	139	(52)	167	(159)	1.4	305	56	185	89	377	(231)
20	143	(46)	183	(135)	1.5	327	59	181	101	348	(211)
21	132	(52)	233	(162)	1.6	365	59	192	127	364	(215)
22	130	(52)	293	(191)	1.7	423	55	223	157	400	(227)
23	105	(42)	293	(202)	2.0	398	55	193	161	388	(231)
24	109	(46)	338	(180)	2.1	448	58	222	174	402	(222)
25	103	(52)	355	(176)	2.3	458	55	226	183	402	(230)
26	95	(50)	351	(161)	2.4	445	56	214	179	370	(200)
27	89	(46)	352	(177)	2.5	440	58	197	196	369	(245)
28	86	(37)	396	(206)	2.6	482	56	213	222	372	(265)
29	84	(42)	366	(171)	2.8	450	57	196	204	328	(256)
30	77	(36)	377	(180)	2.9	454	62	188	216	306	(262)
31	75	(42)	389	(203)	2.9	465	56	197	218	295	(190)
32	70	(35)	400	(179)	3.2	470	61	198	218	303	(193)
33	67	(32)	378	(206)	3.4	445	55	178	218	288	(225)
34	70	(34)	402	(185)	3.3	471	51	206	221	295	(227)
35	77	(34)	410	(156)	3.4	487	58	197	239	268	(226)
36	70	(36)	427	(167)	3.4	497	55	214	241	324	(250)

Gains in Vocabulary in Everyday Use

In processing each observation, a computer program listed and counted for each speaker all of the different words that appeared in the sample. The program compared each word with the dictionary compiled so far for the speaker and added any word from the sample that was not already listed.

The dictionaries compiled in the present study were lists of expressive vocabulary words used during social interaction. Thus, the words recorded were only a portion of all of the words the children knew and understood. The dictionaries, similar to the use of auxiliary verbs and grammatical structures, represented momentary snapshots of the children's learning compiled from samples recorded for an hour once per month.

Table 7 shows two vocabulary accumulations, one based on all of the utterances recorded in an observation and another based on just the first 100 fully recognizable utterances recorded in the hour. Recorded vocabulary size differed depending on how many utterances were examined for different words, so that when based on an hour of recording, larger vocabularies were compiled for the more talkative children. The vocabulary data are more readily compared with findings from other studies, however, when the children are equated for rate of talking, and vocabulary and different words are counted in only the first 100 utterances recorded per hour. Listed in Appendix A are all 2,008 of the vocabulary words recorded in those 100 utterances for all 42 children between 19 and 36 months old.

In the vocabulary based on all utterances, inflected forms were counted as different words. In the vocabulary based on 100 utterances, inflected forms were subsumed in root forms. Proper nouns and nondictionary words (words coded P, L, T, or J; see Table 2) were not counted in any vocabulary. Modifiers were adjectives and adverbs. All noncontentive words were coded as functors, including pronouns, prepositions, and quantifiers. Only after an average of 19 months old did half of the children produce 100 utterances per hour. The CDI is the MacArthur Communicative Development Inventory–Toddlers (Fenson et al., 1993). See Chapter 4, endnote 4, for a description of the CDI.

278

Table 7. Cumulative vocabulary size and different words used per hour

Age of child in months	Cumulative vocabulary in			Different words in					
	All utterances	100 utterances		All utterances	100 utterances				
		Total	CDI words		Total	Noun	Verb	Modifier	Functor
13	6			6					
14	10			10					
15	17			15					
16	27			23					
17	41			29					
18	58			41					
19	81	66	61	57	44	12	10	2	20
20	108	86	77	69	46	13	11	2	20
21	140	107	93	86	50	14	13	2	21
22	176	130	111	105	55	15	15	2	23
23	215	151	126	118	60	15	17	3	25
24	258	173	142	134	60	14	18	3	25
25	304	195	156	143	67	15	20	4	28
26	351	215	168	154	68	15	20	3	30
27	400	232	179	157	73	15	22	4	32
28	448	250	189	179	75	16	23	4	32
29	497	265	197	179	78	15	25	4	34
30	544	280	204	181	80	15	26	5	34
31	591	294	210	201	90	17	30	5	38
32	635	308	216	211	91	18	29	6	38
33	678	321	220	205	96	18	30	6	42
34	718	334	224	220	94	18	30	6	40
35	756	348	228	235	100	19	33	6	42
36	791	360	231	240	98	20	31	6	41

The Normal Pattern of Vocabulary Growth

The children's vocabularies grew gradually during the period of becoming partners (11–19 months old), when their parents were doing most of the talking. During the period of staying and playing (20–28 months old), vocabulary growth accelerated rapidly. The growth rate decelerated only slightly during the period of practicing (29–36 months old), when the children were talking more than their parents talked to them.

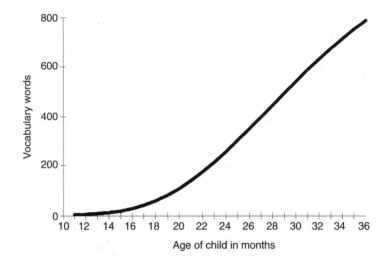

Figure 2. The "normal" vocabulary growth curve created by Dr. David Thissen from the average parameters of the nonlinear curve fit to each child's cumulative recorded vocabulary. See Table 7 for the numbers and Chapter 4, endnote 5, for a description of Dr. Thissen's multilevel model. In each month, the mean vocabulary size obtained from averaging the sum of all of the individual vocabularies was slightly higher than the statistical norm shown in Figure 2. The mean at 13 months old was 9 words, at 19 months old 101 words, at 28 months old 471 words, and at 36 months old 821 words.

The Normal Pattern of Growth in Talking

For 7 months after saying the first word at an average age of 11 months old, the children's frequency of word utterances steadily accelerated without any reduction in the children's frequency of saying nonword utterances. Then in the 2 months when the children were 18–19 months old, the average number of their word utterances became as frequent as the average number of their nonword utterances, after which nonword utterances began a gradual decline. Word utterances increased until at 28 months old the children were talking as much as their parents talked to them, and then the children "settled in" to talking about as much as other members of the family.

In contrast to their parents, though, almost 20% of what the children said continued to be nonword utterances. Their word utterances were generally as comprehensible as those of their parents. Between 33 and 36 months old, 6% of the children's word utterances contained an unidentifiable or inaudi-

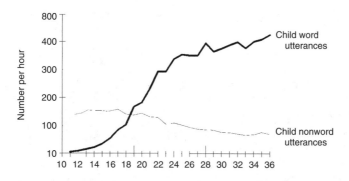

Figure 3.   Average number per hour of child word utterances (heavy line) and child nonword utterances (light line). Word utterances were those containing recognizable words. Nonword utterances were intonational sentences, babble, gibberish, emotive interjections, and strings of nonsense syllables. See Table 6 for the numbers. The vertical line at 19 months old indicates when, on average, children had become talkers: Their frequency of utterances that contained recognizable words had grown to exceed their frequency per hour of nonword utterances. The vertical line at 28 months old indicates when, on average, the children had become speakers: Their frequency of talking (word utterances per hour) had grown to match that of their parents.

281

ble word, as compared with 4% of their parents' utterances. But an average of almost one of every five of the children's utterances was a nonword sound effect ("Boing"), an expression of glee ("Whoopdeedoo") or accomplishment ("Tah-dah!"), or a nonsense refrain ("Let me walk here. Hoohoohoo, ahhooeedoo") accompanying play with toys.

Appendix C

Steps in
Explicating the Social Dance

◆ ◆ ◆ ◆

The Social World of Learning to Talk

During the years they are learning to talk, children are consistently exposed to other people's conversations. Approximately half of the talk children hear is addressed to them, virtually all of it by their parents. Children have innumerable opportunities to hear socially appropriate models of talk and are rarely without competition for parental attention.

The longitudinal data showed that even as the children learned to talk and the pattern of interaction with their parents changed, the overall amount of talk in the family changed proportionately little. Parents, as agents of socialization, always talked to the youngest child more than to anyone else.

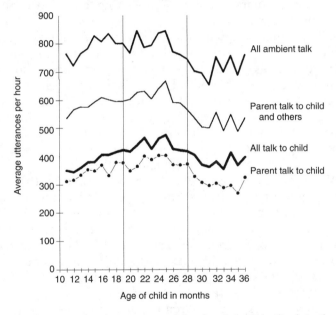

Figure 4. Average number of utterances recorded per hour in the 42 families during the months when the children were 11–36 months old. Added to the average number of utterances addressed to the child by the parents (line with circles) are those addressed to the child by other children and adults (heavy line). Added to this total talk to the child is the amount of other people's talk recorded within the child's hearing: the average number of utterances parents addressed to other children and adults (light line) and added to that the average number of utterances those other children and adults addressed to one another and to the parents (solid line at top). The vertical line at 19 months old indicates when, on average, children had become talkers: Their frequency of utterances that contained recognizable words had grown to exceed their frequency per hour of nonword utterances. The vertical line at 28 months old indicates when, on average, children had become speakers: Their frequency of talking (word utterances per hour) had grown to match that of their parents.

285

Changing Patterns of Parent–Child Interactions

Before their children say words, parents hold the floor and model the behaviors the family as a social group expects its members to learn, and the children contribute smiles, frowns, cooing, and babbling as their part. Then children begin to say utterances with words in them, which promotes longer interactions of prompting and responding until the children are talking as much as their parents. Then the children hold the floor and elaborate more often while their parents begin listening more, elaborating less and initiating fewer of the now more lengthy conversations.

The longitudinal data showed that in the months before the children began saying more than occasional words, much of parent talk was floorholding. A first utterance was followed by more utterances that added to what the speaker had just said before pausing for the listener to respond. The frequency of parent floorholding regularly decreased as the children learned to talk and began holding the floor themselves. The major change in interactions after the children learned to talk was in who listened and who did most of the talking.

Whether the children were babbling or talking, they responded more frequently to their parents' utterances than their parents responded to the children's. Parent and child responses to one another increased as the children began to talk, peaked when the children were approximately 24 months old, and then began to decline. After the children had become speakers who talked as much as their parents, the frequency of parent responses declined further.

Even as babies, the children regularly initiated social interaction more often than their parents, and their average frequency of initiating changed very little during the time they were learning to talk. After the children became talkers whose utterances contained recognizable words more often than nonwords, the frequency of parent initiations began to decline very gradually.

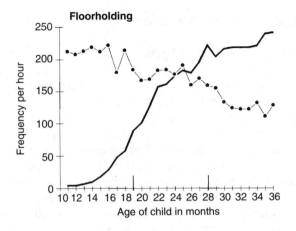

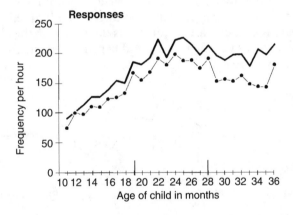

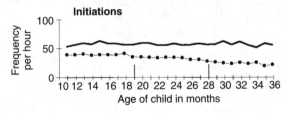

Figure 5. Average frequency per hour of child verbalizations (word plus nonword utterances; solid lines) and parent utterances (lines with circles) that were floorholding (top), responses (middle), and initiations (bottom) recorded in 42 families when the children were 11–36 months old. Vertical lines indicate when, on average, children became talkers (at 19 months old) and speakers (at 28 months old; see Figure 4).

Changes in Prompting and Imitation

When parents stay and play with children who are novices at making conversation, they ask questions that encourage their children to practice answering, naming, describing, and remembering. They imitate to confirm the topic, and they prompt the children to imitate.

The longitudinal data showed that the parents imitated more often than the children. The parents began imitating the children's first words and asking the children to imitate them. The children's imitations increased until the children were an average of 22 months old and then steadily decreased.

The number of parent questions, similar to the number of parent responses and parent utterances, increased in frequency nearly every month until the children were 24–25 months old and began holding the floor more frequently than their parents. Then parent questions decreased as the children gradually took over the talking and began, in effect, answering before they were asked.

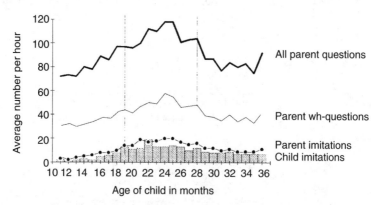

Figure 6.   Average frequency per hour of all of the questions of any kind that the parents asked the children (heavy line), of wh-questions (light line), and of parent (line with circles) and child (shaded bars) imitations recorded when the 42 children were 11–36 months old. Wh-questions were interrogatives containing "What," "Where," "When," "Who," "Why," "Which," or "How." An imitation was defined as a repetition of all of the contentive words (nouns, verbs, modifiers) in an immediately preceding utterance of the prior speaker. Included in imitation in Figure 6 are extensions (repetitions that added words) and expansions (repetitions that recast an utterance into a more grammatically standard form). The vertical lines at 19 and 28 months old indicate the months when, on average, children became talkers and speakers (see Figure 4).

The Pattern of Learning to Talk

When children begin to say utterances containing recognizable words, the entertaining turn-taking interactions between parents and infants begin to be interspersed more and more frequently with a dance between partners who answer one another. Partners stay and play at conversation until the children are talking as much as the family. Then the children graduate to being simply "other children" who practice as speaking members of the family.

The longitudinal data showed that the parents talked to their 11-month-old infants at the frequency per hour that was typical of the amount of talk in the family. The infants verbalized with nonword utterances at a frequency that was unrelated to the amount of their parents' talk. The children's frequency of utterances containing recognizable words accelerated until their combined word and nonword utterances matched their parents' frequency of talking to them. At that point their parents' frequency of talking to the children began to decline, followed by a leveling off of the children's growth in talking.

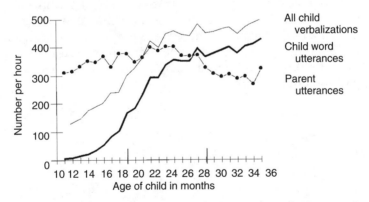

Figure 7. Average number per hour of parent (line with circles) and child verbalizations during the months when the children were 11–36 months old. The light line shows all child verbalizations (word utterances plus nonword utterances), and the heavy line shows child word utterances (utterances containing recognizable words). See Table 6 for the numbers.

The Lawfulness of the Pattern

The extremes in the continuum across the 42 children were most noticeable in terms of whether children became talkers earlier or later than the average and whether at age 3 they were more or less talkative than the average. Across the continuum, patterns of interaction and the children's skill gains were similar. All of the children were competent speakers by age 3 and were talking as much and as well as other members of their family.

A pattern similar to the average of all 42 children was apparent in each of the four subgroups at the extremes. As infants, the children's frequency of verbalizations was similar across all of the groups and unrelated to their parents' amount of talking.

Across all of the groups the children's frequency of talking accelerated until their word and nonword utterances together matched their parents' frequency of talking to them. Then their parents' frequency of talking to them began to decline, and the growth in the children's rates of talking began to level off.

As 3-year-olds, the children's frequency of talking was closely related to the frequency per hour that their parents, their primary partners, had talked to them while the children were learning to talk. Whether children started talking early or late, the children became as talkative or as taciturn as their parents and their family.

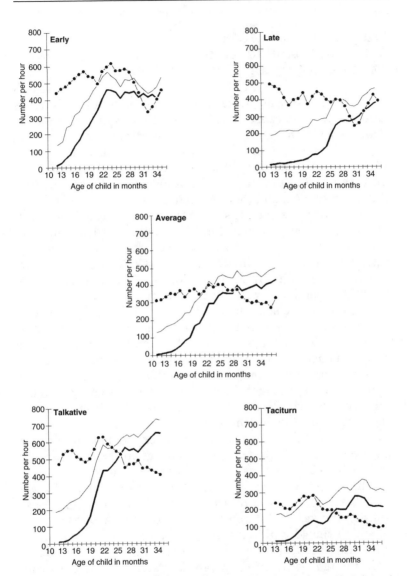

Figure 8.   Average number per hour, in five groups of children, of parent (lines with circles) and child utterances during the months when the children were 11–36 months old. The light lines show all child verbalizations (nonword utterances plus word utterances), and the heavy lines show child word utterances (utterances containing recognizable words). The middle graph is a reduced copy of Figure 7. The four surrounding graphs are identically plotted data from each of the four subgroups at the extremes. At the left are the data from 4 children who became talkers early (top) and 4 others who were most talkative at age 3 (bottom). At the right are the data from 4 children who became talkers late (top) and 4 others who were most taciturn at age 3 (bottom). See Chapter 8 for the selection and demographics of the four subgroups. The data averaged for each of the four subgroups were smoothed to show a running average of 3 months.

Practice and the Total Language Experience of Children from Talkative and Taciturn Families

Practice using language is at least as important as hearing language used. Because of the special circumstances of childhood, practice may even be more important than exposure during the months in which children are learning to talk. When the beginner is a child, learning occurs in a climate of nurture in which there are no strong consequences. Everything is provided, and there is no need to talk. The chief reason for talking is social, so an unembarrassed display by a novice meets an uncritical encouragement of communication, however imperfect. Casual conversation during everyday activities ensures that incidental aspects of experience evoke continual variability in what is said, and the social dance gently guides practice toward cultural norms.

The intimate social dance between children and parents blends practice and exposure in language development. Children's practice displays the growth of cognitive functioning that influences the complexity of parents' responses and the frequency of interactions that lead children to refine and elaborate symbolic competencies. Practice improves children's fluency and flexibility as dance partners. The social dance of the family establishes the sociability seen in the frequency with which children recruit language experience from other people and seek opportunities to engage in the more varied and sophisticated dances of school and peer culture.

In our prior book, *Meaningful Differences in the Everyday Experience of Young American Children* (1995), we examined the vastly different amounts of language experience to which the 42 children were exposed by their parents. We noted that the talkativeness between family members was a prominent feature of each family culture. When, in this book, we examined the children's practice, we discovered that a child's talkativeness grew rapidly until it matched that of the child's parents and then stopped increasing. In each family the child's talkativeness came to be similar to

292

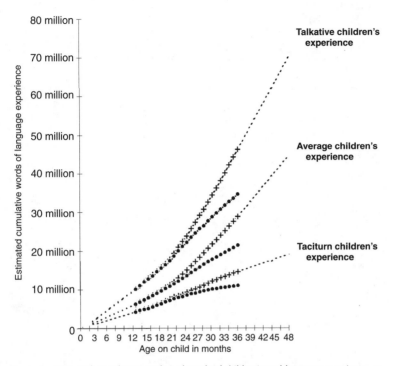

Figure 9. Estimated cumulative number of words of children's total language experience, assuming 14 waking hours per day or approximately 100 hours per week of experience time. Exposure from the parent (lines with circles) is the cumulative number per hour of words said to each child by their parents. Added to exposure from the parent is the children's practice (lines with plus signs), the cumulative number per hour of words said by each child during each of our monthly in-home observations when the children were 12–36 months old. The dotted line trajectories were extrapolated back to birth from the parent exposure slopes and forward to 48 months of child age from the combined parent exposure and child practice slopes, to display an estimate of the increasing differences between talkative and taciturn families in the cumulative total language experience of their children. The talkative and taciturn children are the children in the talkative and taciturn subgroups (see Figure 8).

the talkativeness of the family. There was a highly significant association between the number of words a child said and the number of words said to the child per hour ($r = .64$, $p < .001$). When the children's practice in using language was added to their exposure to language from their parents, the differences between the total language experience of children in talkative and taciturn families could be seen becoming ever greater as the children learned to talk.

Index

◆ ◆ ◆ ◆

Page references followed by *t*, *f*, or *n* indicate
tables, figures, or endnotes, respectively.